SHADOWS
OF
HOPE

SHADOWS OF HOPE

◼

A Freethinker's Guide to Politics in the Time of Clinton

Sam Smith

Indiana University Press   Bloomington & Indianapolis

Sam Smith is editor of the *Progressive Review* and has been an alternative journalist in Washington, D.C., for three decades. He was editor of the *DC Gazette* and one of the founders of the D.C. statehood movement. His book *Captive Capital: Colonial Life in Modern Washington* (also published by Indiana University Press) is still regarded as a major source on non-federal Washington twenty years after its publication.

The paper used in this publication meets the minimum requirements of American National Standard for Information Sciences—Permanence of Paper for Printed Library Materials, ANSI Z39.48-1984.

Manufactured in the United States of America

Library of Congress Cataloging-in-Publication Data

Smith, Sam, date
    Shadows of hope : a freethinker's guide to politics in the time of Clinton / Sam Smith.
        p.   cm.
    Includes bibliographical references and index.
    ISBN 0-253-35284-3 (alk. paper)
        1. Clinton, Bill, 1946-   2. United States—Politics and government—1993-   I. Title.
    E886.S65   1994
    973.929—dc20   94-2852

1 2 3 4 5 00 99 98 97 96 95 94

Contents

ACKNOWLEDGMENTS

In writing this book I have been greatly aided by a number of the finest kind, those with whom one can comfortably exchange unsorted ideas, seminal speculations, exploratory theses, new books, and old stories—much as others trade baseball cards or recipes. They are the sort who will telephone to convey nothing more than a thought or will slip a magazine article to you in the mail without comment, knowing that you will quickly find what moved them and be moved as well.

Among those who shared their cards and recipes to enlighten or enliven this book are Jonathan Rowe, Mike Pertschuk, Gene McCarthy, Conrad Martin, Mort Mintz, Anne Heutte, Rod French, Mark Plotkin, Keith Rutter, Harris Gleckman, Nadi Savio, Larry Smith, Matt Donohue, and David Bowes. Jane Hardin's assistance on Victorian welfare policies was especially helpful. Tom Martin's writings on devolution both educated and inspired me. Sam Wiebenson researched several critical points. My editor, John Gallman, once again provided wise and gentle guidance. The resources of Peacenet (where my Internet hangout in the global village is ssmith@igc.org) proved invaluable. And the incisive efforts of Nick Constantinople, Steve Dejter, and Ian Spence proved both timely and effective.

My wife Kathy remained calm and loving throughout it all. The views expressed in these pages do not necessarily, or in some cases even remotely, reflect her own. On the other hand, I hope this book does to some degree reflect the influence of her lifetime faith in, and practice of, history's relevance to our current concerns. Finally, my sons Nathaniel and Benjamin retained their usual tolerance and good humor in the face of the idiosyncrasies of their paternity.

Some of what follows appeared originally in the *Progressive Review*, the *D.C. Gazette*, and Washington's *City Paper*.

SAM SMITH
Washington, D.C.
December 15, 1993

INTRODUCTION

If this were a conventional book about national politics, it might rarely leave Washington except aboard Air Force One. Much that is written on the subject stays comfortably within the two-by-three-mile area in which one finds the White House and the Congress, the Supreme Court and the State Department, the Pentagon, the Watergate, and the National Press Club. As typical pasture in the American West, this spread could support about 120 cows and their calves.[1]

The tendency to concentrate our view of politics and of our collective selves upon this tiny enclave has accelerated in recent decades, in part because of a dramatic shift in power away from fifty "united states" toward an increasingly centralized and powerful federal government. But it has also been encouraged by a conglomerated media that requires news topics as ubiquitous as its own expanding corporate structures yet which still can be distilled into a single face or story.

Thus Congress has lost power relative to the White House not merely for various political reasons, but because 535 legislators are simply too many for the media to handle. TV, in particular, treats politics much as it does wide-screen movies; it snips off the right and left sides until the frame fits comfortably within the more equilateral shape of its eye. The edges of our experience are lost, and we find ourselves staring at a comfortable center—which in the case of politics means we find ourselves endlessly watching the president while much of the rest of American democracy passes unnoticed.

This preoccupation with the presidency not only exaggerates

the importance of the position, it distorts the constitutional division of political power, denigrates the significance of state and local government, and creates pressures for presidential action when such action may be neither wise nor even lawful. We cannot, even out of seemingly harmless celebrity worship, imbue our president with supra-constitutional virtues or powers without simultaneously damaging the Constitution and the democratic system it was established to protect.

Besides, our presidential fetish badly skews our view of our country and the changes occurring within it—not only elsewhere in government but beyond politics entirely. It trivializes our own collective and individual roles in creating social and political change. And, conversely, it can create the illusion of great change when far less is really happening.

Bill Clinton has said that he is "reinventing government." This hasn't happened, which isn't surprising since Clinton ran for president as a centrist, and centrists don't reinvent things. It is probably more factual, and more important, to say that with a new administration, America starts reinventing itself. Or at least reinventing what it says about itself—because, as with presidents, talking about change is sometimes all we can handle.

Change certainly has occurred under Clinton and will continue. It will not, however, emanate only from the White House like the once-imagined brilliant pebbles of Star Wars, but as a result of the American people and their president trying to figure each other out, manipulate each other, and mythologize each other. A new administration is something that happens not just *to* us but *with* us and *because of* us. Bill Clinton could not have been elected, for example, had not the country itself changed prior to his election. Did Clinton bring this about, or did he merely seem to represent the best choice for carrying out the change the country wanted? Was Clinton's success to be found in what he proposed or in his ability to perceive what the voter would like proposed?

Or maybe we really wanted change more than we wanted Clinton. Perhaps it was as Washington Irving noted in *Tales of a*

Traveller: "There is a certain relief in change, even though it be from bad to worse; as I have found in traveling in a stage coach, that it is often a comfort to shift one's position and be bruised in a new place."

To understand the changes that come with a new administration, we must observe not only the president but ourselves. There is a lot going on.

Some change can be substantial: witness the sudden shift in the relative power of gays and anti-abortionists. It can also be slight but noticeable: playing the saxophone means something different than it did a few years ago, and someone has counted at least twenty men in the White House wearing earrings.[2]

Change means new symbols, new myths, and new language. We don't necessarily like them, but their omnipresence makes them a part of our life anyway. We stop hearing the word *patriotism* so much and find even ourselves occasionally using the word *infrastructure.* We pay less attention to Saddam and more to Sarajevo and Somalia. We trade in some of our fears about drugs in order to fret about the deficit.

A change of administration can also change our views about change. In 1992, environmentalists were seeking to prevent Bush from undermining the whole regulatory structure of ecological protection; in 1993 they were complaining that Clinton was not moving fast enough on programs about which, for more than a decade, they had hardly dared dream.

Reactions vary. The banker is wary. The farmer—part of a rare constituency that stuck with Bush—is skeptical. The entrepreneur sees opportunity. The homeless man wonders whether the country will come to care. The lobbyist reorganizes her Rolodex. The student decides to become a teacher rather than an investment banker.

Some of the most important changes in America have nothing to do with the president or even politics. Television, which would eventually swallow politics, was created without its assistance. The Post-It Note was the result of a technological accident. The decline in the birthrate never made it to a political platform. Younger Americans are eating less meat without the advice and consent of the Senate. And so forth.

Other change is intentional and political, but occurring far from Washington, at the state and local level where financial shortfalls provide encouragement, a shorter distance between the governing and the governed provides a prod, and smaller and more human organization permits the serendipity of individual inspiration to flourish as it seldom can in the federal capital.

Change can also occur because of what the president does, or it can occur because of what he gets us to do. The latter cannot be judged by bills passed, or wars avoided, but by our own actions and thoughts. Sometimes, at least on the personal level, the impact can be substantial: I met my wife because John F. Kennedy had inspired her to move from Wisconsin to Washington. Sometimes the impact can be unclear, even split within one's own head. An architectural student said to me early in the Clinton administration, "I feel good about being a Democrat again. I feel like the white male Republicans have finally been stalled." She paused a moment before adding, "But I have to admit that what I feel and what I read are different."

Finally, but not least, a change in administration can bring us hope. It can be the Easter morning of our politics, the crocuses in the national garden, the sun breaking through the clouds scudding over our souls. It doesn't always happen, but this time it did—for a little while. In the weeks before Clinton's inauguration the word *hope* was everywhere, and only the cynical noticed how seldom anyone said *expect*.

So this is a book not about Bill Clinton but about Clinton and us. It is about the Clinton we read about and the Clinton we feel, the Clinton who is, the Clinton we would like him to be and the Clinton he would like to be. It is about why Clinton matters and, less noticed, why he doesn't. It is about our power and his, our attempts to manipulate him and his to manipulate us. It is about our periodic ritual of renewal called an election and how we use it to move on and to stay very much the same. It is also about lies and myths and about an America still groping for its own perestroika after decades of political racketeering and abuse of its democratic systems. And it is, finally, about some things we might do about it.

There is no easy way to approach this. The time has not been long enough for the historian; the data are too slim for the sociologist; the American tribe is too large for the anthropologist, the story too messy, with too much myth competing with fact, for the journalistic literalist.

But it is in the nature of democracy that we are constantly being called upon to act before we have all the facts. It should not surprise us that writing about democracy is as incomplete as its subject. Journalism, after all, is to thought and understanding as the indictment is to the trial, the hypothesis to the truth, the estimate to the audit. It is the first cry for help, the hand groping for the light switch in the dark, the returns before the outlying precincts have been heard from.

Most books of this sort posit the author as expert. There are several problems with this, not the least of which being the growing symbiosis between the Washington politician and the Washington journalist. Go back forty years and you will find that more than half of America's reporters had only a high-school degree. Journalism in those days, to borrow a phrase, looked more like America. As the media has risen in social status, it has become increasingly a companion rather than a critic of power. Here's how UPI Washington correspondent Helen Thomas put it: "We do mix and mingle. It's important that we get to know these people. To think of people as friends and colleagues." It is difficult to write with precision and dispassion about one's friends and colleagues, and too many Washington writers long ago passed the point of even having occasional doubts about it.

There is also the problem created by the implicit presumption that what happens to America can be adequately described by what happens in Washington. If the experience—such as that with a new president—is shared throughout the United States, then surely the knowledge and expertise is dispersed as well. We are all, it has been noted, experts in our own self-interest.

There is finally the conundrum that while the analyst deals in facts and logic, these play a relatively small part in American politics. What increasingly drives our politics is myth, propaganda, and fantasy. The facts, the polls, and the data leave us, in the end, feeling empty. A more impressionistic approach to the matter, relying on reasoned subjectivity rather than the crypto-ideology of pseudo-objectivity, may help to bring us within range.

And so this writer proposes to serve not as an expert, but rather in the more modest and, I would argue, more constructive journalistic role of being the surrogate eyes and ears of the reader. Consider me simply someone who has traveled this trail several times before and thus might remember where the clean water is to be found, the names of some of the rarer plants, and possibly even a shortcut home.

The trail of this book begins with Bill Clinton, but that is only the beginning. We shall look at the ideas that inform him and the capital culture that envelops him. Eventually, as it must in a democracy, the trail leads back to us. It does no good to speak of a president's power but ignore the source of that power, to chastise his lies but not our own myths, or to question a president's stewardship of the country without considering our own. When we elect a president, we not only choose a leader, we describe ourselves. And so when I speak of Bill Clinton, it is sometimes a shorthand for talking about the rest of us as well.

I have, in fact, traveled this trail before. I was born in Washington and have lived here much of my life. They called my generation the "silent" one, the one America skipped in moving from George Bush to Bill Clinton.

Maybe some of us were quiet because we were trying to figure out how to avoid becoming the man in the gray flannel suit or part of the lonely crowd. The struggle, we thought, was about individuality, and no one spoke of movements. Our cultural heroes didn't organize anything. They hit the road. Our goal wasn't to overthrow the establishment, someone would say a decade later, but to make it irrelevant. Or, like Miles Davis in concert, play with your back to it. In the 1960s, when we were in our thirties, we were told that we already were too old to be trusted. It wasn't really true; in many ways the sixties was just the mass movement of something that had started in the fifties with our coffeehouses, music, and conscious political apathy.

Some of us made Humphrey Bogart an anti-hero in part, I think, because we already suspected that America was our own Casablanca, a place of seductive illusions and baroque deceptions, where nothing was as it appeared. After all, we had been taught that if we crawled under our desks, we would be safe from The Bomb. Even our teachers lied to us. Bogey knew how to live in a time of lies.

I covered my first national story during the Eisenhower administration as a nineteen-year-old radio reporter. I also covered the attempt by D.C. police to restore public safety and tranquility by closing down a coffeehouse called Coffee 'n' Confusion. It would be the last time anyone in Washington would be afraid of poets.

These were also the last days of the great postwar American myth. Already it was starting to unravel with the Gary Powers spy plane incident, the quiz show scandals, the stench of McCarthyism, the genesis of the civil rights movement, and the growing sense that we had been badly misinformed about the dangers of nuclear power.

Over time, I found myself no longer believing in Washington. When the sixties showed up, I was ready to join. Since then I have had what may be the longest-running act on the off-Broadway of Washington journalism, editing several alternative journals, actively engaging in a variety of causes, and being guided by H. L. Mencken's dictum that the liberation of the human mind has been best furthered by those who "heaved dead cats into sanctuaries and then went roistering down the highways of the world, proving to all that doubt, after all, was safe."

So while I live well inside the Beltway, I have also lived well outside the loop—more as a laptop-toting guerrilla hidden in the hills of Rock Creek Park than as a member of any elite, cultural or otherwise, that is said to dominate this city. And it is with this perspective—that of a subversive native, of a consummate Washington outsider—that I offer you my services. Welcome to Casablanca.

SHADOWS
OF
HOPE

Audition

When millions of Americans first saw Bill Clinton on television, he bored them. While nominating Michael Dukakis at the 1988 Democratic Convention, Clinton talked so long the crowd started interrupting, yelling, "We want Mike." According to biographers Charles Allen and Jonathan Portis, "It was clear to television viewers that Clinton was confused and frightened." The governor pleaded for patience, but when he said the words "In conclusion," the conventioneers broke into cheers. One disgruntled delegate observed, "He wrote eight drafts but forgot to throw out the first seven."[1]

To those who had heard about Clinton, it was somewhat surprising. After all, a myth was already beginning to form around the Arkansas governor. His advance notices had been uniformly favorable: he was bright, capable, and above all articulate. He was still considered a young rising star ten years after he had first been elected governor.

Clinton had also been the beneficiary of what one journalist has called the Great Mentioner. He had already been noted, remarked upon, and welcomed in the smokeless salons where national politics are created. Clinton mattered.

How one comes to matter in Washington politics is guided by few precise rules, although in comparison to fifty years ago the views of lobbyists and fundraisers are far more significant than the opinion, say, of the mayor of Chicago or the governor of Pennsylvania. This is a big difference: somewhere behind the old bosses in their smoke-filled rooms were live constituents; behind the political cash lords of today there is mostly just more money and the few who control it.

Thus coming to matter has much less to do with traditional politics, especially local politics, than it once did. Today, other things count: the patronage of those who already matter, a blessing bestowed casually by one right person to another right person over lunch at the Metropolitan Club, a columnist's praise, a well-received speech before a well-placed organization, the assessment of a lobbyist as sure-eyed as a fight manager checking out new fists at the local gym. There are still machines in American politics; they just dress and talk better.

There is another rule. The public plays no part. The public is the audience; the audience does not write or cast the play. In 1988, the 1992 play was already being cast. Conservative Democrats were holding strategy meetings at the home of party fundraiser Pamela Harriman. The meetings—eventually nearly a hundred of them—were aimed at ending years of populist insurrection within the party. They were regularly moderated by Clark Clifford and Robert Strauss, the Mr. Fixits of the Democratic mainstream. Democratic donors paid $1,000 to take part in the sessions, and by the time it was all over, Mrs. Harriman had raised about $12 million for her kind of Democrats.

The play was also being cast by a group that called itself the

Democratic Leadership Council. Although lacking any official role in the Democratic Party (and often appearing more a Democratic Abandon Ship Council), the DLC claimed it was the voice of mainstream party thought. In fact, it was primarily a lobby for the views of southern and other conservative Democrats, yet so successful was its media manipulation that it managed with impunity to call its think tank the Progressive Policy Institute.

In such places the important Democratic politics of the late 1980s was being made. Clinton may have bored millions of Americans on TV that night, but Clifford, Strauss, Harriman, and the DLC found him intensely interesting, extremely intelligent—an appealing pragmatist, willing to compromise, and fully at home with the policy jargon of the capital. He was not the only horse in their stable—Pamela Harriman, for example, also liked Al Gore and Jay Rockefeller—but he was as good as any they had.[2]

The appeal of Clinton to these matchmakers went beyond mere political calculations. Clinton was not only politically realistic, he was culturally comfortable. He projected the image of an outsider, yet had adapted to the ways of capital insiders. Official Washington—including government, media, and the lobbies—functions in many ways like America's largest and most prestigious club, a sort of indoor, East Coast Bohemian Grove in which members engage in endless rites of mutual affirmation combined with an intense but genteel competition that determines the city's tennis ladder of political and social power. What appears to the stranger as a major struggle is often only an intramural game between members of the same club, lending an aura of dynamism to what is in truth deeply stable.

The Yale law degree, the Rhodes scholarship, the familiarity with the rhetoric of the policy-pushers all helped Clinton fit into the club. But perhaps most of all, Clinton knew when to stop thinking.

Just as the Soviets tolerated free thought only within the limits of "socialist dialogue," so debate in Washington is circumscribed by the limits of what might be called Beltway discourse. Ideas that adjust or advance the conventional wisdom are valued. Those that challenge it are ignored or treated with contempt. Beltway discourse is informed by a number of disciplines but tends to ignore others. The teachings of law and political science as well as those of economics and similar pursuits of quantification are considered important; those of history, anthropology, religion, literature, philosophy, and the arts tend to be discounted.

Clinton had a fine sense of the limits and the language. The media, the major enforcer of Beltway discourse, naturally found Clinton appealing. Clinton not only spoke the policy patois the Washington media understood and appreciated, he shared their orthodoxy about the future of the Democratic Party. By the late 1980s there was a widespread consensus among both the press and the Democratic leadership that the party's problems could be traced to several factors:

- The loss of control by party bosses due to excessive democratization of nomination and convention procedures.
- Undue pandering to such traditional constituencies as blacks, liberals, and women.
- The need for a new and far more conservative Democratic platform.

By the 1988 convention, this consensus had taken root. *U.S. News & World Report* reported:

> That the Democrats went beyond all bounds to appear bland and "normal" is incontrovertible. The brief, boring and bullet-proof platform gave "platitudinous" new meaning. "Notice," complained New York Senator Daniel Patrick Moynihan, offering only one example, "that the word *city* does not appear in our platform. We talk about *suburban hometown America* and I figure that doesn't mean the South Bronx."

With the rise of this orthodoxy, the media's language changed. What was once a civil rights cause now became "demands of special interest groups." The conservative Democrats' self-definition as "moderates" or "mainstream" was uncritically adopted. And "liberal" began to be used, even in purportedly objective articles, as a pejorative. It made someone like Clinton look very good.

By the time of the 1992 New Hampshire primary, the press would be overwhelmingly in the Clinton camp. Hendrik Hertzberg in the *New Republic* reported that he had surveyed several dozen journalists and found that all of them, had they been New Hampshire voters, would have chosen Clinton. Hertzberg noted that this was a change from previous elections when the press had tended to split their primary choices, sometimes sharply. He suggested that the "real reason members of the press like Clinton is simple, and surprisingly uncynical: they think he would make a very good, perhaps a great, president. Several told me they were convinced that Clinton is the most talented presidential candidate they have ever encountered, JFK included."

While the most that even reasonably informed Americans knew about Bill Clinton when he spoke in Atlanta in 1988 was a string of favorable adjectives from the Great Mentioner, the governor himself was well enough positioned to have already given serious consideration to running for president. He had reflected, waffled, and finally backed out, citing among other things his responsibilities to his daughter Chelsea. But now, in the wake of his convention debacle, he faced a big political problem anyway. He had gone national and flopped.

The incident provided a glimpse of a personality America would not really begin to understand until some months after Clinton had been inaugurated:

• There was, for example, the elaborate but futile preparation—multiple drafts of an effort that would ultimately misfire.

• There were the nineteenth-hole rationalizations—ranging from valid complaints about the failure to dim the lights in the convention hall to a disingenuous claim that he had plowed ahead out of obligation to Dukakis.

• There was the sense that Clinton perceived the speech—much as he regarded politics itself—in intensely personal terms. It was not the disservice to Dukakis that seemed to matter, but the fact, as he put it to a reporter, that "I just fell on my sword." This was not the comment of a second banana—of the warm-up act— but of a man who, like so many successful individuals of the eighties, found himself in a lonely battle against the rest of the world and who was, in the end, his own best hero.

- Finally there was the recovery, the comeback. Our country loves comebacks, perhaps because they help keep the American Dream alive by giving everyone another chance. They are entertaining, moving, and inspiring. Few question whether such mercurial swings, whatever their appeal in sports or entertainment, serve any national purpose. The political comeback is just assumed to be a virtue canceling any failure that necessitated it.

The speech quickly became a joke. Johnny Carson ridiculed Clinton, calling him a "windbag." But Clinton managed an invitation to the show and not only proved an ingratiating guest but played sax with Doc Severinsen's orchestra. In doing so, he received postmodern America's equivalent of a presidential pardon: laughter and applause on late-night television. Clinton went on that evening to a party given by Harry Thomason and Linda Bloodworth-Thomason. There was a sign there depicting the White House. On it was a slogan: ON THE ROAD AGAIN . . . CLINTON '96.

Even in this small incident, four years before the election of Clinton as president, we find the outlines of the Clinton style, of the meat of myth, and of a politics so personal that politics seems almost an afterthought. We would be seduced into the Clinton saga again and again not because it was noble or tragic, not because of its political substance or ideological appeal, but simply because we wanted to know how it would turn out: *Days of Our Politicians' Lives,* starring Bill and Hillary Clinton.

The beginning of TV-era politics is generally traced to the Kennedy-Nixon debates. In his book *The Fifties,* David Halberstam quotes Russell Baker describing the battle between a sweating

Nixon and the cool Kennedy: "That night image replaced the printed word as the natural language of politics."

Adlai Stevenson had seen it coming. A few months earlier he gave a speech in which he observed: "If freedom is really the organizing principle of our society, then we cannot forget that it is not an illusion, propaganda or sedatives, but truth alone that makes us free. Under the influence of the politics of sedation and the techniques of salesmanship, I believe that in recent years self-deceit has slackened our grip on reality."[3]

True enough, but Kennedy and Nixon remained essentially traditional politicians manipulating a new electronic world. They would each learn to use it well but in the end would still unmistakably possess their own virtues or failings.* It would be a couple of decades before we felt the full power of television to create the reality of our politics. Ford, Carter, and Reagan were all televised, but television, for better or worse, could not change their natural state. Reagan seemed to have been born in syndication, and neither Ford nor Carter was willing or able to adapt to the great eye.

George Bush was another matter. Without television, Bush would have been just one more dull country club Republican. His media handlers, however, transformed him from a stiff flop in the early primaries into a television version of a president. To be sure, Bush was to JFK as Connie Chung is to Edward R. Murrow, but that was irrelevant because television no longer needed or wanted JFK or Murrow. It had discovered that complex, well-developed characters actually conflicted with the brutal simplicity of its message. It wanted primal symbols, Punch and Judy characters, myths, and comfortable "concepts." If politics was to make full use of the medium, it could not remain baroque theater occurring outside of television. It had to become simple enough for the camera to explain. It had to *become* television, each campaign another series pilot.

By the end of the 1980s, television, it seemed, was more

---

* In our enthusiasm for Kennedy's telegenic ability, we tend to forget that the reason Nixon was able to debate Kennedy at all was because of his own remarkable "Checkers" speech, perhaps the only television address to single-handedly save a political career.

important than anything. Newspapers were hurting. Peter Teeley, press secretary to then Vice-President Bush, had described cynically but honestly a critical difference between the media: "You can say anything you want during a [presidential] debate and 80 million people hear it. [If the newspapers later correct the record] so what? Maybe 200 people read it or 2,000 or 20,000." In the midst of the Gulf War, one poll reported that 81 percent of Americans were getting most of their news from television. By 1993, as United Nations troops searched for clan leader Muhammad Farah Aidid, the Somalian general was insisting on staying only in those safe houses that received CNN.[4]

Television's secret was that it was more important than many of the people appearing on it because, while they could not exist outside of the tube, television had plenty more where they came from. Bush falters; bring on Clinton. In fact, it seemed you didn't even need live politicians anymore. In August 1993, a correspondent appeared on the CBS morning show to discuss the relative power of senators and the White House. On his lap, to assist in his report, was an enormous voodoo doll in the likeness of Senator David Boren.

It is true that Clinton had been reelected many times by the people of his state, had been judged the best governor in a newsweekly poll of his peers, was demonstrably personable, well-informed, and intelligent, and far from being the political equivalent, say, of some eminently replicable network weatherman. Still, there were important things about the man that were missing.

Such as history.

In its darkest corners Clinton's past is his enemy, something to have overcome and to overcome still. In the Clinton campaign story there was talk of family, but his mother and half-brother remained in the shadows. There were those older than he who helped him on his way, such as Senator Fulbright, but they too appeared far on the periphery of his story. His most moving tale was of challenging his abusive stepfather. His daughter is named not after a relative, but for a popular song. He has good friends, but apparently hundreds of them. He has no home and no vacation home. He left the place of which he has spoken most often, Hope, Arkansas, when he was seven; his family moved to Hot Springs, a resort with flourishing illegal brothels and casinos, whose patronage included Chicago and New York mobsters.

Clinton's convention documentary would try to suggest roots yet, carefully crafted as it was, there was a void. Clinton was there and people were there, but they seemed around him, not with him. He reaches out of the crowd at Boys' Nation to touch Jack Kennedy's hand, just as during the campaign tens of thousands would reach out to touch his. A touch. A moment. A moment gone.

It was the normal work of the politician, but with Clinton there seemed too much. Too many hands, too many friends, too many words, too many hours before he went to sleep, too many hours on C-SPAN solving the nation's problems with too many industrialists and economists—and, in the end, too little else. It was as though he were afraid that if he excused himself from the public eye he might no longer be real. It was not surprising that Clinton said he wanted to run his administration like a campaign. His whole life had been one.

Politics used to be about remembrance. The best politicians were those who remembered and were remembered the most— the most people, the littlest favors, the smallest slights, the best anecdotes tying one's politics to the common memory of the constituency.

Politics was also about gratitude. Politicians were always thanking people, "without whom" whatever under discussion could not have happened. You not only thanked those in the room—as many as possible by name—you even thanked those without, for "having prepared the wonderful meal which we have just partaken of." The politician was the creation of others, and never failed to mention it.

Above all, politics was about relationships. The politician grew organically out of a constituency and remained rooted to it as long as incumbency lasted.

Today, we increasingly elect people about whom we have little to remember, to whom we owe no gratitude, and with whom we have no relationship except that formed during the great carny show we call a campaign. Dallas coach Jimmy Jones spoke for many contemporary politicians when he answered a question about his memories of Thanksgiving Day football games by saying, "Memories? That's not my style."

At the beginning of the 1992 campaign, few of us knew, let alone remembered, anything about Bill Clinton. If we were not from Arkansas, we had nothing for which to thank him. And our whirlwind relationship, our arranged marriage, was under the constant control of the great American matchmaker: the media. Clinton's past was unimportant not only to him, but to us as well.

In an earlier time, Clinton's non-history would have been an enormous limitation. Now it wasn't, because Clinton had one huge edge over his opponents: he looked good and acted well on TV. Tom Harkin moved and spoke as mechanically as the Energizer bunny; Kerry's personality and platform remained a cipher; Tsongas talked funny; Brown was didactic; but Clinton was at home.

Against this advantage, facts faltered. The facts said that Clinton had been an unexceptional governor. He could claim better prenatal care programs and a decline in infant mortality, but at the same time the Center for the Study of Social Policy would rate the state only forty-first on children's issues in general. Arkansas also ranked, according to the Southern Regional Council, in the bottom 10 percent of all states in average weekly wages, health insurance coverage, state and local school revenue, unemployment, blacks and women in traditional white male jobs, environmental policy, and overall conditions for workers.

An examination of his record raised warning flags, not the least of which were rocky relationships with labor and environmentalists. At the beginning of the campaign Clinton came under attack by his state's AFL-CIO president, who (before the national union ordered him to shut up) sent around a highly critical report on Clinton's record. Labor, said Bill Becker, should expect Clinton's help only 25 to 30 percent of the time. And the League of Conservation Voters ranked Clinton last among the Democratic candidates on conservation issues.

Greater attention to Clinton's record also might have brought to more prominent notice the major tax increases during his tenure. Or the comment by the union official who said that Clinton would slap you on the back and piss down your leg. Or the tendency to waffle on issues. Early in the campaign, David Maraniss of the *Washington Post* cited Mrs. Clinton's reflection on the death penalty: "We go back and forth on the issues of due process and the disproportionate minorities facing the death penalty, and we have serious concerns in those areas. We also abhor the craze for the death penalty. But we believe it does have a role."[5]

Acting on the latter part of this circumlocution, Clinton left the New Hampshire campaign to oversee the execution of a lobotomized black murderer named Rickey Ray Rector, a man so removed from reality, reported Richard Cohen, that "at his last meal, he set aside a slice of pecan pie so he could have some later."[6]

Similarly, in February 1992 Clinton said, "I supported the Persian Gulf war because I thought it was in our national interest," while one year earlier he had said, "I guess I would have voted with the majority [of the Senate on the war] if it was a close vote. But I agree with the arguments the minority made."

Perhaps the most revealing story of this sort did not appear until after the election. According to the *New York Times,* it seems that following five days of agonizing over a higher-education bill, Clinton finally vetoed the measure with a stamp that read DISAPPROVED. The bill was delivered to the clerk's office, but because it was after closing time it had to be slipped under the door. Clinton then called the state's university presidents to explain his decision. They convinced him that he had made a mistake. The *Times* continued:

> So the Governor summoned a state trooper in his security detail and asked him to go back to the clerk's office and retrieve the vetoed bill. The trooper could see through the locked glass

door that the bill was lying on the floor. He took a coat hanger, slipped it under the door and slid the bill out. He brought it back to Governor Clinton, who simply crossed out the letters DIS and sent it back as APPROVED.[7]

Although each of these stories appeared somewhere in the American press, journalistic traditions lessened their impact. In the first place, most papers prefer to run their own stories and downplay any other paper's contribution. As a result, the aggregate investigative output of American journalism is unavailable except to those who subscribe to expensive clipping or computer search services. Secondly, as a campaign progresses, the past becomes less and less important. There is a foreshortening of concerns; media attention is focused on what happened yesterday or the day before. Basic information about the candidate developed early in the campaign inevitably fades, is considered stale and irrelevant, and we are left to judge by only the most recent standards.

There is also a compression of language. A once-complex investigative story gets reduced to a candidate's "controversial relationship" with someone, a seventy-five-page policy position to a "detailed jobs proposal." In 1993 even the candidates, as though bored with their own rhetoric, compressed their pitches dramatically, creating a sort of pidgin politics.

Here is Paul Tsongas:

"Twinkie economics. Tastes good. No nutrition."

"Cold War? Over. Japan won."

And Jerry Brown on the North American Free Trade Agreement:

"Clinton: jobs there. Brown: jobs here. It's real simple. Don't complicate this vote."

There are other journalistic factors that affect campaigns, not the least of these being peer pressure. George Orwell once noted, "At any given moment there is a sort of all-prevailing orthodoxy, a general tacit agreement not to discuss some large and uncomfortable fact."[8] A journalist wishing to challenge this orthodoxy faces not only the resistance of sources but the ridicule of peers, well described by D. D. Guttenplan in the *Columbia Journalism Review:*

> Polls, fundraising, media strategies—that's what the [media] insiders on the road want to know about. Ask a candidate a detailed question about health care and you're instantly marked as a yahoo. Ask about day care or job creation or the racial makeup of his staff, and you're tagged as a fanatic—some kind of "ideologue." Why this should be so is difficult to explain, except that "on the bus," naiveté is the worst possible offense. The best way to seem sophisticated is to ask the shallowest questions, preferably with a sneer in your voice.

Why this should be so is perhaps explained in *The Evolution of Cooperation,* in which Robert Axelrod describes how German and English soldiers in the trenches during World War I tacitly developed a mutually protective relationship, right down to eliminating salvos during lunchtime and timing other gunfire so the opposing side would know when to stay under cover. He quotes a British officer facing a Saxon unit of the German Army:

> I was having tea with A Company when we heard a lot of shouting and went out to investigate. We found our men and the Germans standing on their respective parapets. Suddenly a salvo arrived but did no damage. Naturally both sides got down and our men started swearing at the Germans, when all at once a brave German got on to his parapet and shouted out, "We are very sorry about that; we hope no one was hurt. It is not our fault, it is that damned Prussian artillery."[9]

Axelrod cites this analysis by Tony Ashworth: "In trench war, a structure of ritualized aggression was a ceremony where antagonists participated in regular, reciprocal discharges of missiles, that is, bombs, bullets and so forth, which symbolized and strengthened, at one and the same time, both sentiments of fellow-feelings and beliefs that the enemy was a fellow-sufferer."[10]

A similar bonding—complete with "regular, reciprocal discharges of missiles"— occurs in the trenches of politics between the media and those it covers. In such a closed reality, the reader or viewer, not the news subject, becomes the one left out.

The single-mindedness of the press can be astounding; witness this from the *Washington Post* of May 26, 1993: "White House spokeswoman Dee Dee Myers claims to have won a press office betting pool on how many [questions about the mass firing of White House travel office employees] would be asked at yesterday's daily briefing. She guessed 127 and the tally came in at 118."

Orthodoxy can also be reinforced by the bias of words used to describe something, as in this query from an ABC News poll: "Which of these statements comes closer to your view? Beneath it all, Clinton is an old-style, tax-and-spend Democrat; OR Clinton is a new-style Democrat who will be careful with the public's money."

It can be even more blatant. *Extra!*, a progressive media watchdog magazine, for example, listed a few of the terms that purportedly objective journalists used during the campaign to describe Jerry Brown, one of Clinton's opponents:

Annoying—Ted Koppel, ABC News.

Weird—Cokie Roberts, NPR.

A pain in the you-know-what—Bernard Shaw, CNN.

Flailing about, spewing out charges like sparks from a Fourth of July pinwheel—R. W. Apple, *New York Times.*

He's a chameleon, a character assassin and a first-class cynic—John Alter, *Newsweek.*

Brilliant, self-absorbed, friendless, idealistic, erratic, opportunistic, cold, hypocritical—*New York Times.*

Jerry Brown's more corrupt than the system—Eleanor Clift, *Newsweek.*

The nature of politics has also been affected by the decline of descriptive journalism in the wake of Watergate and television's rise. Real reporters now prefer smoking guns—stories that offer the potential of major victory or defeat, if not of resignation, impeachment, or indictment. Stories that merely reveal character or style, or open a window on our political experience, are downplayed or relegated to gossip or "lifestyle" coverage, especially if there is any suggestion—without formal proof—that something is amiss. In short, a legalistic rather than a literary standard of coverage has evolved. Politics, once the great American novel, has been reduced to a case study.

Absent a smoking gun, editors often favor stories that explain import, perceive perceptions, and reveal meaning. Detailed chronicles of the daily joys, inanities, and mishaps of politics have faded. News, for example, has literally started to disappear from the front pages of the *Washington Post,* replaced in no small part by the reflections of various writers about what the unreported news means to them or is supposed to mean to us. This approach, a futile and often boring attempt to justify the paper's existence in a world of television and *USA Today,* creates some oddities, such as the *Post* commissioning a presidential poll and then failing to reveal the results for nine full paragraphs, during which one has waded deep into the story after a tedious trek through E. J. Dionne Jr.'s analysis of the facts we might learn if we only hang on long enough.

Further, a priggishness has infected a generation of self-consciously respectable journalists. This can be easily seen by comparing the exuberant reportage of H. L. Mencken or A. J. Leibling with the stolid work of today's analysts. The former was intensely descriptive, while the latter is written in a ritualistic and abstract style that sucks life from politics and which, by making it all seem so boring, may actually be a cause of electoral apathy. If democracy is no more exciting than David Broder would have us believe, why bother to vote? When, rarely, today's columnists do go after a politician with vigor, the target is almost always someone on the political edges like Jerry Brown or Pat Buchanan rather than an establishment figure such as Clinton and Bush.

Here, on the other hand, is an example from the 1920 presidential coverage of Mencken. It clearly violates just about every canon of contemporary objective journalism yet, with the benefit of hindsight, hardly suggests that Mencken misled his readers about the choice before them:

> No one but an idiot could argue seriously that either candidate is a first-rate man, or even a creditable specimen of second-rate man. Any State in the Union, at least above the Potomac, could produce a thousand men quite as good, and many States could produce a thousand a great deal better. Harding, intellectually, seems to be merely a benign blank—a decent, harmless, laborious hollow-headed mediocrity. . . . Cox is quicker of wit, but a good deal less honest. He belongs to the cunning type; there is a touch of the shyster in him. His chicaneries in the matter of prohibition, both during the convention and since, show the kink in his mind. He is willing to do anything to cadge votes, and he includes in that anything the ready sacrifices of his good faith, of the national welfare, and of the hopes and confidence of those who honestly support him. Neither candidate reveals the slightest dignity of conviction. Neither cares a hoot for any discernible principle. Neither, in any intelligible sense, is a man of honor.[11]

With the current more somber and "responsible" approach often comes a bowdlerized view of the candidates and the politics surrounding them. This doesn't mean that the coverage is better. The media, in its desire to avoid unsubstantiated political allegations, can easily find itself instead providing unsubstantiated exonerations. The most prominent example in the Clinton campaign involved Gennifer Flowers's claim to have had an affair with the governor. Flowers backed up her allegation with tape-recorded conversations between the governor and herself. Most of the major media declined to run excerpts from the tapes, some using the argument that the tapes did not prove the existence of a sexual relationship. (Clinton himself gave substance to the recordings by apologizing to Mario Cuomo for pejorative remarks made on one about the New York governor.)

While it was true that the tapes could be interpreted in a number of ways, they did suggest that Clinton and Flowers were covering up *something,* and at the very least provided an enlightening view of the ethical calculus of the candidate.

Clinton was never pressed by reporters for the inner meaning of his comment that if "everyone hangs tough, they're just not gonna do anything. They can't. . . . They can't run a story like that unless somebody says, 'Yeah, I did it.'" Certainly, when Richard Nixon had similar reflections on the Watergate tapes, we thought it of more than passing interest. A year and a half later, Adam Nagourney of *USA Today* admitted to *Vanity Fair,* "Nobody pursued it. You could have taken those tapes and gone to town."[12]

Back when the Gary Hart story broke, a public-relations man suggested how he would have handled the scandal: put up billboards featuring photos of FDR, Eisenhower, JFK, and Hart. Underneath would be the single phrase HART: IN A GREAT TRADITION.

In a similar vein, some reasonably made the argument that if Hillary had bought her husband's explanation, that was good enough for them. Still, the Flowers story, and the way Clinton handled it, went directly to concerns about the man other than adultery. There were times during the campaign when Clinton's versions of his past reminded one of the Raymond Chandler character: "smart, smooth and no good." Tracking a Clinton explanation, whether of past actions or present policy, could be like trying to dance on a floor covered with marbles. As Paul Greenberg of the *Arkansas Democrat Gazette* put it: "Bill Clinton *is* a presidential debate."

Further, in the Flowers case the media seemed to be having it both ways. The *Washington Times* pointed out, for example, that Clinton's alleged affair got far kinder treatment from the media than had similar stories involving others. The Flowers story quickly disappeared from the mainstream press. In contrast, said the *Times,* the 1980 story about Dan Quayle—then just a congressman—sharing a Florida cottage with Paula Parkinson and several other members of Congress was the topic of eleven stories in the

New York Times and sixteen in the *Washington Post* all in one week. During the same period, the major networks ran thirteen stories.

When John Tower was nominated to be secretary of defense, the networks ran thirty-two stories concerning his alleged sexual improprieties. The *Washington Post* ran a story by Bob Woodward that accused Tower of having "appeared to be drunk" during two visits to a Texas Air Force base and having fondled two women. The only source for this story was one former Air Force sergeant. And during the nine days before the Senate voted to confirm Clarence Thomas, the networks ran ninety-nine stories—the *New York Times* ran sixty-three and the *Post* sixty-one—about Anita Hill's allegations, though they were not backed up by anything so substantial as a tape recording. In the politics of sex, politics count at least as much as the sex.

If the media merely reported the public actions of politicians, there would be a strong argument for avoiding a story like Flowers's. But that's not what happens. The Washington press, for example, consistently projects a halcyon, virtuous, and lovable image of our presidents at play, which then inevitably colors our reaction of them at work. The now mandatory White House tour, in which a network anchor fawns over the presidential couple, their pets, furnishings, and knickknacks, is only the beginning.

A double standard develops. If the recipe for Barbara Bush's or Hillary Clinton's chocolate chip cookies is important, then at least equally true the tale of Gennifer Flowers. If it's okay for the children of a politician to be up on the nationally televised stage, why not the politician's mistress as well? Besides, the umbrage taken at the Flowers allegations must be considered in light of Hillary Rodham Clinton's swipe at George Bush's own friend named Jennifer and the Clinton team's post-election snooping into Bush personnel files. As it turned out, someone had been expecting them. The Jennifer Fitzgerald file was empty.

It may be that the media, deep down, does not believe that the American people are wise enough to be trusted with the truth that their leaders are often not what they would seem. In any event, the result is an expurgated version of politics which creates the very sort of lie from which the media claims to be protecting us.

Even beyond Flowers, the press was little interested in stories that scraped the presidential patina from the Clinton campaign. The major exception was the draft controversy.

Here Clinton discovered the outer boundaries of media tolerance. That this line should have been drawn between marital and national fidelity may reflect the self-protective instincts of those on the road covering a presidential campaign for months on end. In any case, the media pursued the draft story with considerable diligence, missing only a few ancillary matters such as who paid for Clinton's stay in an upscale Moscow hotel at a time when the Oxford student was supposed to be broke.

In the end, Clinton survived the story, but would suffer from this account as much as any that grew out of the campaign, leaving many with sour reactions over his manipulation of the draft system as well as its suggestion of underlying arrogance not unlike that of British scholar Heathcote William Gerard, who explained his absence from World War I by saying, "I am the civilization they are fighting to defend."

In other matters, Clinton fared far better. His precipitous mid-spring interest in fairness as he went after black and labor votes, for example, attracted little media attention. *The Nation* quoted Bob Borosage, a Jackson aide in 1988: "You have to be a political junkie to remember that Clinton now is not how he positioned himself for the last four years. The irony is that Clinton is now using a major theme of fairness against Tsongas when fairness was the word the [Democratic Leadership Council] was going to banish from the Democratic lexicon. The DLC said it was for growth and told people they had to stop talking about fairness. It's hilarious."

Only a few sharp-eyed reporters caught Clinton filching ideas from other campaigns. Gwen Ifill of the *New York Times* was one, noting Clinton's use of Kerry's cry for "fundamental change," Harkin's demand for increased use of ethanol and his "real Democrat" line, and the anti-corporate rhetoric of Jerry Brown. Later, Christopher Georges, an editor of the *Washington Monthly,* would point out in a *Times* op-ed that many of Clinton's ideas—including thirty-nine of the forty-nine specific proposals in his economic plan—were virtually identical to programs advocated by Michael Dukakis in 1988. Included among the Dukakis clones were Clinton's apprenticeship program, worker retraining initiative, and planned assault on tax cheaters.

Although the national press blanketed Arkansas early in the campaign, the effort proved only marginally informative. Thus the public heard about Clinton's success in attracting new business to the state but little about the wage differential that was far more appealing to industries than the governor's charm or skill. It heard about his economic development efforts, but little about how Clinton's development agency had favored friends of the governor. There was virtually nothing in the mainstream press about Mena, Arkansas, a Contra training and drug-running center, nor of Clinton's curious reluctance to investigate what was going on there. Only a handful of reporters took an interest in Worthen Bank, although its $2 million line of credit kept Clinton alive in the early stages of the campaign.

Only fleeting attention was given the fact that Bill Clinton's wife had represented a client and co-investor before a regulatory agency of her husband's government. Or that federal and state agents, while wiretapping Clinton's half-brother Roger, heard him describe the governor's mansion as a favorite trysting place. Or that at the beginning of the campaign Clinton's personal security chief was being sued in a Contra-connected case in which a federal judge ruled that "an unlawful conspiracy may exist." This story required no digging; the *Arkansas Democrat-Gazette* had reported it in January 1992. Yet the tale barely made it out of Arkansas, Alexander Cockburn's coverage in *The Nation* being a rare exception.

Similarly, the media quickly and uncritically accepted the opinion of the Clintons' attorney friend that there was nothing amiss with the candidate's investment in the Whitewater Development Corporation, a judgment that would be badly shaken by the end of Clinton's first year in office.

Some stories providing a useful view of the political and social culture in which Clinton operated would appear in one media outlet but be ignored by others. For example, *Money* magazine reported that Clinton annually received about $1.4 million in admissions tickets to the state-regulated Oaklawn racetrack to hand out to campaign contributors and others. *Money* couldn't find another major racing state that allowed such gifts and quoted an authority on government ethics as saying, "It creates appearances of impropriety." Said the expert, "I'm stunned frankly at the amount. It's a staggering amount." The Clinton campaign's reaction to the story was that the passes, which have gone to the state's governors since the 1950s, are a "great nuisance," adding, "I guess the potential is there for a conflict of interest, but we never let it be a conflict."[13]

Nor were such practices a fluke. According to Brooks Jackson of CNN, the commission that regulates Arkansas's only greyhound track—the nation's largest—held its regulatory meetings several times a year at the track's exclusive Kennel Club, with the Southland Greyhound Park paying for the commissioners' food and booze.[14]

Once the media has bestowed *gravitas* upon a candidate it is reluctant to let contrary facts get in the way. Thus the media portrayal of Clinton quickly lost its Arkansas flavor. It was Clinton the Rhodes Scholar, Clinton the man of policies, who came to the fore, and Bubba Bill began to fade.

As simple political narrative this was a disservice. If there was one thing that made Clinton stand out among his political contemporaries, it was the complexity of his character, friendships, and past. Without such full—even if contradictory—details, the portrait of Clinton was destined to be more myth and propaganda than reality.

As such it was left to the conservative *Washington Times* to tell the story of how a convicted Arkansas drug dealer got pardoned in the middle of the Washington inauguration, complete with allegations that Clinton had reneged not only on payments to the dealer's father (who had worked on Clinton's last state campaign) but on his promise to help market the father's recipe for sweet potato pie.

The alleged deal provoked considerable discussion in Arkansas, but the national media was otherwise engaged, installing with proper sobriety the next president of the United States. To any aficionado of southern politics, the story roots Clinton in a long and engaging if not entirely honorable tradition. One southerner to whom I told the story remarked, "I didn't believe you until you said the part about the sweet potato pie."

But this tradition is at odds with what national statesmen are supposed to be about, and so was let pass by a media which, reported the *Washington Journalism Review,* was busy using the phrase "defining moment" seven hundred times over an eighteen-month period.

Not all the myths of the Clinton campaign were for public consumption. There were also the myths it created for and about itself.

Every campaign has them. It's one of the things that keep people working eighteen-hour days for little or nothing. When a campaign turns out to be a winner, these myths move easily out of the campaign boiler rooms and into the public consciousness. Camelot actually began in grimy halls in West Virginia, for it is on the campaign trail that the most mundane activities start to gain an almost sacred quality.

At the center of the Clinton team's internal mythology were some of the values that characterized America's upwardly mobile minority of the 1980s. Most Americans lost ground in this decade; the real income of a male worker with only a high-school education dropped some 15 percent. Gaps showed up everywhere. According to economist Robert J. Samuelson, the difference between the best- and the worst-paid college graduates grew, as did that between the best- and the worst-paid lawyers.

But there was a small group of winners, and the Clinton peo-

ple were among them. They had gone to the best undergrad-
uate schools and the best law or business schools. A few had
made millions during the eighties. They possessed boundless self-
confidence, a strong sense of entitlement, a willingness to work
extremely hard and long to win admission to the society of the
hypersuccessful, and were neither burdened nor blessed with no-
table institutional, family, or community ties.

Clinton and his team had grown up as many of the communal
support systems of society were disintegrating. Family, church,
and neighborhood were all on the ropes. Politics was also
breaking down: not only had the old machines faded, but the
parties were faltering and Congress was splintering. Extraordinary
national common symbols were gone as well: the Kennedys, the
Reverend King, and—just as the eighties began—John Lennon.
Young America entered the decade very much alone.

Thus the egocentrism of yuppie America did not originally
spring from greed, but from an apparent reality; it truly seemed a
struggle between oneself and the rest of the world. Quietly, and
unnoticed at first, the economy was following community into
disarray, and a Darwinian imperative took hold. Winning became
its own justification.

The Clintonites' sense of entitlement stemmed from qualities
they valued in themselves and others: intelligence, skill in communications, and a managerial ability to rise above the factions and
ideologies of everyday life.

The intelligence they admired was not that of the philosopher
or the artist, nor even that of a good street politician or business
entrepreneur. It was of the sort that excelled in the accumulation
and analysis of information and data. It was the skill of the lawyer
or academician who could find every defect in an argument and
compose every possible counterargument. As congressional aide
and former *Washington Monthly* editor Jonathan Rowe would say
during Clinton's first year, "The proposals they send up here are
term papers; they have no politics in them."

Politics has many traps for those who rely on rationality and
analysis, for it requires not only objective calculation but a blend-

ing of experience, morality, and knowledge into judgments that cannot be parsed and decisions that cannot be charted. And it frequently demands choices before all their implications can be calculated.

Further, skillful campaigners, no matter how brilliant their account of the inadequacies and injustices of current affairs, will not necessarily become wise or intelligent incumbents. The jobs are so different that one politician, burdened with the newly discovered problems of office, remarked, "Hell, I didn't want to *be* governor; I just wanted to be *elected* governor." When Clinton, the lawyer, became president, some of the decisions he faced seemed to propel him toward catatonia. In contrast, Harry Truman, the haberdasher, directly and simply made even tougher choices and yet slept well the same night. Clinton, seeing the possible flaws in a policy, would hesitate, pull back. Roosevelt, on the other hand, understood that government was a constant act of experimentation, and that experimentation included failure.

The second virtue, the ability to communicate, is one common to all animals. What distinguishes human beings, it has been noted, is that they can also think. This is not a mere quibble, because people who use the verb *communicate* a lot tend to mean something closer to a frog's *baroomph* than an essay by Emerson. In response to their communications they seek not thought nor an articulated response, but a feeling. We are supposed to *feel* like having a Michelob, *feel* like the president's bill will stimulate the economy, *feel* like all our questions about health care have been answered.

The rhetoric of contemporary "communications" is quite different from that of thought or argument. The former is more like a shuttle bus endlessly running around a terminal of ideas. The bus plays no favorites; it stops at every concept and every notion, it shares every concern and feels every pain, but when you have made the full trip you are right back where you started.

Consider again Mrs. Clinton's comment on the death penalty: "We go back and forth on the issues of due process and the disproportionate minorities facing the death penalty, and we have serious concerns in those areas. We also abhor the craze for the death penalty. But we believe it does have a role." She paused dutifully at major objections to the death penalty yet finished her homily as though she had never been to them at all. In the end, the president would propose fifty new capital crimes in his first year.

The approach became infectious. As the Clinton administration was attempting to come up with a logical reason for being in Somalia, an administration official told the *New York Times,* "We want to keep the pressure on [General] Aidid. We don't want to spend all day, every day chasing him. But if opportunity knocks, we want to be ready. At the same time, we want to get him to cooperate on the prisoner question and on a political settlement."[15]

If you challenge the contemporary "communicator," you are likely to find the argument transformed from whatever you thought you were talking about into something quite different— generally more abstract and grandiose. For example, if you are opposed to the communicator's proposed policy on trade, you may be accused of being against "change" or "fearful of new ideas" and so forth. Clinton is very good at this technique. In fact, the White House made it official policy. A memo was distributed to administration officials to guide them in marketing the president's first budget. The memo was titled: HALLELUJAH! CHANGE IS COMING! It read in part: "While you will doubtless be pressed for details beyond these principles, there is nothing wrong with demurring for the moment on the technicalities and educate the American people and the media on the historic change we need."

Philip Lader, creator and maitre d' of the New Year's "Renaissance" gatherings attended by the Clintons for many years, liked this sort of language as well. Said Lader on PBS: "The gist of Renaissance has been to recognize the incredible transforming power of ideas and relationships. And I would hope that this administration might be characterized by the power of ideas. But also the power of relationships. Of recognizing the integrity of people dealing with each other."[16]

There is a hyperbolic quality to this language that shatters one's normal sense of meaning. Simple competence is dubbed "a world-class operation," common efficiency is called "Total Quality Management," a conversation becomes "incredibly transforming," and a gathering of hyperambitious and single-minded professionals is called a "Renaissance" weekend.

Some of the language sounds significant while in fact being completely devoid of sense, such as "recognizing the integrity of people dealing with each other." Some of it is Orwellian reversal of meaning, such as the president's pronouncement after his first budget squeaked through: "The margin was close, but the mandate is clear."[17] This is the language not of the rationalists that the communicators claim to be, but straight from the car and beer ads. One might ask, for example, exactly what has really been transformed by the "power of ideas and relationships" at Renaissance other than the potential salaries, positions, and influence of those participating.

The third virtue claimed by the Clintonites is the ability to rise above the petty disputes of normal life—to become "post-ideological." For example, the president, upon nominating Judge Ginsburg to the Supreme Court, called her neither liberal nor conservative, adding that she "has proved herself too thoughtful for such labels." In one parenthetical aside, Clinton dismissed three hundred years of political philosophical debate.*

Similarly, when Clinton made the very political decision to name conservative David Gergen to his staff, he announced that the appointment signaled that "we are rising above politics."

"We are," he insisted, "going beyond the partisanship that damaged this country so badly in the last several years to search for new ideas, a new common ground, a new national unity." And when Clinton's new chief of staff was announced, he was said to be "apolitical," a description used in praise.

Politics without politics. The appointee was someone who, in

---

* In fact, the *Legal Times* found that while on the Court of Appeals Judge Ginsburg had sided only 55 percent of the time with liberal judge Patricia Wald, but 85 percent of the time with conservative Robert Bork.

the words of the *Washington Post,* "is seen by most as a man without a personal or political agenda that would interfere with a successful management of the White House."

By the time Clinton had been in office for eight months, he appeared ready to dispense with opinion and thought entirely. "It is time we put aside the divisions of party and philosophy and put our best efforts to work on a crime plan that will help all the American people," he declared in front of a phalanx of uniformed police officers—presumably symbols of a new objectivity about crime.[18]

Clinton, of course, was not alone. The Third Millennium, a slick Perotist organization of considerable ideological intent, calls itself "post-partisan." Perot himself played a similar game: the man without a personal agenda.

The media also likes to pretend that it is above political ideology or cultural prejudice. Journalists such as Leonard Downie Jr. and Elizabeth Drew don't even vote, and Downie, executive editor of the *Washington Post,* once instructed his staff to "cleanse their professional minds of human emotions and opinions."

"What part of government are you interested in?" I asked a thirty-something lawyer who was sending in his résumé to the new Clinton administration. "I don't have any particular interest," he replied, "I would just like to be a special assistant to someone." It no longer surprised me; it had been ten years since I met Jeff Bingaman at a party. He was in the middle of a multi-million-dollar campaign for the U.S. Senate; he showed me his brochure and spoke enthusiastically of his effort. "What brings you to Washington?" I asked. He said, "I want to find out what the issues are."

If you got the right grades at the right schools and understood the "process," it didn't matter all that much what the issues were or what you believed. Issues were merely raw material to be processed by good "decision-making." As with Clinton, it was *you*—not an idea or a faith or a policy—that was the solution.

This purported voiding of ideology is a major conceit of postmodernism—that assault on every favored philosophical notion since the time of Voltaire. Postmodernism derides the concepts of universality, of history, of values, of truth, of reason, and of objectivity. It, like Clinton, rises above "party and philosophy" and, like much of the administration's propaganda, above traditional meaning as well.

Like Clinton, the postmodernist is obsessed with symbolism. Giovanna Borradori calls postmodernism a "definitive farewell" to modern reason.[19] And Pauline Marie Rosenau writes: "Postmodernists recognize an infinite number of interpretations (meanings) of any text are possible because, for the skeptical postmodernists, one can never say what one intends with language, [thus] ultimately all textual meaning, all interpretation is undecipherable."[20]

She adds: "Many diverse meanings are possible for any symbol, gesture, word. . . . Language has no direct relationship to the real world; it is, rather, only symbolic."[21]

Marshall Blonsky brings us closer to Clinton's postmodernist side in *American Mythologies:*

> High modernists believe in the ideology of style—what is as unique as your own fingerprints, as incomparable as your own body. By contrast, postmodernism . . . sees nothing unique about us. Postmodernism regards "the individual" as a sentimental attachment, a fiction to be enclosed within quotation marks. If you're postmodern, you scarcely believe in the "right clothes" that take on your personality. You don't dress as who you are because, quite simply, you don't believe "you" are. Therefore you are indifferent to consistency and continuity.[22]

The consistent person is too rigid for a postmodern world, which demands above all that we constantly adapt and that our personalities, statements, and styles become a reflection for those around us rather than being innate.

Later, Blonsky (perhaps illuminating why Gennifer Flowers and the draft and ever-changing policy positions don't matter) writes:

Character and consistency were once the most highly re-garded virtues to ascribe to either friend or foe. We all strove to be perceived as consistent and in character, no matter how many shattering experiences had changed our lives or how many persons inhabited our bodies. Today, for the first time in modern times, a split or multiple personality has ceased to be an eccentric malady and becomes indispensable as we approach the turn of the century.[23]

Other presidents have engaged in periodic symbolic extrava-ganzas, but most have relied on stock symbols such as the Rose Garden or the helicopter for everyday use. Clinton, on the other hand, understands that today all power resides in symbols and devotes a phenomenal amount of time and effort to their creation, care, and manipulation. Thus the co-chair of his inauguration an-nounced that people would be encouraged to join Clinton in a walk across Memorial Bridge a few days before his swearing-in. "It signifies the way that this president will act," Harry Thomason said. "There are always going to be crowds, and he's always going to be among them."

As a postmodernist, Clinton is in some interesting company—such as Vanna White, of whom Ted Koppel remarks, "Vanna leaves an intellectual vacuum, which can be filled by whatever the predisposition of the viewer happens to be." Blonsky reports that Koppel sees himself as having a similar effect and says of Bush's dullness: "You would think that the voter would become frustrated . . . but on the contrary he has become acclimated to the notion that you just fill in the blank." And then Koppel warns: "It is the very level of passion generated by Jesse Jackson that carries a price." Clinton understands the warning and the value of the blank the viewer can fill in at leisure.[24]

Of course, in the postmodern society that Clinton proposes—one that rises above the false teachings of ideology—we find our-selves with little to steer us save the opinions of whatever non-ideologue happens to be in power. In this case, we may really have progressed only from the ideology of the many to the ideology of the one or, some might say, from democracy to authoritarianism.

Among equals, indifference to shared meaning might produce nothing worse than lengthy argument. But when the postmodernist is president of the United States, the impulse becomes a five-hundred-pound gorilla to be fed, as they say, anything it wants.

Michael Berman describes one postmodernist writer's "radical skepticism both about what people can know and about what they can do [passing] abruptly into dogmatism and peremptory *a priori* decrees about what is and what is not possible." The result, Berman says, can be a "left-wing politics from the perspective of a right-wing metaphysics," not a bad description, it turns out, of President Clinton's health-care policy.[25]

That postmodernism is confusing there is no doubt. Stephen Miller, writing in *American Enterprise,* quotes the editor of a collection of essays on the subject attempting a definition: "I have regarded Postmodernism as a theoretical and representational 'mood' developing over the last twenty years." Novelist and semiotician Umberto Eco says the term appears to be "applied today to anything the user of the term happens to like."

Certainly Mrs. Clinton found the concept troubling. In a speech some have compared to Jimmy Carter's maladroit oration on malaise, she said: "We are, I think, in a crisis of meaning. What do our governmental institutions mean? What do our lives in today's world mean? What does it mean to be educated? What does it mean to be a journalist? What does it mean in today's world to pursue not only vocations, to be part of institutions, but to be human? . . . We lack at some core level meaning in our individual lives and collectively."

Quoting a dying Lee Atwater as saying, "You can acquire all you want and still feel empty," Mrs. Clinton went on: "We need a new politics of meaning. Now, will it be easy to do that? Of course not. Because we are breaking new ground. . . . *It's not going to be easy to redefine who we are as human beings in this post-modern* *age. . . . But part of the great challenge of living is defining your-self in your moment"* (emphasis added).*

Columnist Charles Krauthammer cast a skeptical ear toward all this: "Heavy, as we used to say in college. Yes, there is more to life than power and prestige. Yes, there is more than politics and eco-nomics. Yes, life needs meaning. Most adults, I dare say, have come to these thundering truisms early in life."

Trite indeed, a fast-track lawyer's yearning out of sync with the 94 percent of Americans who say they believe in God. Another example of the current trend toward intellectual cross-dressing in which ministers mess in politics and politicians pretend they are theologians. Yet in the speech was a cry for something to grab, something solid in the moment-driven, symbol-pumped postmodernism of the life she and her husband have known. And she did touch on a common sense that something is missing, bet-ter expressed by UCLA history professor Joyce Appleby in the journal *Liberal Education:* "We live in an era of posts. The build-ings going up around us are postmodern. Our age is postindus-trial. Our literary criticism poststructural. We have postpositivist sociology, postbehavioral political science, and postanalytical phi-losophy: Ours is clearly an age that knows where it has been and senses that it is no longer there."

Later, she says: "We continue to think within a liberal frame of reference even as we chip away at the frame. What we no longer share is liberalism's potent, energizing, cohering faith in progress. The use of 'post' language to locate ourselves in cultural time indicates that we still identify ourselves through the old convic-tions. We have not rejected liberal values so much as we have lost liberal certitude."[26]

Of course, Bill Clinton, as in other matters, is far from pure

---

* Maureen Dowd provided a different view of the dying Lee Atwater in the *New York Times.* According to one associate, Atwater called in friends he had double-crossed and confessed his lies about them. Said the friend, "It was not a true conversion but just the best calculation he could make to settle old scores because he was scared. Lee was spinning his own death."

in his postmodernism. He likes facts and data too much. Writing about the president at the end of his first 100 days, Arkansas columnist Paul Greenberg remarked, "What the clintonized culture hath wrought is summarized pithily in one of the better chapters of Jack Butler's new novel, *Living in Little Rock with Miss Little Rock:* 'People . . . understood reality as machinery rather than God's own dream of existence, intelligence as information rather than judgment.' " Clinton might sell his programs with the postmodernist's flair for symbolism and indifference to truth and consistency, but he would head the most rationalistic government this country has seen since Robert MacNamara and his whiz kids attempted to purify Vietnam.

In *Voltaire's Bastards: The Dictatorship of Reason in the West,* the Canadian historian John Ralston Saul argues: "When the 18th-century philosophers killed God, they thought they were engaged in housekeeping—the evils of corrupt religion would be swept away, the decent aspects of Christian morality would be dusted off and neatly repackaged inside reason." Instead, says Saul, came "a theology of pure power—power born of structure, not of dynasty or arms. The new holy trinity is organization, technology, and information."[27]

Reviewing Saul's work for the *Utne Reader,* Jeramiah Creedon wrote:

> The new priest is the technocrat, someone who interprets events not morally but "within the logic of the system." Saul's point is that reason alone has no inherent virtue; it is simply an intellectual tool. In fact, when reason is allowed to unfold in an ethical vacuum, untempered by common sense, the results are apt to be terrible. The classic example is the "perfectly rational" Holocaust, planned by the Nazis with "the clean efficiency of a Harvard case study." . . . Reason has also created a recurring human type well suited to perpetuating it: the leader for whom calculation is everything.[28]

To embrace all of this—from cold logic to hip logos—and to

create a technicolor technocracy without drowning in the contradictions was a tour de force. To the trinity of organization, technology, and information, the Clinton team had added a spectacular symbolic sound and light show.

In *Work of Nations,* seminal Clintonite Robert Reich described the world's emerging new elite as "symbolic analysts" who spend their time "manipulating symbols."[29] Blonksy goes further: "Connotation today—far beyond advertising phenomenon—is no longer merely 'hidden persuasion' but is in fact a semiosphere, a dense atmosphere of signs triumphantly permeating all social, political, and imaginative life and, arguably, constituting our desiring selves as such."[30]

The Clinton campaign would ultimately become a victim of its own success in manipulating the semiosphere, for it would not only fool us, it would, once in office, delude itself. But in July 1992, everything was still intact, albeit after a few symbolic alterations in which the media gladly acquiesced. The message—what with Ms. Flowers, the draft, and the drifts—had gone awry. The campaign let it be known that the Clintons would be "reintroduced" at the convention. They were, and few seemed to find it at all strange or disingenuous, for we had become postmodern, too.

The convention at times looked more like a leveraged takeover than a political gathering. Clinton operatives were busy spinning off the unwanted assets of the Democratic Party—blacks, unions, the cities, and progressives, as long-time workers of the firm, from Jesse Jackson to Governor Casey, were told they'd have to take a cut in pay or that their services were no longer needed. If you took a loyalty pledge, you got a few moments on the podium and one sentence in the candidate's acceptance speech (where liberals were lumped with the homeless as among the pariahs of America), but after such cameo appearances you were expected to shut up and get out of the way so the lawyer-lobbyist kill-or-be-killed tough guys could turn the party into a lean, mean, and profitable corporation.

They didn't fool around. Even the language had a yuppie

baron's tone to it. One businessman reported getting a call from Clinton fundraiser Rahm Emanuel that began, "The governor's gonna be in Chicago next week, and he wants to see you. Bring $10,000 or don't come."[31] The day before the election, Clinton campaigner Paul Begala told a reporter the campaign couldn't coast, it had to "drive a stake" through the GOP's heart. And *Newsweek* reported Clinton responding to a Bush offensive by saying, "I want to put a fist halfway down their throats with this. I don't want subtlety. I want their teeth on the sidewalk."

After you cut through the talk about a "new covenant" and "inclusion" and so forth, much of the Clinton campaign was about political power in its purest sense. There was mention of "vision," but as they say in Texas, it was all hat and no cattle. These weren't people out to build coalitions or create a movement, only to win and make sure everyone knew they had. Later, *Time* would calculate that phrase "new covenant" had virtually disappeared by the spring of Clinton's first year in office. A check of five major newspapers found it mentioned forty-five times in July 1992, thirty-one times in August, but only four times the following April.[32]

To a few, the convention reintroduction via film and telethon rhetoric was bizarre and tasteless. Imagine, one Democrat suggested, FDR on the podium telling the full story of his struggles with polio or Harry Truman turning offstage *à la* Clinton and saying huskily, "I love you, Bess." But to many more, especially party workers desperate to end their twelve years of exile, it was an appealing and fully credible myth.

It worked, thanks in no small part to the semiotic sophistication of Clinton's glitzkreig, which borrowed from television's disease-of-the-week specials to create the shameless bathos of the candidates' acceptance speeches and then immediately proceeded to evoke every male buddy tale from Huckleberry Finn to Newman and Redford by sending its stars across America together on a bus. It wasn't Greyhound or, as *Washington Post* columnist Tony Kornheiser put it, "891 hard miles with a warm Dr. Pepper and a stale cheese sandwich," but nobody seemed to care. Nothing that would happen in the next three months would quite match it. Fortunately for Clinton, it didn't have to.

The eighties began with the murder of John Lennon. In the early nineties, Mark David Chapman explained it this way: "I wasn't killing a real person. I killed an image. I killed an album cover."

Within days of the election, Ford began running a TV ad using a voice-over that sounded just like Clinton delivering a speech to an enthusiastic audience. Or was it really Clinton delivering a speech to an enthusiastic audience? Or really Clinton selling cars a few days after his election?

We had helped put Clinton in the center of the semiosphere. He knew how it worked and how to work it. But did we?

Showtime

THE LIBERATION OF WASHINGTON. PICK-
ING THE ELECTORAL LOCK. LOOKING LIKE
THE NEW YORK SHUTTLE. THE FIRST HUN-
DRED DAYS: HOIST ON ONE'S OWN CLI-
CHÉ. UNDERRATING THE OPPOSITION.
DON JUAN POLITICS. FOLLOWING THE
BOUNCING RHETORIC. GERGEN TO THE
RESCUE. THE UNCERTAIN TRUMPET OF DEF-
ICIT REDUCTION. GOVERNMENT BY MAR-
KET RESEARCH.

In the last days of the campaign, Clinton ran a television commercial filmed from the window of a moving bus. The voice-over
said:

*Something's happening out there. A feeling. Call it hope. That
a country can move in a new direction. That the future is something to look forward to. Not fear. If that's what you're feeling, you
may have noticed something else. You are not alone.*[1]

The TV ad closed with a shot of Clinton and Gore in a crowd.
It had offered not a single fact, yet was one of the most truthful
documents of the campaign, political haiku catching the mood of
at least a plurality of the nation.

Even if you were one of those who voted for Clinton without
joy, you felt it. I disagreed with him, I did not trust him, but I had

never really doubted that I would cast my ballot for the man despite everything I knew. It was a simple matter of "compared to what?" Besides, I had abstained in the Humphrey-Nixon election and that hadn't helped a bit. So I comforted myself with Mae West's maxim that when faced with the choice between two evils, she always picked the one she hadn't tried before. I went to Precinct 27 and did what I had to do.

It was the sort of politics I knew, the politics of making the best of it rather than the politics of "hope," "renewal," or "meaning." If you grew up in a big American city—I had lived in several—you learned to vote for someone but not to brag about it. There were other things you learned about. Like short-pencil men.* Like the ward-heeler stepping behind the voting booth curtain to "help" my aged aunt. Like the wedding caterers loading the trunk of a police car with a case of champagne. Like in the last days of the last hurrah, the Massachusetts city council member who told me he couldn't decide whether the cops and firemen deserved a raise once you added in the "other money and things" they received. And the fact that I could count on the fingers of one hand the candidates I liked who hadn't turned out to be disappointments or, in one case, in jail.

It wasn't that politics lacked appeal. But if you're going to be serious about it—the way a racetrack aficionado is serious about horses—then the first thing you've got to figure out is what's fact and what's fluff, what you can believe and what you can't. Fantasies are for sex, not politics. And democracies fail not because of excessive skepticism about their leaders, but rather because of a mass illusion that everything is going to be all right.

So I voted for Clinton despite suspecting that he was unfaithful to his wife, his draft board, and his professed political beliefs. I also suspected that he had, at the very least, looked the other way when Oliver North set up his Contra operation in Arkansas, that

---

* A short-pencil man goes to vote early, but instead of casting his ballot, removes the paper in order to mark it inconspicuously with the party slate for the benefit of the next voter. The marked ballot is then cast and the voter gives the blank one to the short-pencil man, who then repeats the operation with each new voter.

the Whitewater Development Corporation wasn't as simple a deal as he made it out to be, and that he could cut ethical corners on two wheels without squealing. He seemed that great American prototype, the genial salesman. As aluminum siding salesman Danny DeVito said in *Tin Men* after losing his license, "Tell, me, where's it written in the Constitution where it says a man can't hustle? . . . All I'm doin' is sellin'. Where's the crime in that?"

Besides, second only to American pride in salesmanship is American pride in being able to resist salesmanship. After twelve years of pathological parsimony toward the needy and obsequious service to the needless, after tripling the national debt and decimating the national morality, Clinton at worst seemed an engaging and manageable hustler. We could handle him.

These were thoughts, however, that I largely kept to myself in the Washington winter of 1992--93. For local Democrats, the long night was over, and with it had departed all doubt. In some ways, the election was even better than Jack Kennedy's. Kennedy was a Massachusetts Irishman who assumed power in a still southern city. He joked about Washington's "northern charm and southern efficiency" and then set out consciously to civilize the capital. Clinton, on the other hand, not only was comfortable with the ways of establishment Washington, he had been its candidate from the start.

There were others—not part of the lawyer and lobbyist elite—who were just as happy. Clinton had selected as his running mate the greenest member of the Senate; environmental activists were delighted. Clinton made the most direct pitch to young voters that anyone could remember, and the city's young—especially those of political families or who had volunteered in the campaign—felt something rare and wonderful was happening. Said one twenty-three-year-old of Clinton's predecessors: "Think of, like, your grandparents running the country."

It was true. For twelve years a remarkably resistant gerontocracy had ruled according to the politics of nostalgia. In the end, it seemed not so much a battle over policies or program as a struggle for power by two generations of white men of the same political herd. As in an animal pack, the younger male eventually won—not necessarily in order to produce change, but perhaps only to renew the vigor and continuity of the pack.

Gays and lesbians had, thanks to their campaign contributions and Clinton's reciprocal commitments, found great cause for hope. By age and lifestyle, the city's young professionals connected easily with the Clintons, with the women among them particularly proud that a peer was in power at last.

In fact, to anyone whose political interests had been stymied for more than a decade by the most reactionary administrations since the 1920s, change and hope had suddenly become possible again.

There was another and much more practical reason to be excited. Whatever stimulus a Clinton administration might provide the national economy, it seemed indisputably a jobs program for Washington Democrats. It would soon develop that the Clinton people were getting résumés not in the thousands but by the tens of thousands, and that they were being scanned by a computer rather than by Vernon Jordan. There were reports that only the correct code (easily manipulated by transition workers trying to place their own friends) could save the average résumé from early dispatch to the paper shredder. Yet even such discouraging rumors failed to stem the flow of applications or the anticipation of their success.

In the midst of such euphoria, it was easy to lose track of what had really happened. Bill Clinton had won the presidency with 43 percent of the vote, the least any national winner has gotten in eighty years.[2] This was four percentage points more than Herbert Hoover received in his contest with Roosevelt, and two points more than Carter got when he was wiped out by Reagan. Election expert Curtis Gans noted that only 23 percent of all eligible voters had actually cast their ballot for Clinton, the smallest percentage since John Quincy Adams ran in 1824.

In January 1992, a *Washington Post* writer had declared, "One thing seems painfully clear: Clinton's candidacy looks kaput." In

March, Fred Barnes wrote a *New Republic* cover story headlined: WHY CLINTON CAN'T WIN. In May I had concluded that Clinton couldn't take the general election. Later, seeking explanation if not expatiation for my miscalculation, I went back over the campaign to see where I had gone astray. One thing seemed clear: the election had probably been decided in March, when growing interest in Ross Perot quickly increased the anti-Bush vote by about 15 percent. For the rest of the campaign, Bush's support stayed within a narrow range whether Perot was in the race or not. Once Perot had made it respectable to reject Bush, the voters never came back. After that it was just a matter of Clinton and Perot double-teaming Bush out of office.

Of course, if Clinton had run in a country with proportional representation, he would have been forced to create a coalition with either moderate Republicans or Perot supporters in order to form a government. Unlike most of the world's democracies, in America you don't need a majority to govern, you only need to be first. So firmly do we accept this notion that we are repeatedly surprised when a minority victor such as Clinton has trouble governing. We attribute the inevitable results of popular disagreement to a "failure of leadership" or "gridlock" rather than to an electoral system that doesn't even try to reach a consensus.

This truth is rarely apparent because American journalists are more likely to believe in the two-party system than they are to trust in God. They thus initially ignored Clinton's intrinsic weakness. Some in the media also credited Clinton with returning various political lost sheep to the Democratic fold. Based on the exit polls, however, Clinton got a slightly *lower* percentage of votes than had Dukakis from the young, independents, moderates, conservatives, and the middle class. While it is true that Clinton, unlike Dukakis, was in a three-man race, it is also true that one of the main arguments for Clinton's nomination had been his special appeal to such groups. And it is also true that against Reagan and Anderson, Carter in 1980 did just as well with the young, and better among conservatives. Where Clinton did do better than Dukakis was with college graduates (40 percent of the voters), white born-again Christians, Jews, and those over sixty. Despite media assumptions about the nature of Clinton's appeal, James Carville was much closer to the truth when he said, "We didn't find the key to the electoral lock. We just picked it."[3]

If Clinton had run his new administration like Carville ran the campaign, he might have had a more pleasant first year. Unfortunately, neither his ambition nor pre-inaugural mythology would permit such a modest goal.

There is a conspiracy of excess that develops at inauguration time. The president, the media, and the public all join in the charade, not unlike youths drawn to mischief that will ultimately result in punishment but seems too much fun to miss. A trifurcated political situation that six months earlier had been seen as possibly headed for a constitutional crisis was thus transformed by January into a mandate, a Mardi Gras, a "season of renewal," the beginning of the best 100 days ever, and one of those rare moments when a poet is actually allowed on national TV.

Clinton added his own touches. His administration was not only going to be visionary, it was going to "look like America." He was not only going to solve the country's economic crisis, but he was going to do it with the largest and most comprehensive domestic economic conference ever.

There were, to be sure, a few jarring notes. Parked at Little Rock's Central Flying Service during the Clinton economic meeting were more than fifty corporate jets. This amounted to about one corporate jet for every seven participants, not including those company planes waiting at other airports around town. It would also turn out that Clinton's cabinet, while diverse in color and sex, was remarkably uniform in other respects. In the fall of 1993, Knight-Ridder Newspapers published an analysis that found that 80 percent of Clinton's first 518 appointees were from the Washington-Boston corridor or the West Coast. More than half came from D.C. or its suburbs. His deputy treasury secretary, Roger Altman, was credited by his firm with the completion of four of the six largest takeovers of American companies by Japa-

nese investors. His commerce secretary, Ron Brown, had represented Baby Doc Duvalier. And major corporations would cough
up nearly $20 million in gifts and loans for the "populist" inaugu-
ral festivities while the inaugural committee was grossing addi-
tional millions from TV airtime, including the selling of the
previously public Lincoln Memorial site for HBO's coverage of the
Clinton musical extravaganza.

University of Pennsylvania communications professor George
Gerner told the *Washington Post,* "This sort of thing sends a message that everything is for sale in our country, even the presidency." A representative of General Motors, on the other hand,
said it was "a real marketing opportunity."

For Clinton, the inaugural pomp created a massive affirmation
of his message of hope and of the people's faith that he could
convert it to reality. It also created expectations well beyond anything that political conditions could justify.

As soon as the inauguration was over, the "100 Days" began.
Neither statute nor sense dictates such a period in presidential
politics. Clinton, still unpracticed in the baroque politics of Washington, certainly didn't need it. On January 12, press aide Dee Dee
Myers tried to declare the 100-days idea merely a figment of the
media's imagination: "People of the press are expecting to have
some 100-day program. We never had one." Unfortunately, six
months earlier Clinton had said, "If I'm elected, I'll have the bills
ready the day after I'm inaugurated. I'll send them to Congress and
we'll have a 100-day-period."

In the end both the president and the vice-president issued
reports boasting of their achievements in the first fourteen weeks
and two days of their administration. Clinton would have been
wiser to have told his aides, as Kennedy said to Ted Sorensen, "I'm
sick of reading how we're planning another 'Hundred Days' of
miracles." Or to have quoted from JFK's inaugural: "All this will
not be finished in the first 100 days. Nor will it be finished in the
first 1000 days. . . . But let us begin."[4]

He might have also considered the competition. During the

100-day session of Congress that gave the term its modern meaning, Franklin Roosevelt pushed through legislation that rescued the banking industry, slashed government pay, established the Civilian Conservation Corps, passed the National Industrial Recovery Act, provided relief for millions of citizens, regulated Wall Street, created bank deposit insurance, and set up the TVA.

Clinton, in comparison, reversed a number of anti-abortion regulations, signed a motor voting bill and a family leave act, and agreed to the global biodiversity treaty. While admirable, these were boilerplate decisions most incoming Democratic presidents would have quickly made. Other matters were underway but far from complete: a major change in the way that college loans were financed, a national service corps, and a deficit-reduction plan which, while somewhat slowing the growth rate of the national debt, was of highly uncertain economic effect. Clinton also proposed a timid "jobs package" (grandiosely calling it a "Vision of Change for America") that even before it was eviscerated by Congress would have disappeared with barely a trace into the gross national product. Meanwhile Clinton waffled on whether gays could join the military, and reversed campaign positions on a middle-class tax cut, the return of Haitian refugees, and Bosnia. Despite this modest and mixed record, Clinton asserted that his was "the most action-oriented administration in our memory."

Given political realities, there was no particular reason for Clinton to claim anything other than that he had made the best of a difficult situation. As GOP pollsters Fred Steeper and Christopher Blunt would point out some months later, the average new president starts out in office with a public disapproval rating in single digits. Clinton's, however, was 24 percent. Said Steeper and Blunt in the *Polling Report:*

> New presidents take office with a certain reserve of public trust and good will. Until a president does something to breach that trust, most Americans seem willing to give him the benefit of the doubt and report that they either approve of or are undecided about his performance. Disapproval becomes the "harder" rating;

voters will give approval without a specific reason, but increasing disapproval will have a specific reason.[5]

Clinton had started well behind the curve. Further, while the new Senate appeared to be comfortably Democratic, the chamber was actually divided ideologically into three parts. In 1992, based on the voting scorecard of Americans for Democratic Action, liberals held thirty-seven seats, conservatives held thirty-nine seats, and centrists (two-thirds of them Democrats) held twenty-four. There was nothing new about this: ten years earlier, near the beginning of the Reagan era, the split had been liberal, thirty-four; conservative, forty-five; and centrist, twenty-two.

Helping Americans understand the true political divisions of their Congress might have mitigated criticism of a president as he tried to bridge the gaps. But hubris got in the way. Michael Kramer in *Time* quoted a Clinton friend as saying, "Bill Clinton firmly believes he can exit any jam and gain any success simply because he's so smart and works so hard." Some months later Lani Guinier's mother would tell the *Boston Globe*, "I've had little boys like him in my classes, who are good looking and very smart . . . and think they can do it all alone. Well, they can't."

Clinton' s bright but arrogant staff tried to take Capitol Hill like an enemy redoubt. Early in the administration, Senate Finance Committee chair Pat Moynihan complained that no one from the White House was speaking to him. Said Moynihan to *Time*, "Not since November. Not a single call. Not from the president or any of his top people. I just don't get it." *Time* went to one of these top people and got this response: "Big deal. Moynihan supported Bob Kerrey during the primaries. He's not one of us, and he can't control Finance the way Bentsen did. . . . We'll roll right over him if we have to."

In April, with his economic bill in trouble, Clinton tried the tough guy approach again. Texas newspapers reported that Rep. Pete Geren couldn't get White House tour tickets for forty senior citizens because he hadn't gone along with the president's economic measure.[6]

Clinton was poorly trained for such tactics. He had come out of a small feudal state with a far more homogeneous legislature than the United States Congress. Accustomed to no more than a dozen GOP members of the legislature, he had never wrestled with a skilled and organized Republican opposition such as he found under the leadership of Bob Dole. And while he knew the general outlines of Washington's power structure, he lacked the personal details and long relationships that make the difference between pleading with legislators and subjecting them to a full-court press. When he tried to bully Senator Shelby, the Alabama senator merely rose in his state's polls.

Clinton also initially appeared to accept the great Washington and national illusion that Congress's primary job is to pass the president's legislation. So twisted have the proper functions of our governmental branches become that Senate majority leader Mitchell felt compelled in the spring of 1993 to remind the media that it is to Congress and not the White House that the Constitution grants the responsibility for raising revenues.

On domestic matters, the Constitution says that the president shall:

- grant reprieves and pardons
- appoint judges and other officers with the advice and consent of the Senate
- from time to time give Congress information on the state of the union
- "recommend to their consideration such measures as he shall judge necessary and expedient"
- "take care that the laws be faithfully executed."

The Congress, on the other hand, holds *all* legislative power, including the power to:

- levy and collect taxes
- pay debts
- provide for the common defense and general welfare

- borrow money
- regulate commerce.

While in the case of taxation, practical politics and common sense suggest that the president propose and the Congress dispose, this chronological logic has been turned into a distorted hierarchy of power in which Congress finds itself bludgeoned, blamed, and bamboozled.

There is, in fact, no reason why Congress cannot and should not alter any piece of legislation the president sends it. Unfortunately, this elemental constitutional principle is so poorly understood by the public and the media that even a president as beleaguered as Clinton initially dared not attempt to write off his troubles to the normal protective inefficiencies of democracy. Despite the personal cost to his own reputation, Clinton persisted in the illusion that he should, as president, be able to *make* Congress do his will. Only after being badly battered did Clinton take public notice of the constitutional balance of powers.

Clinton's ego also pressed him. Clinton, said one of his aides, is "a control freak." At the same time he seems sincerely to want to make everyone happy. This dichotomy helps explain the frequency with which Clintonian dicta turned into political donnybrooks requiring an unseemly and occasionally disingenuous presidential retreat.

The process sometimes worked like this: The president would approach a problem by seeking input from numerous sources whose views were within the bounds of the decision he envisioned. Having accumulated the input, the president then contrived a solution which represented the best compromise *he* could conceive and announced his decision.

The problem was that the compromise had really been achieved only in Clinton's own head. Little had happened politically. That would occur next, as the president leaked or announced his decision. Too often, hell broke loose.

Clinton's approach was modeled on that used by managers and CEOs. But people in business do not need a popular consensus, they only need to be right. In politics, on the other hand, the way you get someplace can be as important as where you're going. To have an effective compromise, the deal must be worked out by those whose interests are being compromised. This requires a more mediating and modest style than Clinton could master. It also required a far keener assessment of the various powers arrayed in battle. From gays to grazing lands, Clinton constantly underrated the opposition to his plans in his first six months, leaving a trail of braggadocio hacked into broken promises and wobbly compromises.

It was one of the oddities of the Clinton administration that a government so centrist in its politics should be so clumsy in reaching consensus. But neither could Clinton easily find ground on which to stand firm. The *New York Times'* Maureen Dowd noted:

> Washington is a city built on the swamp of compromise. But it is also a town that puts a high premium on stand-up, don't-blink, line-in-the-sand politics, a place where a bold image is often more valuable than a correct decision or a bold program. Attorney General Janet Reno learned that within her first days in town, when the city hailed her as a heroine merely for taking responsibility for the conflagration at the Branch Davidian compound near Waco, Tex., while Mr. Clinton stayed out of sight in the White House.

By reaching compromises only at the last minute and in an often unflattering manner, Clinton achieved credit for neither consensus nor courage. A D.C. cab driver remarked, "Everybody hits on Clinton for not being in the Army. I wouldn't want him there; he'd just cut and run."

What was perhaps most curious about the administration's first six months was that while it had doggedly sent its image and "message" out over every information highway and electronic dirt road it could find, it ended up with the worst popularity rating of any modern president at a similar stage and with headlines as damaging as *Time*'s June 7 cover, which showed a tiny Clinton looking up at huge type that read: THE INCREDIBLE SHRINKING PRESIDENT.

Other journals made the same point less dramatically:

ANOTHER FAILED PRESIDENCY, ALREADY?—*Washington Post.*

CLINTON SPUTTERS—*USA Today.*

AFTER DEFT FALL CAMPAIGN, PRESIDENT IS STUMBLING IN OFFICE—*New York Times.*

About the same time someone sent me a fax:

What's the difference between Bill Clinton and David Koresh?
Some people still believe in Koresh.

The Clinton people had ignored a few basic rules of Washington. They had missed the ubiquity of what the wily James Carville calls the "splat ceremony" in which "they run you up the flagpole and then you fall and everyone goes, 'Gee, what a shame.' There seems to be a cycle. You get built up and you crash."

And they had neglected to pander to a White House press that could match the Clinton staff ego for ego. As *Esquire* columnist Walter Shapiro put it, the former displayed a "puffed up self-importance" and was angry at a president who "could not pick them out of a police lineup."

The Clintonistas had learned during the campaign how to leap over the traditional media by such means as appearing on the television talk shows. "Larry King has liberated me by giving me to the American public directly," Clinton carelessly bragged at a correspondents' dinner early in his presidency. Writing in the *Washingtonian,* Barbara Matasow reported: "The Clinton treatment has come as a shock to White House regulars, who had grown used to the high standard of care and feeding established by the Reagan administration. 'Our reporters would come back from a briefing with Jim Baker or Dick Darman looking like they'd been to Elizabeth Arden, all manicured and pampered,' recalls *Newsweek*'s Evan Thomas."[7]

While the campaign and White House press might be miffed at their lesser role, the nature of the media was in fact rapidly changing. After all, during Walter Cronkite's last season, 75 percent of the public had watched the evening news. By 1993, according to *U.S. News & World Report,* the figure was only 57 percent. Further, the actual news portion of the CBS evening news was down to 19.5 minutes, 1 minute less than in 1990.

The Clinton people understood this and had discovered both the new media and the importance of local television. Matasow noted that the Clinton administration had an aide in charge of developing "new avenues of communications" such as MTV and computer bulletin boards. Clinton also invited state anchors and reporters to the White House for locally focused interviews. On one Saturday in March 1993, Clinton met with thirteen Miami journalists and news readers, then had similar sessions with others from California and Connecticut. Some months later, the Clintonites, in an extraordinary array of political and journalistic egos, would hold what amounted to a talk show fair on the White House lawn. This was also an administration, the *Washington Post* reported, where "each morning, communications director George Stephanopoulos anchors a conference call during which the far-flung press secretaries of the executive branch discuss the message of the day."

It was with no little irony, then, that in announcing the hiring of David Gergen as a top aide, the White House should suggest that it was trying to correct a failure of communications. Once again the very skills of which the Clinton people were most proud had let them down. As *Spy's* Nina Burleigh wrote of the Clintonites' love of polls: "These scientific forays are supposed to help Clinton appease lunatic Perotists; the fact that they haven't has only seemed to increase the polling frenzy of White House wonks, who, like well-trained rats, keep furiously pressing the bar long after the treats have stopped coming."[8]

Reviewing some of the matters being communicated, Clinton's problems were not all that surprising. For example: who did the president think would believe him when he said his appointment of Gergen showed "we are rising above politics"?

What reaction was a normal *Washington Post* reader to have upon finding the following concerning firmly promised cuts in the White House staff: "[George] Stephanopoulos said getting programs through Congress and establishing an effective White House operation take priority over an absolute 25 percent staff cut, which now seems to have fallen into the category of a goal."

Did Clinton really think no one would check when he said: "One of the things that no one notices is that I was the first president since anybody could remember that had every member of his cabinet confirmed the day after I took office. That was a manifestation of competence, getting them all up and getting them all confirmed the next day. That hadn't happened in anyone's memory."

(The *Washington Times* did check and found that Kennedy's entire cabinet was confirmed the day after he took office, and Nixon's was confirmed on inauguration day.)

And how were we to judge a president who claims to be both "mainstream" and "pro-change" in the same sentence?

Sometimes the president's self-serving "communications" bordered on parody, as when he bragged in Honolulu of his achievement in Korea: "I walked out further than any American president ever had, onto the Bridge of No Return, about ten yards from the line separating North and South Korea."

The dissonance between his statements and substance didn't help the new administration's reputation, either. This, of course, was not unique to Clinton. Dwight Eisenhower declared his administration's first 4th of July a national day of penance and then spent Independence Day morning catching four fish, the afternoon playing eighteen holes of golf, and the evening playing bridge. In 1992, Unitarian senator Bob Packwood wrote his Jewish constituents: "You and I must help Israel resist pressure to trade our historic Jewish homeland for Arab promises. Only during the Diaspora, when we were dispersed to other homelands, did the Jewish people become a minority in our own homeland." Packwood later insisted he never intended anyone to think he was Jewish: "It is not uncommon for me to speak in a personalized sense. I felt so swept up in the legitimacy of Israel's cause."[9]

The gap between Clinton's words and actions tended to be

less colorful, and more stealthily concealed. For example, he was able to blame a changed economic policy on the new realities of a revised deficit estimate—even though the revision had appeared in plenty of time to have been incorporated into his campaign rhetoric. Clinton's backtracking was also encouraged by his habit during the campaign of casually predicating a future he could not control, such as his promise to remove the ban on gays in the military, something that clearly would require negotiations by Clinton the president.

Then there were the simple inconsistencies. In May 1992 Clinton said, "I don't like to use the word *sacrifice.*" In January 1993 he said, "It will not be easy. It will require sacrifice." Throughout the campaign, Clinton attacked Tsongas for proposing an energy tax, cuts in entitlements, and a middle-class tax increase. As president, Clinton adopted these policies. As a candidate Clinton ran an ad in January 1992 that said, "I've offered a comprehensive plan to get our economy moving again . . . It starts with a tax cut on the middle class." That same month, he said, "I want to make it very clear that this middle-class tax cut, in my view, is central to any attempt we're going to make to have a short-term economic strategy." Almost precisely one year later, just before his inauguration, Clinton said, "From New Hampshire forward, for reasons that absolutely mystify me, the press thought the most important issue in the race was the middle-class tax cut. I never did meet any voter who thought that."

The swings continued after inauguration. On April 1, 1993, Clinton said of Bosnia: "We have a national interest in limiting ethnic cleansing." On June 3, his secretary of state said, "Bosnia involves our humanitarian concerns, but it does not involve our vital interests."

While Clinton and his aides provided earnest and at times convincing arguments as to why a particular promise had not been carried out, the quantity of these explanations became troublesome in itself. By spring 1993, *Spy* magazine had counted 100 Clinton lies, including the fact that the president said he wore a suit one size smaller than was actually the case.[10]

The media and the public seemed reluctant to call Clinton to account for his dissembling. Part of this hesitance came from the moral exemption often granted the sufficiently charming—the curse of uncritical forgiveness that can be to the recipient what a tumbler of vodka is to the alcoholic. Clinton, it appeared, had enjoyed this exemption his entire life. If he ever had paid a substantial price for not telling the truth, it is not on the public record. But beyond this was an almost desperate desire for things finally to be right, for the country to regain its course, for the words Clinton was saying to prove true. As much as the president, we needed the myth of Clinton, and when contrary facts intruded, one sensed at times more annoyance toward the facts than toward the president. Clinton was the music man coming to River City after twelve tough years.

Sometimes it appeared that Clinton couldn't keep a promise for more than a few days. Becoming an appointee or near-appointee of his administration turned out to be almost absurdly problematical for some. On the other hand, while less well-connected nominees found themselves digging up social security records for years past, Lloyd Bentsen—known on the Hill as Loophole Lloyd—flew through confirmation so fast that the Senate committee didn't even get around to questioning him before it voted. Only eleven of its twenty members were present, and those arriving a little late found to their amazement that their proxy had already been cast.

The arrogance and insensitivity with which Clinton exposed potential candidates for high office to public scrutiny only to unceremoniously dump them reached a nadir with the case of Judge Stephen Breyer, who was called to Washington from his hospital bed presumably to be named to the Supreme Court. A day later, Clinton named Ruth Bader Ginsburg to the job and then stomped out of a news conference when Brit Hume tried to question him on his erratic manner of making a decision. Said the hapless Judge Breyer, "The doctors took a fourteen-inch tube out of my chest for me to come down here and go through this?"

Except for the fact that she was in good health, the treatment of Lani Guinier was little better. After picking her to be assistant attorney general for civil rights, Clinton wavered and then ran for cover in the face of right-wing and southern Democratic assaults. Guinier had written a number of law review articles that challenged conventional voting rights enforcement efforts. Her grounds were solid; after all, the traditional tactic of creating minority legislative districts amounts to a revival of the separate-but-equal philosophy that brought on the civil rights movement in the first place.

Guinier had suggested a number of remedies, including a form of proportional representation, the use of super majorities (such as the Senate uses to end filibusters), and the rotation of legislative offices. While these suggestions were certainly debatable, they were hardly radical, having a provenance ranging from the practices of other western democracies to the civil rights arguments—in thirty-two cases—of the Reagan and Bush administrations. Guinier's logic, however, was ignored not only by white southern members of Congress (those most directly threatened by the proposals) but by much of the media and by the president himself, who called her ideas "inappropriate" (a standard Washington brush-off) and added the patently false claim that they were also "anti-democratic."

Ms. Guinier, unlike Clinton, had gone beyond the limits of Beltway discourse. She had applied logic and intelligence to an important problem and recounted where these had led her. To some this is called thought; in Washington it makes people nervous. It's that kind of town.

Harvard Law professor Randall Kennedy said: "I think this is one of the most vivid examples of the dumbing down of American politics I've ever seen. [Guinier] asked very tough questions about our democracy . . . and we're supposed to be against somebody for asking questions."[11]

Jesse Jackson asked his own question: "If one's previous writings or words were the basis for rejection, then how could one . . . drop Lani and accept as chief spokesman David Gergen?"

Part of the answer could be found in polling data. Within one month of the hiring of Gergen, Clinton had twice turned to the Reagan-Bush remedy for electoral discomfort, namely launching military assaults against despised minor world figures, in this case those resident in Somalia and Iraq. The bombing of third world countries had its usual calming effect on the administration and its critics and boosted Clinton's ratings a few notches. This was all that was necessary for another reassessment of his presidency by journalists, revisionism that was happily encouraged by Clinton's spinmeisters. The *Washington Post* quoted one senior Clinton aide as saying after the assault on the Iraqi intelligence center: "That's always an issue for a new president—'Are you willing to use force?'—and he left no doubt on that score." Bragged another administration official, "We were showing that Bill Clinton can take the challenge."

It was now time for a round of reportage admiring the president's turn to the right. The illusion that the president's troubles were due to an undefined "lurch" leftward had become one of the most popular journalistic clichés of the first year. After Clinton sacked Guinier for Gergen, *Newsweek*'s Eleanor Clift could barely contain herself, praising the president's "shift to the right" and calling upon him to have "the backbone . . . to make it stick."

(A few reporters identified the leftward lurch as a myth. *Time*'s Barbara Ehrenreich compared it to the "stab in the back" invented by right-wing Germans after World War I: "an instant myth designed to discredit all one's political enemies in one fell swoop. Ask anyone who hangs out in left field . . . and they'll tell you there hasn't been any lurching in their direction." And the *Washington Post*'s E. J. Dionne Jr. wrote, "The assertion about leftward drift is flatly wrong.")

In any case, the reassessment and the air raids provided only temporary relief; Clinton was headed for a showdown with Congress over the budget that even foreign distractions couldn't mitigate. Guided by his new mentor Gergen, Clinton began rephrasing the struggle, even suggesting to reporters from time to time that he was *only* the president and reminding them that Congress had a role in these matters as well.

Now no one took swipes at Pat Moynihan even off the record. The chair of the Senate Finance Committee and his House peer, Danny Rostenkowski, held the key to whether Clinton's budget bid was to be accepted or not. Although the story on the Hill was that Moynihan had written more books than Rostenkowski had read, the latter gave the White House a lesson in handling the New York senator. Rostenkowski admitted to the *New York Times* that Moynihan used a lot of those "linguistic words," but that they had both come from ethnic neighborhoods and walked in "the same field of eggs."

As the budget had worked its way to and through the Hill, it drifted far from whatever initial coherence it might have possessed. When Clinton had first announced his economic plans in February, he had, with typical restraint, said: "We have heard the trumpets. We have changed the guard. And now each in our own way, and with God's help, we must answer the call."

But what call? Rudolff Goldscheid, a sociologist in the early decades of this century, wrote, "The budget is the skeleton of the state stripped of all misleading ideologies."[12] If so, Clinton's budget and supporting legislation reflected a government torn between pandering and progress, austerity and stimulus, nastiness and compassion.

There were good things, often attracting the least notice, such as the president's educational loan program and the significant increase in the earned income tax credit—a direct subsidy to the working poor. There was more money for various social programs, a reversal of Reagan-Bush miserliness, and action on gun control. And there was even a reduced request for the office of the drug czar that hinted there might be a quiet retreat from the futile, brutal, and often unconstitutional war on drugs.

On the other hand, there was also a massive military still plodding along at average Cold War fiscal levels and a continuing deferral of attention to the nation's cities. And there were fifty new

justifications for executing someone, not to mention judicial short-
cuts making it easier and speedier to accomplish.

But most of all, the issue with the first Clinton budget was
dollars. As on many matters, Clinton had ducked and weaved
about this throughout the campaign. If, as Clinton later suggested,
support for his economic policies was a sign of patriotism, then it
is fair to say the president himself displayed disloyalty during the
primaries when he took a number of positions contrary to what
national fealty was now apparently demanding. The strength of
his post-inaugural economic convictions could be gauged by his
own declaration that he would not determine their nature until
as late as possible. Thus the Congress was being called upon to
reinvent America based on ad hoc political choices reached only a
few weeks earlier.

In the rhetoric of a previous age, we might have said that
Clinton had lied to us, just as, if not more so than, Bush did when
he asked us to read his lips. The preferred contemporary euphe-
mism, however, was that he was "addressing new realities."

And what exactly were these new realities? A somewhat higher
projected deficit than that readily available to Clinton from the
Congressional Budget Office in August, and, far more important,
an extraordinarily slow economic recovery.

At a similar point after the 1982 recession, over 6 million new
jobs had been created. At the same point after the 1975 recession,
nearly 4 million. But in 1993, well less than a million new jobs had
turned up in the wake of the latest downturn.

The public knew this, and polls consistently showed that it
preferred job-creating action before cutting the deficit. Even Clinton knew it. In October 1992 he had said, "You could raise taxes
a lot and try to balance the budget. You just make the unemployment problems worse." Nonetheless, after the election, Clinton would become a convert to the deficit-mongering school of
economics.

This school has been effective in obscuring what should be
obvious: reducing the deficit will not cut the multi-trillion-dollar
national debt responsible for the level of our interest payments;

rather, it will only slow its growth. To actually reduce the national debt, and therefore the cost of carrying it, our government would have to make a profit and apply the surplus to retiring the debt. Should such an unusual event occur, however, there would be massive pressure—including much from the same sources now complaining about the deficit—to send the surplus back to the citizens in the form of tax reductions. Given the nature of American politics, it is difficult to perceive of a time when a serious reduction in the national debt would be considered politically practical. Thus the real argument was over a politically unacceptable question: at what rate should the national debt increase?

It is also worth noting that even if Clinton had, say, raised public investment expenditures to $100 billion (comparable to British levels, but still well behind the Germans and Japanese), it would have added only about 2.5 percent to the national debt under the worst—and highly unlikely—possibility that it produced no new national income at all.

In truth, one of the most effective ways to lower an annual deficit is to make it easier for people to pay taxes—by creating new jobs and better incomes. A study in Maine, for example, found a decline of 15 to 20 percent in state income and sales tax revenue during the recessionary years. Even the best-run state can't handle that sort of retreat.

In March 1992, 100 economists (including 6 Nobel Prize winners) wrote George Bush and asked him to spend $50 billion on public works and education, to provide investment tax credits, not to raise taxes or cut government expenditures, and to forget about the deficit until the economy was back on track. On balance, Clinton chose a markedly different course, a choice based not on a coherent alternative theory, but on ad hoc political calculations.

The Clinton policy was not being driven so much by deficit figures as by a desire to capture those voters who went for Perot and those who think we are just one balanced-budget amendment away from nirvana. It was influenced more by fear than by logic, and thus we found Clinton hyperventilating over the federal debt with the best of the reactionaries.

Ironically, even Perot voters had a better handle on the situation than Clinton. Queried by the president's own pollster, three-quarters of Perot voters failed to mention the deficit as a first- or second-place concern. The economy was first. According to Stan Greenberg, these voters thought the deficit represented massive irresponsibility, but that "the solution is not austerity; the solution is responsibility."

Admittedly, many Americans are really quite ambivalent on the matter. Sen. George Mitchell tells of a real-estate group that visited his office with a nine-point list. The first item was to balance the budget. All the rest of the proposals increased government expenses. One member of the group explained that the first item was just "sort of like a letterhead."

Clinton's initial reaction was similarly to have it both ways: spend money to stimulate the economy *and* cut the deficit. Each segment of his program had another that worked against it. But Congress was beginning to stampede, and even Clinton's modest economic stimulus program was slashed to less than a billion dollars.

Clinton responded by becoming a convert to austerity. The inconsistency was nicely summarized by John Makin of the American Enterprise Institute in a *New York Times* op-ed:

> After arguing . . . that $30 billion more in stimulus spending would improve the economy, [the administration] has pushed for a package of advertised tax increases and spending cuts, which would average $100 billion a year for five years, as the key to a healthy economy. . . . There is no way to claim that if $30 billion in government spending is good for the economy, $500 billion in taxes and spending cuts would be better.

With Clinton's conversion to deficit-slashing, a three-way race developed between the Democrats, Republicans, and Perotistas to see who could starve the economy faster. Clinton, however, was at a disadvantage, since even with his stimulus program in tatters, he still needed money for various promised domestic programs. This meant new taxes. And while Perot had glibly advocated tax increases, that had only been talk. Clinton's taxes would actually be collected.

Clinton was, in fact, following in the footsteps of Franklin Roosevelt, who had come into office a would-be budget balancer. Before the year was out Lord Keynes, the economist, wrote to chide him:

> [As] the prime mover in the first stage of the technique of recovery I lay overwhelming emphasis on the increase of national purchasing power resulting from governmental expenditures which is financed by Loans and not by taxing present incomes. . . . The setback which American recovery experienced this autumn was the predictable consequence of the failure of your administration to organize any material increase in new Loan expenditures during your first six months in office.[13]

Increases in expenditures (and in the deficit) would become a hallmark of subsequent successful efforts to deal with recessions. What was extraordinary about 1993 was the lack of a political constituency for such a traditional approach. An economic McCarthyism had come over the country. Thanks to Perot, Robert Dole, and finally even Bill Clinton, to question austerity was to trifle with disloyalty. This time it was the national debt and not communism that lurked behind every tree.

In such an atmosphere, it is perhaps not surprising that none of the presidential candidates had tried to straighten out Marisa Hall, who asked at one of the presidential debates: "How has the national debt personally affected each of your lives? And if it hasn't, how can you honestly find a cure for the economic problems of the common people if you have no experience in what's ailing them?"

Bush was confused by the question, and in attempting to clarify, the woman said: "I've had friends that have been laid off from jobs. . . . I know people who cannot afford to pay the mortgage on their homes, their car payment. I have personal problems with the national debt."[14]

Each of the nation's economic problems had, in this voter's mind, been caused by one factor, one figure, then running about 4 trillion dollars. And while Clinton did gently suggest that her problems might not *all* be due to the debt, none of the candidates truly confronted her underlying misapprehension.

The national debt has a long history of causing trouble. Soon after the founding of the republic, Connecticut firebrand Abraham Bishop railed against a government then costing $42,000 a day. Washington, he declared, "begun on a system rivaling in expense and magnificence ancient Babylon, has been a sink for your money." And that was only 1801.[15]

According to Thurman Arnold in his classic *Folklore of Capitalism,* prior to the First World War "sound economic opinion estimated that a national debt of $500 million was all that our economy could safely absorb." By the end of World War I, the debt was up to $26 billion, so the Republicans set about to reduce it. In ten years they had cut the debt to $9 billion, an achievement that was shortly followed by the Great Depression.

FDR had run for office on the "tried and true principle of balancing the budget." Wrote Arnold:

> It was not lack of purchasing power but rather lack of business confidence that was supposed to be the cause of prolonging the great depression. Roosevelt was forced to abandon his devotion to the principle of a balanced fiscal budget in favor of measures which were absolutely required to keep people from starving.

Arnold added:

> Government spending creates a great deal of activity. It builds concrete things such as houses, which the economist calls "wealth." The country is not poorer for each additional house which is built. Yet it is thought to be poorer in terms of budget balancing.[16]

World War II, with its obligatory deficit-spending ending

the Depression, suspended the debate over whether purchasing power or "business confidence" was the key to a healthy economy. But with Eisenhower, the budget-balancers returned in force, resulting, Arnold wryly noted, in "the greatest peacetime deficit in our history and the greatest peacetime inflation."[17]

Although deficits, according to popular lore, are something created by Democrats, Republican administrations since World War II have added to the national debt at a rate five times that of Democratic administrations. Despite all the talk about "tax and spend Democrats" blindly parroted by the press, it was a top Reagan aide who explained indifference to the then $2 trillion national debt by saying, "You just don't see people running the streets to have the deficit cut." And Reagan himself once joked that the deficit was big enough to take care of itself.

With the single exception of Kennedy, every administration that has more than doubled the average budget deficit of its predecessor has been Republican. In fact, the much-maligned Jimmy Carter has the distinction of being the only postwar president to have cut the average deficit. One of the reasons for this is that Democrats, prior to the current president and Congress, have been willing to increase purchasing power by government spending during economic downturns.

American levels of public investment, in fact, remain well below those of other developed countries. Meanwhile the 1993 U.S. budget deficit, as a percentage of gross domestic product, was about the average for a G7 country, below the European Community average, and significantly below that of Italy and the United Kingdom.

Describing the Clinton budget as "about as humane an austerity program as a mainstream politician could devise," the *Left Business Observer* still projected depressed economic growth rates— "meaning lower incomes and higher unemployment—for years to come."

This was far from just a leftist view, although you had to root around in the media to find it. For example, the *New York Times* on May 29, 1993, briefly let readers in on some of the potential downside of deficit reduction while quoting several establishment sources:

- "The deficit reduction is an important drag on the economy and as it gets larger as years go by it becomes a heavier drag. Offsetting that is the benefit of lower interest rates associated with more coherent fiscal policy and lower deficits." —Donald H. Staszheim, chief economist of Merrill Lynch
- "Deficit reduction puts a drag on the economy in the near term; there is no way of escaping that. There never seems like a good time to do it." —Economic consultant Laurence Meyer
- "On the face of it, huge tax increases and huge spending cuts spell contraction." —John P. LaWare, a governor of the Federal Reserve Board

The odd thing was that the public seemed to understand the economics of the situation better than the politicians. Although not consistent on the matter, when asked to rank the relative priority of cutting the deficit and stimulating the economy, the voters regularly chose the latter. Immediately following passage of the president's budget in 1993, a *Time* poll found 72 percent of the voters declaring economic stimulus as more important than deficit-cutting.

The politicians, stampeded by Perot, didn't pay much attention to such matters, nor were they interested in applying their austerity principles to the Pentagon. The media played its usual role, which was to ask bankers for advice and worry incessantly about the reactions of the "markets." A typical *Washington Post* analysis before the inauguration fretted: "There are pitfalls for Clinton if he goes too far in trying to speed up the economy, however. Already, markets are afraid that he will seek to boost spending but not make a serious effort at reducing the deficit."

The truth of the matter was that the "markets" don't like social welfare programs and never have. If we couldn't engage in such programs at a time of extremely low inflation and interest rates, there would probably never be an occasion when they would be acceptable to the "markets."

Writing in *The American Prospect,* in the fall of 1993, Richard Rothstein gave a strong defense of Clinton's budget tactics and final results. He pointed out not only the political realities that Clinton faced but that the final budget contained about $24 billion in new revenues, mostly from the rich, that would be transferred to the poor through food stamps, immunization programs, and an expanded earned income tax credit that would rise 27 percent in 1994 and still more the following year. As Rothstein rightly said of the EITC: "This is the beginning of nonpunitive welfare reform, since the EITC rewards the poor for working; it does not create social service bureaucracies but fights poverty by increasing poor people's income. And since the poor are more likely to spend it quickly than the rich, the EITC expansion is simulative."[18]

Rothstein chided liberals for failing to observe what Clinton was really up to and for not giving him credit for progressive policies. It was an appealing argument until one backtracked to find the source of the impression that Clinton was a fiscal conservative strongly opposed to traditional liberalism. The source, it turned out, was not disgruntled liberals, who in fact had tended to be as mushy and timid in the face of their party's conservative juggernaut as they were in standing up to Joe McCarthy. No, the headwaters of these ideas were right in the White House itself. Rothstein was attacking liberals for believing what Clinton and the White House Office of Communications had told them. It was the White House that was obsessed with the deficit at the expense of explaining the merits of the earned income tax credit. It was the White House that chose to downplay educational loan reforms even though they were far more important than its showboating national service scheme.

While the White House and its journalistic admirers were quick to instruct liberals on why they should be satisfied with what they got, their tone became far more conciliatory with those on the right such as the DLC. Once again, the politeness of the party's liberals earned them nothing but scorn and lectures, while the right and the extremist middle got into the serious bargaining. The liberals were told, in effect, to take their earned income tax credit and their biodiversity treaty and shut up, and to understand that no matter what the president might actually say about them, he really loved them. It was a politics more suited for a John LeCarre novel than as a basis for a lasting alliance.

Following passage of his budget and a Jackie Kennedy–graced vacation on Martha's Vineyard, Clinton returned to the capital to find that views of his administration were as erratic as some of his policies. On October 2 we were told by the Associated Press that Bill Clinton was on a rebound: "Highlighted by the launch of its health care plan, the administration is enjoying its smoothest stretch yet, beginning with the narrow budget victory and continuing through the introduction of Vice President Al Gore's 'reinventing government' initiative and the hosting of the Israeli-Palestinian peace accords signing."

Less than two weeks later, *U.S. News & World Report* headlined a major story: DISASTER IN WAITING. EVEN FRIENDS WORRY THAT CHAOS IS GRIPPING BILL CLINTON'S WHITE HOUSE. Said *USN&WR,* "Many now worry that Clinton's basic operation is so flawed that it is incapable of handling a truly serious or sustained crisis."

When Washington journalists speak of a "truly serious or sustained crisis," they are usually referring to something foreign. God produces *disasters* such as floods and earthquakes. Domestic policies produce homelessness and high unemployment and similar *persistent problems,* but it usually takes another country to produce a *serious crisis.*

By such a definition, Clinton was having his share of crises. There was Bosnia and Somalia and Haiti, not to mention a Russian leader whom Clinton hailed as a democrat but whose administration was rife with corruption and who had suspended the national parliament, ignored the highest court in the land, fired the nation's top prosecutor, forced the resignation of the country's top judge, dismantled regional and local legislative bodies, shut down fifteen newspapers, censored others, and banned ten political parties.

Some of Clinton's binds, though, were of his own making. On

September 13, while staying at the White House, Jimmy Carter informed Bill Clinton that Somalian General Aidid had expressed a willingness to cooperate with an investigation into attacks on UN peacekeepers. Carter told the *New Yorker*'s Sidney Blumenthal, "We talked about Somalia at length. Primarily I wanted the UN to get off the military option—stop emphasizing the killing of General Aidid and proceed with a political solution." According to *Time,* Clinton asked national security advisor Tony Lake to debrief Carter. On October 3, eighteen soldiers were killed in Somalia. On October 14, Lake finally met with Carter.[19]

In early November, the *Washington Post* ran a story under the headline: HOW THE WHITE HOUSE RUNS AND STUMBLES.

But then just a few weeks later, the Washington press was standing in awe of a man who had managed to win congressional approval of NAFTA through pure grit and a style that reminded one aide of college: "You screw around, party too much, cut classes, and then you pull an all-nighter and pass. It's government by pass-fail." Clinton had given the media politics the way it wanted it: tough and with the clock going into overtime.[20]

By then even the Washington press had grown tired of using "defining moment," but the *New Yorker*'s Sidney Blumenthal managed to project the notion anyway in a breathless report:

> As [Clinton] committed himself to the fight, the stakes grew enormously. NAFTA was not simply about an accountant's ledger of jobs gained and lost, and it was not only about the future of American relations with Mexico and Latin America. It had come to encompass Clinton's ability to conduct foreign policy on an internationalist basis. . . . In the end, the issue was the power of Clinton's Presidency.[21]

Thus, it appeared, NAFTA *was* about jobs, but really only one. In a strange editorial on November 14, the *New York Times* said that "after weighing the economic pros and cons, NAFTA comes out slightly ahead." So why all the excitement? For the future shape of Latin American relations and "the vitality of the Clinton

Presidency." That same day NAFTA pit bull Al Gore declared that a defeat would be "catastrophic" to the Clinton presidency.

Such hysteria seems remarkable given the modest role that NAFTA had played in Clinton's campaign. Even during the initial debate, both sides spent much of their time arguing about job gain or loss. Toward the end of the battle, however, proponents began de-emphasizing economic arguments and started claiming that killing NAFTA would undermine American foreign policy. Why the sudden surge of geo-politics? According to Thomas L. Friedman in the *New York Times,* "The shift in emphasis is in part a campaign tactic. White House polling experts are convinced that the public and Congress tend to defer more to the President on foreign policy issues than they do on domestic or economic ones."

In this enterprise the White House received the enthusiastic assistance of the American establishment, including all former living presidents as well as Henry Kissinger, who declared that NAFTA was "the single most important decision that the American Congress is going to make in foreign policy in the term of President Bill Clinton. . . . I don't look at NAFTA as a trade agreement. I look at NAFTA as a new political orientation for the United States." If so, America was adopting its new political orientation under rules that prohibited members of its Congress from even offering amendments.

The *Washington Post*'s David Broder, word stylist to the political stars, also put a cosmic spin on the issue. He said that NAFTA opponents were "dramatizing a decade-long struggle to determine whether the Democratic Party will speak for the losers or the winners in the rapidly changing American economy and society." Among the former, Broder included blacks, women, union members, and older Democrats—"unfortunate, unhappy people" in the words of one 1984 focus group participant cited by Broder.

After the NAFTA vote was safely over, *Washington Post* media critic Howard Kurtz wrote a piece pointing out the predominance of pro-NAFTA voices among his colleagues. He cited a four-month study by the media watchdog FAIR that found the *Post* and the *New York Times* quoted three times as many NAFTA supporters as opponents. He then quoted NAFTA critic Sen. Byron Dorgan of North Dakota as having calculated the length of the *Post*'s pro-NAFTA editorials and op-ed pieces since January at sixty-three feet. Anti-NAFTA commentary ran only eleven feet.

Dorgan said, "The *Post* [and other papers] prefer to portray [NAFTA critics] as a bunch of backwards folks who just pulled into town in a pickup truck," while NAFTA backers are "always described as visionaries, statesmen and deep thinkers."

Post editorial page editor Meg Greenfield told Kurtz: "On this rare occasion when columnists of the left, right and middle are all in agreement . . . I don't believe it is right to create an artificial balance where none exists."

What both Kurtz and Greenfield forgot to mention was that Dorgan had tried without success to get his comments into the paper *before* the NAFTA vote, as either an article or a letter, but had been rejected.

FAIR's examination of the *Times* and the *Post* produced some other interesting results. For example, between April and July, only 6 out of 201 sources (3 percent) quoted on NAFTA were environmentalists. No labor union officials were quoted, and representatives of *all* public interest or civic action groups—whether for or against the treaty—were quoted only 7 percent of the time. This didn't stop the *Times* from proclaiming in August that business groups were stepping up their efforts for NAFTA "after months of letting unions and environmental groups dominate the debate."

FAIR found that more than half the sources in each paper were with the U.S. government, another 11 percent were with the Mexican and Canadian governments, and 13 percent were with corporations.

Although the corporate media were overwhelmingly pro-NAFTA, some perceptive comment did trickle into the mainstream. For example, the *Boston Globe*'s Steven Stark pointed out in September that the split between the country's establishment and its outsiders might be more cogent than that between Republicans and Democrats. NAFTA, said Stark, was "the quintessential Establishment cause." The political problem is that all presidential elections since 1976 have been won by the candidate who portrayed himself as an outsider, a trick Reagan managed to accomplish even when seeking his second term. Clinton, who ran as an outsider, proceeded to alienate liberal and conservative populists in a variety of ways: supporting gays in the military, hanging out with Hollywood types, and finally with NAFTA. What's more, wrote Stark two months before the vote, if NAFTA passes, Clinton and the treaty "will be blamed for every weakness in the economy for years to come."

Following the NAFTA win, establishment Washington breathed more easily. Although it was estimated that Mexico had thrown $30 million into the battle, and American corporations had donated a similar amount, the credit went largely to Clinton, who worked obsessively using every perk, penny, and platitude at his command in order to sway wavering legislators. It was generally conceded that such was a president's privilege; unlike similar alleged acquisitions of New Jersey black ministers, the purchase of members of the U.S. House of Representatives was still considered acceptable.

Since the media regarded NAFTA as a good thing, its passage—along with the subsequent cliffhanger approval of the Brady Bill—was cited as grounds for yet another revision of the conventional view of Clinton. As Congress adjourned, the media joined in the White House spin that declared the session a stunning victory. Pronounced Bruce Buchanan of the University of Texas, "He has a batting average that puts him up with the heavy hitters of the century."

As is its wont, Washington's hand was once again in the hyperbole jar. Much of the quantitative productivity of the first year—the Clinton people tended to evaluate legislation as though it were sacks coming out of a flour mill—was clearly the result of ending the party split between the White House and Congress. After all, most any Democratic president with a Democratic Congress would have passed such measures as family leave, motor voting, and gun control.

Meanwhile, not only was the problem of jobs and downward wage pressure exacerbated by the passage of NAFTA and the failure to approve a jobs stimulus package, but an ineffective, obnoxious, and cruel crime bill was making its way through Congress with the president's approval. It provided for a significant increase in the number of capital crimes and greater use of mandatory sentencing despite its clear injustices, including discriminatory treatment of minority drug users and de facto transfer of judicial power from the courts to the prosecutors.

But if the president had muffed foreign affairs and underfed the economy, if he had toadied to the domestic right in crime policy and to the multinationals in foreign affairs, it was also true that his attorney general had told the National Women's Political Caucus that "America would rather build prisons than invest in a child, and we've got to change that."

And if Joycelyn Elders had told the truth about legalization of drugs, it is also true that the rest of the administration rose as one to tell her she shouldn't have.

And if Al Gore was working hard to introduce new governmental efficiencies, it was also true that the Congressional Budget Office estimated that these improvements were not likely to produce even a third of the savings loudly claimed by the Clintonites.[22]

And if Clinton failed to cut the military budget significantly, it was also true that he was being undermined by a Pentagon that was circulating documents claiming that his slight trim job would leave the Army "substantially weakened."[23]

And if the president spoke often and loudly about his concern for jobs, it was also true that the administration had told economists in an off-the-record briefing that the nation would continue to have high unemployment until 1998.[24]

In short, almost anything one might say about the Clinton administration might be true for only one day, one agency, or one official. Its centrist politics were deeply postmodern—not those of steady moderation, but rather something one could derive only by computing the average of the various swings, leaps, and spasms of a government trying to hang ten on each wave of public opinion.

There were, to be sure, those in the administration whose politics had grown straight and strong and who, for better or worse, spoke in words and not echoes—Reno, Elders, Cisneros, and Babbitt stood out in the first year. But for the most part it was an administration built not on leadership, nor even compromise, but upon obsessive market research, a compulsive desire to win, and a working contempt for consistency and principle. It was, in many ways, a continuation of the 1980s by other means.

In Search of Clintonism

It is tempting to see all politics in terms of techniques, tactics, symbols, and strategies. This is how much of the press views the matter, a practice that tends to project Washington as an Olympics for political athletes whose performances are judged not by their value to the country but in comparison to their peers. As in conventional sports, the differences can be exceedingly small yet produce a cascade of journalistic superlatives.

It is for this reason that few Americans realized that the difference between all the budgets proposed by Reagan and Bush and all the budgets finally approved by the Democratic Congress was less than 1 percent. Or that the deficit reduction sought by Clinton and that sought by moderate critics ultimately varied by a similar amount compared to total spending. Grown journalists proclaimed—in the cataclysmic fashion of a play-by-play announcer describing the microseconds dividing a first- and second-place luge—that the presidency was at stake over these momentous gaps.

Political journalists, like sports writers, are enthralled by the mechanics of action, a fascination that results in our knowing much more about how a bill was passed than about what it contains. Such journalists, were they to cover a cross-country drive, might well do so by describing only what had occurred under the hood.

In Clinton's case there are other distractions: his charm, his emotional reaction to events, the unusual ease with which he moves among the country's various constituencies, his bouts of indecisiveness, the unpretentiousness of his style, the informality with which he wears power, and the sincerity of his unguarded moments.

Finally, as some of his admirers have repeatedly reminded me, there is for them the persistence of hope, a hope that has repelled months of bad news, bad moves, and bad luck. They see this hope, in the words of Erich Fromm, as being "like the crouched tiger, which will jump only when the moment for jumping has come." We are not wrong to be affected by such things or, despite their often gossamer form, to grant them a place in our view of Clinton, to enjoy and remark upon them.

But such considerations, like the mechanics and the scoreboard of politics, shed little light on the underlying beliefs, values, and philosophy of a president and his administration. The problem is not that techniques, tactics, style, symbols, and strategies are unimportant, but that in Washington such considerations tend to crowd out others, including the substantive nature of the change (or lack thereof) occurring as a result of the political activities so lovingly detailed. At best, these details can only describe the weather in which our experience happens. The experience itself is another, and less told, story.

Admittedly, in Clinton's case a philosophy can be hard to discern even on a sunny day. As the *Arkansas Democrat-Gazette* noted at the end of the presidential campaign, "It is not the com-promises [Clinton] has made that trouble so much as the unavoid-able suspicion that he has no great principles to compromise."

There is sometimes a dizzying ad hoc quality to Clinton's poli-cies. Perhaps this should be expected of a president who may be the first to have cited Machiavelli as a defense. Clinton often seems a political Don Juan whose serial affairs with economic and social programs share only the transitory passion he exhibits on their behalf. At times Clinton reminds one of the Right Hon. James Hacker MP, protagonist of *Yes, Minister,* the BBC's brilliant satire on British government. In a book version of the series, the "edi-tors" note:

> Hacker himself processed events in a variety of ways, and the readers will have to make their own judgment as to whether any given statement represents
>
> (a) what happened
> (b) what he believed happened
> (c) what he would like to have happened
> (d) what he wanted others to believe happened
> (e) what he wanted others to believe that he believed happened.[1]

The common defense of Clinton is that he is a pragmatist. In Washington, political pragmatism and political ideals are seen as mutually exclusive. The typical formulation of centrist politicians is that since they are criticized by both liberals and conservatives they must be doing something right, although they would never accept the corollary that a liberal must be doing something right for having achieved the wrath of both centrists and conservatives.

G. K. Chesterton, the British liberal and populist, was closer to the truth when he argued that the only place a practical politician could start was with the ideal. Any other commencement of the political journey invites the creation of illogical and unsatisfactory remedies. The ideal provides a constant and necessary naviga-tional marker from which one can compute a compromise's true cost in distance and time. Without such a marker, a purposeful trip becomes mere random motion. In politics, this can—over the years—produce things as baroque as our current health-care system, in which directionless compromises have been lumped one upon the other, leaving us finally, as health activist Dr. Jerry Liebman has noted, with a system that *nobody* wanted.

A politics as pragmatic as Clinton's easily becomes a process without a point. That there is nothing that can be simply identified as Clintonism may help to explain why the Clinton administration got off to such a rocky start. Yet while it may be presumptuous to ascribe a philosophy to a man so dedicated to avoiding one, even a politician of such intensely situational values and policies leaves clues. Here, then, is a preliminary taxonomy of Clintonism:

The Taxonomy of Clintonism

The Politics of Better Than

Bill Clinton is better than Bush, his administration is better than Bush's, his policies are better than Bush's, his budget is better than Bush's. For Clinton supporters this is the line in the sand. Nothing has been said to me more often in the president's defense. But why does one feel compelled to profess what in earlier Democratic administrations would have been a foregone conclusion? And why does the case for Clinton then seem to peter out? In the early months of the Clinton administration, Christopher Hitchens described the atmosphere in Washington as being like that in *Peter Pan,* in which the children are told that if they stop clapping, Tinker Bell will die.

Voting for a candidate does not carry with it a vow of silence. Certainly conservative supporters of Clinton like Senators Nunn and Boren have felt no such compunction. While progressives and liberals tried faithfully not to rock the boat, Clinton's conservative constituency clomped about, happily jettisoning every progressive policy it found hidden in the bilge or forepeak. While the left was biting its tongue, the right was playing for keeps.

They're Trying

Where it doesn't do better, it is argued that the Clinton administration is at least trying. This is often true. As one activist who has spent many years battling the federal government put it: "With the right sort of information you can shame them into action. The former administration had no shame. . . . You'd catch those folks and they would be proud of it."

Changing Places on the Bus

Clinton is more committed to sexual and ethnic equity in high public office than were any of his predecessors. Of his first 518 appointees, 36 percent were women, and 22 percent were minorities. His attempt to provide equity for homosexuals in the military represented a sincere if badly bungled effort to correct a serious wrong.

On the other hand, there have been few policies or proposed measures that would empower the masses of American minorities the way Clinton has empowered a handful of their elites. Clinton's legislative approach can be most kindly described as that of a moderate Republican. He has shown minimal interest beyond the symbolic in urban America or in the specific problems of minorities. His domestic programs sometimes seem little more than efficient Reaganism: enterprise zones that work better, the real abolishment of welfare, and so forth. He has moved some people to the front of the bus, but is the bus going anywhere?

An Environmental Haze

Clinton's environmental policies will surely be better than anything seen in the U.S. in over a decade. This, however, will only be an average. There will be plenty of environmental causes that will feel, in the manner of one of cartoonist Bill Mauldin's foxhole characters, "like a fugitive from the law of averages."

Environmentalists are divided on what can and should be expected from Clinton and Gore. There are a number of theories as to what is going on. In one, Al Gore is seen as being to the environmental movement what Dan Quayle was to the Republican right. Quayle served to neutralize the right because it couldn't attack Bush without embarrassing Quayle. Gore presents a similar obstacle to the greens.

Another and more optimistic thesis is that the Clinton administration is essentially saying: Look, we're not going to talk about the environment that much, but watch all the little things we do. An example of this is the unheralded attempt by Interior's Bruce Babbitt to institute important biological and ecosystem mapping of the U.S.

It's confusing. I asked one major environmental activist whether Al Gore was an honest broker, whether he was just sitting in the Veep's office feeling miserable, or whether he was playing both sides of the environmental issues. Probably some combination of all three, she told me.

While a division in the environmental movement—perhaps mirroring social class and sources of funding—has developed over NAFTA and some other issues, even the president of the well-mannered National Wildlife Federation denounced Clinton's back-tracking on grazing fees by saying of the greens' relationship with the White House, "What started out as a love affair [has turned into] date rape." And Defenders of Wildlife president Rodger Schlickeisen said, "Simply doing better than Bush isn't good enough. This can't be as good as it gets."[2] On the other hand, when *Mother Jones* asked various environmental leaders to score Clinton, the Rainforest Action Network's Randy Hayes gave him a solid B, although noting, "The earth needs an A+ or we're still in trouble."

The Return of Progressivism

Clinton's political philosophy is heavily influenced by old-style progressivism, with its faith in efficiency and in government by experts. The strength of this approach can be seen in Al Gore's attempt to reduce waste in government. It can also be observed in the quality of many of Clinton's appointments.

There is no doubt that, if rigorously and enthusiastically applied, efficiency can make a difference. Labor Secretary Robert Reich, for example, accomplished the following within eight months: eliminated 8 of 13 advisory committees not required by law; eliminated 8 of 14 internal reports; eliminated 165 of 359 interagency committees; and ordered the use of departmental credit cards for purchases to bypass the government's complex purchasing system.

On the other hand, the weakness of this approach can also be seen in Al Gore's attempt to reduce waste in government. Behind this effort is an assumption that government's problems are those of management, efficiency, or—in the current cliché—governance, rather than those of policy, program, and purpose. Improving the efficiency with which the Pentagon buys redundant equipment or speeding up the ease with which corporations gain permits to cause environmental damage is ultimately an unproductive efficiency.

The weakness can also be seen in the quality of many of Clinton's appointments. Not only is there a strong strain of elitism, but there is the expert's tendency to propose policies that have no popular provenance. One of the most striking characteristics of the "managed competition" idea in health care was that no one other than a small elite of academicians and corporate lobbyists had ever heard of it, let alone tried it out, before it became a major political issue. Clinton's health plan was a theory in search of proof, politics from the top down.

The Farley Factor

The late Democratic Party chair Jim Farley said that his father taught him a fundamental principle of politics: Just remember, son, that behind every Democratic president, no matter how bad, are other Democrats, and behind every Republican president, no matter how good, are other Republicans.

Whatever the faults of Bill Clinton, no matter how far the Democratic Party has strayed from its former politics of decency and justice, there remain those other Democrats, often in little-noticed places, keeping their piece of the faith alive.

Thus we can, for a while at least, expect relief from such cant as the judgment of the Bush Justice Department official who said that "with environmental crimes, you have decent people doing bad things." Gone are the platoons of mean, puerile little men stoking the policy fires of the Reagan-Bush years. In their place we find increased AIDS funding, the arts once more treated with integrity, a man who likes his trees vertical running the Forest Service, and immigrants once again being encouraged to become U.S. citizens.

Even Clinton, despite a compulsive urge to rid the party of anything that might annoy Sam Nunn, retains enough traditional Democratic clay to go sometimes into battles that a meaner pol might avoid, and to weep occasionally at the thought of what really needs to be done. There is plenty that is false about Bill Clinton, but this is not part of it. The good and the not-good-at-all are constantly in battle within the man and, unusual for a politician, the struggle is close enough to the surface of his personality and his speech that it serves as a metaphor for the similar conflict within the collective mind of America. That Clinton can embrace a black minister while, on another occasion, gaining cheap mileage with a slap at a black rapper, that he can so strongly support both capital punishment *and* day care, reflects accurately, if brutally, the unresolved conflicts of America itself.

Make Profits Not War

Bill Clinton's problems have seemed to intensify with their distance from Washington. It appears that we have had an infinite number of intractable foreign affairs, but without a foreign policy to handle them. There were, for Americans, uniquely humiliating scenes such as the fleet turning back from Haiti in the face of a small gang of island thugs and our near-total impotence during the Bosnian massacres.

Part of the problem, it seemed, was the president's impatience with and indifference to non-domestic matters. Yet even this might not have mattered so much if he could have successfully delegated foreign concerns to his secretaries of state and defense and to his national security advisor. All three of these men, however, were products of the Cold War. They were trained in the macro-politics of a conflict that each side wished to maintain just short of actual battle, rather than in the micro-skills required to end the gratuitous violence of guerrilla warfare. They were accustomed to the orderliness of great power disputes and not the viciousness of freelance ethnic cleansing. And they seemed somewhat at a loss in a world that no longer gave them a despised ideology. Coleman McCarthy quotes Georgy Arbatov, one of Gorbachev's assistants, as saying during the rise of détente that the Soviet Union was planning something horrible for Americans: "We are going to deny you an enemy."[3]

The problem, however, went far beyond Clinton and America. On any scale that mattered, there simply was not a profession of peace. What existed seemed random, as when a Norwegian brought the Israelis and Palestinians down from their battlements or when a lone French general in Bosnia accomplished more than all of NATO combined. There is literature, scholarship, and empirical experience in making peace, but it just hasn't interested us that much.

This absence of a protocol of peace, combined with Clinton's unfamiliarity with foreign affairs, clearly caused problems. At the same time, the president's instincts seemed, on average, more soundly placed than those of his immediate predecessors. Perhaps what was most encouraging was Clinton's apparent willingness to share the world with others, to at least experiment with something other than unquestioned American preeminence in multinational peacemaking, and to at least be willing to negotiate the complaints of other countries on issues such as the environment.

Thus, despite the considerable and obvious foreign-affairs troubles of the Clinton administration, despite sporadic displays of machismo designed more for domestic than foreign consumption, there has been at least a probing for something more reasonable and decent in international dealings than that to which we have become accustomed.

Yet if one wishes to find a real Clinton foreign policy, such places as Bosnia, Somalia, and the UN are the wrong places to look. The real Clinton foreign policy is simply this: there are no foreign countries anymore, there are only undeveloped markets. The slogan has become "Make quarterly earnings growth, not war!" Trade has replaced ideology as the engine of foreign affairs.

At one level this should be celebrated, since it is far less deadly. On the other hand, this development also means that politics, nationhood, and the idea of place itself are being replaced by a huge, amorphous international corporate culture that rules not by force but by market share. This culture, in the words of French writer and advisor to François Mitterand Jacques Attali, seeks an "ideologically homogenous market where life will be organized around common consumer desires."

It is a world that will become increasingly indifferent to local variation. Marshall Blonsky, writing of the Disneyland outside of Paris, noted the absence of Babar. And when Attali speaks of American influence he says: "We have to build a word which would be 'New York–Hollywoodization.' Because we are not Americanized in the sense that we are not going to be closer to St. Louis, Mo., or some place else. These countries are far from us and we are far from them. They are less in advance, less influencing than New York and Hollywood."[4]

Here is a world in which Babar loses out to Mickey Mouse in France and where a sophisticated Frenchman speaks of St. Louis—but not Hollywood or Manhattan—as a foreign country. It is the world of what Blonsky calls International Man.

International Man—and *he* is mainly just that—is unlocalized. He wears a somewhat Italian suit, perhaps a vaguely British regimental tie, a faintly French shirt and shoes—says International Man Furio Columbo, president of Fiat USA—"with an element of remembering New England boats and walking on the beach." As Blonksy puts it, "You self-consciously splice genres, attitudes, styles."[5]

International Man thrives in Washington. At the moment you call, though, he may well be in Tokyo, Bonn, or London sharing with colleagues who are nominally Japanese, German, or British their common heritage in the land of the perpetually mobile.

It is this unnamed country of international law, trade, and finance, with its anthem to "global competition in the first half of the 21st century," that is increasingly providing the substance and the style to our politics. It is their dual citizenship in America and in the Great Global Glob that characterizes the most powerful among us, now more than ever including even our own political leaders.

International Man dreams of things like NAFTA and GATT and then gets them passed. And he knows that he, as a corporate executive or licensed professional, will pass quickly through Mexican customs in his somewhat Italian suit and shoes with a hint of a New England beach because the agreement he helped to draft and pass has declared him entitled to such consideration. The union worker, the tourist from St. Louis, are, under the new world order, from far countries, and so it will take a while longer. This, then, is the Clinton foreign policy: it is the policy of International Man, a policy that brings Mexico City ever nearer and starts to make St. Louis a stranger in its own land.

Faith in the Meritocracy

While Clinton believes in a meritocracy, it is far from clear what happens to those not skilled or lucky enough to join it. Nothing that Clinton has proposed to date suggests real concern over the growing disparities in the American economy and the failure of sainted "market forces" to correct them. Here is what Clinton said in an interview in *Rolling Stone* during the campaign: "We are going to have to reconcile ourselves not to being a hard-work, low-wage country but to having a higher percentage of people at lower wage levels." Clinton understands this sort of economy. It is why businesses flocked to Arkansas. Clinton bragged of a 19 percent increase in jobs there, but what he didn't add was that the average manufacturing wage in his state put Arkansas forty-eighth in the nation.[6] Arkansas is also where, according to *The Nation,* a much-touted industrial development commission bragged to prospective corporations about the state's anti-union climate and gave one company a $300,000 loan guarantee so it could build up inventory against a possible UAW strike.

The Clinton people not only don't seem bothered by a two-tiered economy—a well-paid elite (Robert Reich's "fortunate fifth") supported by low-paid manufacturing and service workers—but consider it inevitable in view of competitive pressures from abroad. This may be why so many in the Washington establishment speak of layoffs as "dislocations" in tones suggestive of a mosquito bite. And it may be why Clinton could go along with a free trade agreement as unfavorable to American workers as NAFTA, with its "downward harmonization" of wages presaging at some distant time a "level playing field" when we become competitive once more.

Civil Liberties in Storage

Clinton has barely mentioned civil liberties. They do not seem to be of much concern. The president has, in fact, engaged in the worst kind of politics, namely the kind that trades human life and suffering (e.g., capital punishment and mandatory sentences) for popular support. He appears willing to ignore the great residue of Reagan-Bush offenses, especially those growing out of the war on drugs and attempts to gag and intimidate government and defense workers. And he seems similarly disinterested in unclosed cases of political racketeering such as those involving BCCI and BNL. Said one activist lawyer who has met with Attorney General Reno: "She's closing her ears to all of that."

Reno, who was clearly more interested in protecting law enforcement agencies than in finding the truth about the Waco massacre, also early bought the Bush administration line in the BNL bank case. She agreed to a plea bargain by Christopher P. Drogoul, the former Atlanta manager of the Italian bank who had claimed that U.S. intelligence officials were aware of loans made to Iraq. Reno declared that she did not think the case had been mishandled by the Bush administration, despite a federal judge's charge that Drogoul and his Atlanta bank colleagues were "pawns and bit players" in a secret deal to provide arms for Iraq and that the Clinton administration's exoneration of its predecessors was possible only "in never-never land."[7]

The Clinton administration was also doing little to reform the Bush administration's urban pacification program known as "Weed and Seed." In theory, the program was meant to weed out the worst criminal elements in a community and then seed the neighborhood with social services. In fact, social services made up only a fifth of the budget, and the program is primarily used as one more weapon in America's paramilitary occupation of its inner cities. Further, even the social services were hostage to police purposes and involvement. Eight out of ten social service proposals from the city of Seattle, for example, were rejected for being soft on crime or not having a big enough police component.

In recent years the police have increasingly widened their influence over local politics. New York City's new police commissioner, William J. Bratton, saw nothing strange, for instance, in promising to keep the public schools open at night to serve as sanctuaries for neighborhoods. However worthy the idea, this formerly would have been a matter for school officials and not the police. In other cities, activists have expressed concern about the commingling of community policing and the delivery of social services, with its potential for withholding these services to those who, for example, refuse to become police informers. We can expect little help from Clinton in such matters.

Organizing the Economy

Clinton favors using the state to organize the economy and subsidize the oligopolies that increasingly control it. His stances on trade, research and development, and health care all provide examples of this predisposition. The enormous underlying premise—that the bonding of political and corporate America is a virtue—is not even subject to debate. We shall return to this matter shortly.

Regimenting the Poor

Finally, there is a coercive edge to some of Clinton's programs. The only way that many so-called New Democrats can justify social programs is to give them a punitive quality. The Clintonites love to say that rights must be balanced by responsibilities, although they consistently avoid the latter term when referring to business and campaign contributors. Under the New Democrat paradigm, the government becomes a giant nanny. It is not enough to be poor to receive assistance; one must be poor *and* responsible.

It is an insistence at odds with the spirit of the Declaration of Independence and the Constitution, whose authors had considered our rights "unalienable" and who were quite willing to assign specific tasks to elected officials but did not even require the ordinary citizen to vote. It is not that citizens do not have moral or social responsibilities, it is just that it diminishes a democracy to have the state judge and assign them. When a right is contingent on good behavior, it is no longer a right but a privilege. The goal ceases to be life, liberty, and the pursuit of happiness and instead becomes good deportment.

Clinton seems to believe in an innocent poor and a not-so-innocent poor. The former include children, for whom his administration is prepared to provide considerable assistance in the form of education and health care. On the other hand, Arkansas parents who fail to attend meetings with their teachers can be fined fifty dollars, and students below a certain grade level can be denied a driver's license. Clinton has also backed boot camps for minor offenders and national exams for students in order to push them to "meet world-class standards," and favors a form of workfare for welfare recipients. While Clinton was governor, the Arkansas welfare office even gave its women clients a questionnaire that asked about their sexual partners.[8]

It is true that Clinton is not out of step with the American public on such issues. A majority of the American public would drop welfare assistance after a specified time, even in areas of high unemployment. Overwhelming numbers favor what amounts to forced labor for the poor.[9]

But the public reached this dismal state in no small part because politicians like Clinton repeatedly cheered such misanthropic inclinations in their campaigns and enacted them into law once elected. Added to endemic political cowardice and demagoguery has been the failure of politicians to correct the chronic unemployment that is the primary cause of both large welfare rolls and the paranoia over them. The aggregate effect has been the growth of a paternalistic authoritarianism in which the state becomes *in loco parentis,* even—as in the case of welfare recipients—for parents.

The potential for variations on this theme is stunning. For example, the state of Wisconsin has introduced a form of "workfare" requiring that some recipients attend motivational workshops and withholds part of the monthly welfare payments to parents whose children are chronic truants. Maryland cuts payments if children miss health checkups or shots. New Jersey gives a bonus to women who get married, then effectively docks them for having children. The state's governor, Jim Florio, proposed in his unsuccessful reelection bid that welfare benefits be denied any woman who refused to identify the father of her child, a plan that was too much for even his Republican opponent.[10]

Real welfare reform would mean raising welfare payments to nearer the poverty level. Real welfare reform would mean regarding current chronic levels of unemployment as a crisis and not economic normalcy. Real welfare reform would be instituting something along the lines of the pay vouchers advocated by Jerry Brown in order to ease the transition from dependency to employment. Real welfare reform would repeal disincentives to work— such as unrealistic limits on income and assets—that were imposed not by "welfare queens" but by politicians. Real welfare reform would be a shorter workweek to open up new jobs. And it would assume, as did a study by Christopher Jencks and Kathryn Edin, that "single mothers do not turn to welfare because they are pathologically dependent on handouts or unusually reluctant to work—they do so because they cannot get jobs that pay better than welfare."[11]

As Mimi Abramovitz and Frances Fox Piven noted in the *New York Times:* "In fact, the welfare rolls stabilized in the early 1970s at about 3.6 million families and began to grow only with the 1989 recession. Even now, Aid to Families With Dependent Children accounts for only one percent of the federal budget, or about $22 billion a year. . . . No state brings families up to the poverty line, even when food stamps are included."

Clinton has pandered to the worst stereotypes and myths about welfare. It is here that he has turned the most cynical, aggressively adopting the code language of the racial and economic neo-segregationists. When a viewer proposed during a *CBS This Morning* broadcast that the standard should be "if you don't work, you don't eat," candidate Clinton replied, "I agree with you. If people don't work, they shouldn't eat."

This is probably the first time a candidate of either party has suggested starvation as a form of welfare reform, but then Clinton may just have been kidding us. In fact, his touted Arkansas "Project Success" did not put all those who could work off welfare after two years as he claimed. The *New Republic* found that out of 27,000 welfare recipients, only 194 were actually engaged in community service. Only 4,000 were even participating in the program, and 78 percent were protected by education and job search programs. It's not that surprising. Senator Moynihan estimated that 1.5 million jobs would have to be created—half the size of the federal government—to find employment for welfare recipients if they were dropped from the rolls after two years. And assuming that all women on welfare went to work, it might require up to $15 billion a year just in day-care costs.[12]

Further, Clinton's own Labor Department had discovered that the existing job training program for employees hurt by foreign trade simply didn't work. The workers in this $200 million program were to be retrained in computers, nursing, accounting, or various trades such as welding. In fact, of over a thousand workers in the program, only one in five found a job paying at least 80 percent of previous wages.[13]

As I write this, it appears that reality may force Clinton back toward a more traditional and reasonable welfare policy, but whatever plan eventually evolves will undoubtedly continue to blame the poor for their condition.

It won't be the first time. In the last century, the industrial revolution caused an eruption of the social and economic system not unlike what the post-industrial revolution and the end of the Cold War have brought us. The Victorians were truly shocked by some of the effects of what was taking place and attempted to mitigate and rationalize them by reviving a sort of feudalism in which the beneficiaries of the new world order looked after its refugees according to a complex system of rights and responsibilities. One early response in this country, for example, found New England factory owners creating dormitories for their young women workers so their morality and training might be better attended to.

By the end of the century, however, there also developed a more objective approach to the problem, producing, among other things, the then novel argument that it cost a certain amount to live in a certain place, a sum that actually varied by location and not by moral worth. Thus were we introduced to the idea of the cost of living.

By the early twentieth century, however, many English liberals and socialists came to speak increasingly of the need to regiment the poor. A Liberal MP, Charles Masterman, recommended a form of workfare consisting of "the double system of labour colonies for those who desire work in temporary employment, acceptable by free men, carrying none of the degradation of charity and State relief, and of penal colonies for those who do not desire work, as humane as may be, but deliberately designed for the elimination of the 'loafer' and the 'cadger.' "[14]

Margaret Canovan, in *G. K. Chesterton: Radical Populist,* notes that among both Liberals and Socialists in the early part of the twentieth century there was "an astonishing unspoken consensus . . . that the poor had no right to liberty, and that bureaucratic regulation was perfectly acceptable when applied to them." As Lloyd George put it, "If these poor people are to be redeemed they must be redeemed not by themselves. . . . They must be redeemed by others."

The main difference between the Chesterton and the moralistic welfare reformers, wrote Canovan,

> was his vivid sense of common humanity with the poor: his conviction that, physically and spiritually, the poor were just the same as the rich and that they too desired not regimentation but the right to lead their own lives with their own families in security and privacy: The essence of his position was that the rights which the upper and middle classes had gained for themselves should be rights for the poor as well. His generation was coming to realize that poverty and unemployment were often in no sense a man's own fault, but imposed upon him by circumstances outside his control; but instead of altering these conditions the reformers, Liberals and Socialists alike, added to the injury of exploitation the insult of regimentation . . . .
>
> He fought against the Liberal advocates of social welfare because, while they knew the value of liberty and property for themselves and to their own families, they were prepared—on the best philanthropic grounds—to regiment the poor.[15]

Chesterton attacked "the huge modern heresy of altering the human soul to fit its conditions, instead of altering human conditions to fit the human soul": "If soap-boiling is really inconsistent with brotherhood, so much the worse for soap-boiling. If civilisation really cannot get on with democracy, so much the worse for civilisation, not for democracy."[16]

Chesterton and his kindred spirits would eventually prevail, and they would have more in common with the New Deal and most pre-Reagan social welfare programs (including those of

Nixon) than do New Democrats like Clinton. Eighty years later, the "astonishing unspoken consensus" that the poor have no right to liberty is making a huge comeback in American politics. Where once programs such as the CCC, the WPA, and Head Start were instinctively voluntary, now many Americans assume we must order the poor to do right. The welfare mother is to be assigned to a forced labor pool and her son, should he step out of line, to a boot camp.

Where Ideas Come From

If Clinton possessed Rooseveltian charisma, if his congressional margin had been more comfortable, and if the nation had been suffering very badly rather than just badly, it is conceivable that the neatly balanced inertial forces of the capital city might have been knocked asunder, permitting a rare period of great political change. Many Americans say they would welcome such a time, and make the not inconsiderable leap of faith that it would be *their* notion of change that would occur once political stalemate had ended.

There is, of course, no guarantee that this would be the case, especially in a country with such major cultural fault lines and with solutions as varied as its complaints. It is at least as likely that those seeking less government or a more moral government or a more just or efficient one would all be disappointed, for the easiest course of change under current conditions is toward a more intrusive and authoritarian system.

Even after the anti-democratic excesses of twelve years of Reagan and Bush, even after three decades of major political assassinations, Watergate, Iran-Contra, BCCI, domestic spy operations, and the numerous constitutional offenses of the war on drugs, Americans are loath to consider the extent to which their democracy has already been compromised and the risk that it might disintegrate entirely. We live in a country that has come to accept unprecedented invasions of privacy, seizures of property without trial, and searches without warrants, but in our political rhetoric we profess that nothing has really happened to us. Yet in the quiet of the pollster's question, we do share our doubts: since 1964 the percentage of Americans who say they trust the U.S. government to do what is right most of the time has declined from over 60 percent to nearly 10 percent. More than half of this drop has occurred in the last ten years.[17]

Recognizing the danger poses a huge dilemma. Once you can no longer guarantee the competence, democratic instincts, and goodwill of those in power, how does one approach the idea of change itself? It's not easy, especially when the propaganda armies at the disposal of the White House can sweep through the American collective mind like tanks rolling across the Iraqi desert. This power to convince, to distort, and to deceive has become so immense that every president presents the country not only hope but enormous danger.

At the beginning of the Clinton administration, when it looked like much of America might simply turn over the keys of the country to Bill and Hillary, I found myself thinking not of FDR and Eleanor, not of JFK and Jackie, but of Juan and Evita Peron, of his economic nationalism, of the blending of social welfare and corporative economics, of Evita's greater popularity and role as unofficial minister of health and leader in women's issues. Was this unfair to the Clintons? Perhaps, but even distant echoes can carry messages, and it was, after all, as recently as the Reagan administration that serious plans were afoot for the establishment of martial law under poorly defined emergencies. Our reluctance to speak of such things does not lessen their relevance. Besides, I was thinking as much about how much we might be willing to surrender as I was about how much the Clintons might be willing to take.

In any event, America didn't turn over the keys to the Clintons. Clinton couldn't close the sale, the worry seemed to become moot, and a good number of Americans went back to grousing, comfortably convinced that any change would be for the better. For its part, the capital city returned to its affairs, reasonably assured that the talk of change had, once again, been greatly exaggerated.

For several reasons, however, the failure of Clinton to overwhelm Washington conceals the degree to which change is occurring anyway. For one thing, even without congressional approval, the president has great power to raise the apparent importance of an issue. Reagan, for example, declared a drug crisis in the mideighties, whereupon—in the span of just a few months—the issue rose in the polls from being of minor concern to the most important matter facing the republic. Nothing had changed in the drug market, only in the media. To his own regret, Clinton achieved similar results with the issue of gays in the military, which—prior to his public commitment on the matter—had not been high on the agenda even of many gay groups. Meanwhile, with little discussion or objection, the drug issue went into semi-eclipse.

You don't even have to be president to cause change. By the time the president's first budget passed, H. Ross Perot was not only the country's most popular politician, he was arguably the most successful one as well. The budget was a reflection not of what Clinton had initially promised the voters but of what Perot had demanded of the politicians.

The press can also change the agenda. For example, although the deficit had been publicly and dramatically rising over the twelve years of Reagan-Bush, a review of news talk show topics reveals that only twice during this period did television give the subject more than casual attention: during the two months of the 1990 budget debate and during the opening months of the Clinton administration.[18] In other words, for more than 90 percent of the period of extreme deficit growth, these major programs ignored the story. Then, during the other 10 percent, TV turned the issue into a crisis, contributing substantially to the panic with which politicians responded to matters at the beginning of the Clinton administration.

How Ideas Grow

The Federalization of Community Virtue

Ideas can also arise in Washington in much the manner that politicians do—through an elite examination, discussion, and winnowing in which the greater public has little role until choices have been greatly narrowed. Thus the idea of national service has been on the elite agenda for years, with Clinton simply being the politician fortunate enough to be able to oversee its introduction. Had it failed in Congress, say for fiscal reasons, it would undoubtedly have been revived in better times by another administration, and not necessarily even a Democratic one.

For most of our history, community service has been a central cultural trait. In 1630 John Winthrop told his flock as it moored in Salem, "We must delight in each other, make others conditions our own . . . always having before our eyes our community as members of the same body." Later, de Tocqueville would notice: "I have often admired the extreme skill with which the inhabitants of the United States succeeded in proposing a common object for the exertions of a great many men and inducing them voluntarily to pursue it." From barn raising to volunteer fire departments, the American tradition of cooperation is ingrained in American culture.

In the 1980s, however, strange things began happening to community service. Some of the transformation was due to a Reagan White House that declared "volunteerism" a reasonable substitute for governmental action, at least for the duration of a political speech. In other quarters, it became an alternative form of punishment: the convicted, for example, were assigned "community service" rather than being sent to prison.

Quietly the concept was also being federalized, part of a covert socialism of the soul enveloping the country as politicians substituted proselytizing for policies and moral lectures for money. In Congress, bills sprouted that proposed what was now "national service." Some of these measures still assumed people would volunteer, but others felt that citizens, especially younger ones, would have to be drafted into goodness. A group of well-cushioned think-tankers declared themselves communitarians—a merger of *community* and *authoritarian* perhaps?—and began dreaming up ways of bringing "responsibility" to the masses, grandly taking it upon themselves to prescribe the moral duties of others in society. One of their ilk, Amitai Etzioni, typically proposed that marriage be improved by what he called "the heavy hand of the law," i.e., using premarital contracts of the sort already popular in those arrangements where there is more money than love. Soon average politicians, especially conservatives such as the then governor of Arkansas, had picked up the cry. As the White House and the Congress became more mired in their own corrupt irresponsibility, politicians began implying that the real problem was the indifference and sloth of the public.

The 1992 campaign further confused matters. By the end of it, Clinton had added several layers of meaning to the concept of community service. Now, it seemed, community service would be a way students could pay off part of the college loans the campaign had promised them. Further, the venture into virtue by these students was to be substantially subsidized.

Not that Clinton's national service was going to be all fun and games. He spoke of some of the community servants working as cops. And news stories touted a prototype in Boston in which participants started off the day with mass calisthenics, a paradigm of community service apparently borrowed from the Chinese. Other advocates even suggested that the military should be enlisted in community service, thus preparing it for a peacetime economy—or at least for urban pacification.

By this point it was hard to know just what community service meant anymore. To mind came the image of discharged Marines, recently graduated Yale English majors, and drug addicts diverted from incarceration, all doing pushups in front of city hall at 6 A.M. before marching off to solve the urban crisis.

Just what was community service now? Still a natural part of our cultural heritage? A by-product of our moral and religious beliefs? An indulgence to be paid by prospective investment bankers and corporate lawyers? A subsidy to potential members of the 20 percent of America that will form an economic elite under the Clinton paradigm? A form of punishment? A way to get welfare mothers to stop driving around in their Cadillacs? A tactic for peacetime conversion? A cheap means to get more cops on the streets? A symbol that somebody up there cares about the cities? A reference to social conscience on the résumés of future politicians? Part of the compulsive urge by those in power to control ever more aspects of American social life?

It was hard to tell. In any case, there was no particular evidence that national service was the best way to support the country's voluntary activities. After all, more than half of all American adults already volunteered an average of four hours a week, and nearly two-thirds of youths twelve to seventeen gave at least three hours—for an estimated total of 2.1 billion hours annually.[19] The L.A. city government has more than 14,000 volunteers. The town of El Cerrito, California, is run by 100 paid employees and nearly 500 volunteers. When Lafayette, California, got into fiscal trouble, it asked for help from volunteer accountant and management consultants, who came up with a plan to save about a tenth of the city's budget.[20]

There is a strong argument to be made that volunteer agencies really need not more volunteers but more facilities and equipment and logistical support. There is a strong argument to be made that there are better ways of encouraging community service than by spending more than thirty dollars an hour for it, as the Clinton program will do in its early stages. There is a strong argument that moneys might be better expended on the nearly two dozen existing national service plans such as VISTA, Teach for America, the Student Literacy Corps, and the Youth Conservation Corps. Finally, there are the considerable political and social implications of replacing *community* service with *national* service. What exactly is the reason for this federal co-optation of local virtue?

Such issues, however, were not a significant part of the discussion of national service. To most of the country, national service was presented as an unmitigated good, and even the Republicans could effectively challenge it only on cost grounds. Undoubtedly, the national service trust fund will support worthy projects, providing valuable and, in some cases, transformational experiences for those involved. But whatever its salutary effects on individual participants and those they assist, the national service program will have little effect on the country's social and economic problems, will not greatly increase the number of America's community service volunteers, and will not likely create a rush to public service careers. As a Clinton administration official pointed out, the president's program for direct loans to college students "is the real national service program." These loans will be repaid based on a percentage of income, and thus—unlike earlier loan plans that used financial institutions as conduits—do not penalize one for entering a lower-paying occupation. As Rep. Robert E. Andrews put it, "We are shifting from an entitlement to banks to an entitlement for students."[21]

Yet because of its ubiquitous symbolic utility, national service was early destined to have a life much grander than its actual product could warrant. To the young the service program offered a chance to do something meaningful for society. To the country it was an outward and visible—and relatively inexpensive—sign of caring, devoid of such complications as the potential political and economic empowerment of the poor that undermined support for VISTA. For the Clinton administration and congressional supporters it represented a commitment to social values, concern for the poor, and a bit of regimentation for the unruly and undirected young. One might even catch a whiff of a generation that once avoided the draft using its children to atone for its own lack of national service.

A number of the new-style community service programs do, in fact, include paramilitary overtones. Buried in the national service scheme is a plan for a Civilian Community Corps that would use ex-military personnel to run boot camps for urban community service teams.[22] (Apparently young urban blacks get boot camps whether they commit offenses or not.)

Few have raised questions about the civil liberties implications of such militarization of urban policy, although Ray Flynn, when he was mayor of Boston, did argue that "a military solution is not the problem of the cities of America. The solution is a commitment of resources for poor and needy people." More typical, however, was the favorable comparison drawn by St. Paul's mayor Jim

Scheibel between U.S. military intervention in Somalia and military involvement in American cities.[23]

The Clinton plan clearly seeks echoes of the Kennedy Peace Corps. But the Peace Corps was the product of a far less cynical and intrusive federal government. And even it was eventually perverted, as when Ronald Reagan announced that there were 900 Peace Corps volunteers in the field ready to implement the Caribbean Basin Initiative—three-quarters of which turned out to involve military aid to the notorious government of El Salvador. A similar symbolic transfer of virtue appears to be occurring under national service as the president's staff integrates the program into its highly politicized crimefighting effort.

The president and his supporters have hardly been modest in describing national service. Clinton said, "National service will take on our nation's most pressing unmet needs while empowering a new generation to serve as leaders for change." Al From, president of the conservative Democratic Leadership Council, even took credit for reinventing civic spirit: "National service, the cornerstone of the New Democrat agenda, replaces the two dominant ethics of the 1980s—every man for himself and something for nothing—with a simple philosophy that calls for a new spirit of civic obligation and participation in America."[24]

To declare national service a cornerstone of one's domestic policy reveals the paucity of the New Democrat agenda. Even the normally less malleable Mary McGrory in the *Washington Post* declared the program "the best of Bill Clinton," and blandly asserted that "if successful, it could demonstrate a new Democratic philosophy, giving people to problems rather than money."

Poverty, joblessness, the urban health and housing crises are not, however, the product of too few college sophomores giving to the community. How such people—however well motivated—will provide housing, health services, food, and jobs to America's cities without money remains a mystery.

Still, making us all better persons has considerable appeal to some politicians, journalists, and policy hustlers. For one thing, it is inexpensive. In an age of austerity, politicians have limited options: they can prohibit and they can exhort. Much of what passes for politics in a time of budget deficits falls into one of these categories. Unfortunately, these two temptations tend to turn government into a great overbearing prig offering little but supercilious advice, lots of new prisons, and the prospect of still more layoffs.

In the end, the national service program will provide an aura of administration concern much as is achieved by a redlining bank president who serves on the board of a public charity. And it will provide grist for interminable rhetoric about the nobility of the young, matched only by that praising those in public office brilliant enough to have thought of the idea in the first place. Cheap, virtuous, and non-ideological, it is just the sort of program that Washington loves most.

The Politics of Toys

If the truth be told, though, many politicians would just as soon avoid ideas altogether. They are much happier providing constituent services than trying to resolve divisions within their own constituencies or, worse yet, between constituents and contributors. In fact, it is reasonable to assume that the appeal of constituent problems is so great that it has become a problem in itself. This thought first occurred to me when I heard a city council member brag that the number of citizen complaints he handled annually had mounted from 7,000 to 10,000 over the course of his term. What seemed to me statistical evidence of failure was in his eyes tremendous progress. The man apparently not only did not want the city's problems to go away, he was reveling in their accumulation. It suddenly struck me that legislators all over the country, albeit in a more discreet manner, had a tremendous vested interest in the government not working right.

Unfortunately for them, however, ideas and issues do arise, and candidates are all expected to have a few of their own. Hence at the national level the origins of some of our most expensive and wasteful programs.

These programs are to politicians roughly what a BMW is to a young stockbroker. Ronald Reagan's political toy was Star Wars, a theory that wasted tens of billions of dollars without producing anything that worked. Jerry Brown's political toy of the last campaign was high-speed trains, while Bill Clinton preferred to talk about information highways. Such programs tend to share a number of characteristics: they are very expensive, are very complicated, have virtually nothing in common with the major issues facing the country, and will rarely encounter an ordinary voter. To lessen this last disadvantage, the public is usually assured that the program in question is essential for the national defense, or for successful "competition in a global economy," or for the production of incalculable spin-off benefits implicitly including, but not limited to, the cure for cancer.

The high-speed train is a good example, especially since even though Jerry Brown was defeated, the train survived. In April 1993, the Clinton administration announced a $1.3 billion plan to construct a high-speed train system in densely populated areas. Of this, $300 million was to go for developing a train that would float above its tracks on magnetic cushions. To put these figures into some perspective, the most that Congress was willing to appropriate to pull the nation out of its recession was $900 million.*

Although the high-speed project would clearly benefit only a handful of urban corridors, Transportation Secretary Federico Pena, with classic Washington disingenuousness, claimed it would "improve the quality of life of Americans throughout our country."[25] There was, at least, precedence. In 1993, Washington's subway system had received an annual federal subsidy that was twice as large as that given all the nation's rural transit systems combined.

Nothing is intrinsically wrong with high-speed trains. In the best of all worlds every self-respecting urban corridor would have them. We live in a country, however, that has let its generic rail

---

* One of the best ways to keep such figures straight was laid down by journalist Tim Weiner: One thousand seconds is about seventeen minutes. One million seconds is about eleven and a half days. One billion seconds is about thirty-two years.

system deteriorate to a degree that even some third world countries can boast better passenger rail coverage. In India, for example, 41 percent of all travel is handled by rail; in the U.S. it is .4 percent. In Greater Calcutta, 1.7 million persons use suburban rail, as opposed to 300,000 in New York City.[26]

Worse, many communities now lack not only rail but bus service as well. American transportation policy has consistently favored the ritzy and the glitzy, a bias that has produced not only geographical inequities but racial and economic ones. By favoring subsidies for air over those for bus and rail, and by favoring suburban-oriented mass transit like Washington's Metro and San Francisco's Bart over light rail and urban bus transport, we have created a two-tiered and discriminatory transportation system.

The high-speed train exacerbates this bias. An article in *Urban Transport International* points out that for the price of building high-speed rail between London and the Channel Tunnel—without considering the cost of rolling stock or station facilities—one could construct two new subway lines under central London and replace every bus in the London fleet.

Wrote *UTI:*

> There is a substantial body of evidence to show that investment in high-speed systems is of questionable benefit. People use higher speeds not to cut down on the time spent traveling, but to go further. And what do they achieve when they get there? "Those who do travel further do not do anything very different from before: all traffic statistics show that the main change in behaviour is not a change in the purpose of moving around but in the distance to destination," maintains Helmut Holzapfel, a Dortmund based academic who has studied this question . . . .
>
> To quote another authority, Dr. John Whitelegg of the University of Lancaster: "Putting money into high-speed rail only benefits those groups who use it most, and they are predominantly male, between 25 and 45, and more likely to have their journey costs paid out of someone else's pocket."

What helps to drive such programs is the need to find work for defense contractors. The high-speed train is not so much about transportation as it is about employment. The Cold War's end has played havoc with the entire defense industry, but no place more so than with R&D firms, many of which grew up as welfare dependencies of the Pentagon and which might well collapse if required to face the exigencies of true "market forces."[27]

Managed Competition, Even More Managed Debate

While national service and high-speed trains are relatively benign examples of the sort of policy manipulation that occurs in Washington, they suggest the potential for mischief when the federal propaganda state turns its attention to something as important as national health care. During the first months of the Clinton administration, one of the biggest national policy changes of the past fifty years was being forged by a secret committee led by Mrs. Clinton under procedures that periodically defied the courts and the Government Accounting Office, and whose public manifestations consisted of highly contrived media opportunities, carefully staged "town meetings," and similar artifices.

Despite the contrary evidence of public opinion polls, the concept of Canadian-style single-payer insurance was dismissed early. Tom Hamburger and Ted Marmor in the *Washington Monthly* tell of a single-payer proponent being invited to the White House in February 1993. It was, he said, a "pseudo-consultation"; the doctor was quickly informed that "single payer is not politically feasible." When Dr. David Himmelstein of the Harvard Medical School pressed Mrs. Clinton on single-payer, she replied, "Tell me something interesting, David."

In other words, write Hamburger and Marmor, "fewer than six weeks into the Clinton presidency, the White House had made its key policy decision: Before the Health Care Task Force wrote a single page of its 22-volume report to the President, the single payer idea was written off, and 'managed competition' was in."[28]

If there was any popular, grassroots demand for "managed

competition," it never appeared. Managed competition had not been tested anywhere. Nonetheless, reported Thomas Bodenheimer in *The Nation,*

> Around Hillary Rodham Clinton's health reform table sit the managed-competition winners: big business, hospitals, large (but not small) commercial insurers, the Blues, budget-worried government leaders and the "Jackson Hole Group," the chief intellectual honchos of the managed competition movement. . . . Adherence to the mantra of managed competition appears to be the price of a ticket of admission to this gathering.[29]

What was finally proposed involved a massive transfer of the American health industry—by some accounts now larger than the military-industrial complex—to a small number of the largest insurance companies and other major corporations. These were companies that had the assets to play the game being offered—a medical oligopoly that would dispense health care under the rules of the Fortune 500 rather than according to those of Hippocrates.

Clinton's position on health care had bounced around in the early months of the campaign, finally settling on a policy that would leave the big health insurers largely unscathed. It was not particularly surprising. Max Brantley, columnist for the *Arkansas Times,* noted that "Blue Cross owns Arkansas, and [Clinton] never did much to fight them."

The stakes would eventually become so high that a number of the biggest insurers—including CIGNA, Aetna, and Metropolitan Life—would leave the industry-wide Health Insurance Association of America. Five of the largest insurance companies formed something called the Alliance for Managed Competition. In this new game one of the first targets of "managed competition" was the smaller insurance companies that now account for nearly half of the health underwriting business. Said managed competition advocate Lynn Etheridge, "Ninety-nine percent of the insurance companies are going to be wiped out because they're only prepared to be insurance companies." Mrs. Clinton, sounding like a

1980s takeover lawyer, said, "It's going to be a Darwinian struggle. Only the best and fittest of them will survive."[30] Similarly, when asked how small businesses were meant to cope with the added costs of her plan, Mrs. Clinton replied, "I can't go out and save every undercapitalized entrepreneur in America."

Her interest lay with the largest companies, i.e., the ones with the ability to purchase or create the health maintenance organizations that would become de rigueur under the Clinton scheme. The new HMOs would be major profit centers for companies, simultaneously subsidized by federal payments for the ailments of the poor, the elderly, and those without conventional insurance.

Not everyone shared the Clintons' enthusiasm for the plan. *Washington Post* columnist Tony Kornheiser wrote:

> I'm sorry if I sound like a snob, but over the years I've developed fairly good relationships with a few doctors, and I have a feeling that if [the Clinton plan] goes into effect, I'll never see them again. I fear I'll end up in the teeming waiting room of an HMO, sitting on a cold folding chair, wearing those hideous paper slippers and a hospital gown that exposes your behind, shuffling down a bleak hallway, waiting to see the one doctor on call. We'll all be milling around, holding numbers in our hands, just like at an Eastern European fish market.

If Ronald Reagan had proposed managed competition, many of its current advocates would have been on talk shows decrying it as a fraud. In fact, it is not unlikely that Reagan might have done just that, given the provenance of the idea. It was the brainchild of Alain C. Enthoven, a former RAND Corporation think-tanker and once chief whiz kid for Robert McNamara. In 1961, he created what became known as the Office of Systems Analysis. As Rep. Peter Stark noted, systems analysis "never worked. The Pentagon has never gotten costs under control. Systems analysis gave us $600 toilet seats." In 1980, Enthoven became part of the Reagan transition team.[31]

While Enthoven was still in Washington, according to labor writer Tim Knaak, his former employer RAND did a study of health care for New York City and concluded that the solution lay in the private sector. In 1970, Joseph Newhouse, a senior economist for RAND, described medical care as a "luxury." By 1975, Knaak reported, Newhouse was recommending a 10 percent deductible "to introduce 'market forces' that would supposedly keep costs down by preventing 'overuse' of the system. By 1989, a major study suggested that a 50% deductible would be needed to keep costs down."

But the price of the "luxury" of health kept going up. In 1988, the Congressional Budget Office looked at Enthoven's managed competition idea and estimated that it would add another $80 billion to the deficit without slowing health-care inflation.

More recently, managed competition was massaged at meetings in Jackson Hole organized by its right-wing inventors and by corporations such as GE, Prudential, Aetna, Metropolitan Life, CIGNA, the Blues, Merck, and the Pharmaceutical Manufacturers Association. The corporations coughed up $33,000 to $100,000 each for the privilege. The convenor was Paul Ellwood, who had invented the term *HMO* in the 1970s and then sold the idea to Richard Nixon as an alternative to Ted Kennedy's universal health-care legislation.[32]

A leader of the Jackson Hole meetings, Thomas O. Pyle, was initially made chair of one of Clinton's task force committees. His résumé offers good insight into the sort of people to whom the Clintons were listening. Pyle was, until 1991, the chief executive of the largest HMO in New England. He was a director of the Millipore Corporation, a firm that sells a variety of products to drug and biotechnology companies, hospitals, and laboratories.

Equally interesting was his role as advisor to, and stockholder in, the KBI Healthcare Acquisition Corporation. KBI describes itself as a "publicly traded buy-out fund organized for the express purpose of consummating a significant acquisition in the health care field"—the sort of practice that would likely become rampant under managed competition.

Pyle's other activities included being a senior advisor for the Boston Consulting Group, which has health industry clients; a director of the Chickering Group, which sells student health insurance policies; and a director of another firm that sells malpractice insurance.

The media either bought heavily into managed competition or described it in antiseptic, comfortable terms. For example, the *Washington Post* on March 9, 1993, wrote: "Each health plan—which could be organized and managed by insurance companies, physicians or others—would group together doctors, hospitals, clinics, laboratories and other providers. Eventually, the marketplace—consumers making selections through their purchasing cooperative—would determine the price."

Skipping neatly over the fact that it was the "marketplace" that got us into this mess in the first place, the description painted a gentle image of people coming together under a fair and equal system. In fact, however, it took Prudential seven years and $2.6 billion to build its HMO network before it made a profit. Not many physicians—even the wealthiest—can compete in that sort of a marketplace. Those doctors who were not financial wizards were actually not likely to fare much better than consumers; many would be forced into the salaried employ of huge health corporations.

Even the *Post* admitted that managed competition would "limit consumers' choice of physicians, make it harder than it is now to see specialists and would put an intermediary—the 'manager' of the plan—between the doctor and the patient. The intermediary's role would be to make sure that physicians and hospitals use their resources in the most efficient way."

This was not a new idea; it already existed under some insurance companies' "managed care," a system which had helped to drive costs up, drove patients and doctors to distraction, and had failed to improve health services. Under managed care, nurses and managers in the employ of insurance companies second-guess surgeons on treatment, mental health professionals are pressured to prescribe cheaper drugs rather than expensive treatment sessions, and medical specialists are forced to accept the insurer's cost-cutting demands at the risk of being thrown off (or never allowed on) a preferred provider list.

Dr. Bertram H. Bernstein of New York City summed up the problem in a letter to the *New York Times:*

> The concentration of power created by "managed care" reform has resulted in disregard for the patient—for his or her longstanding physical relationship or continuity of medical care. . . . Health insurance companies are able to usurp the clinical judgment, experience and diagnostic skills of the physician. The companies have the power to determine if medical treatment decisions are "appropriate." The decisions, often made by inappropriate personnel, may be self-serving for the insurance companies and not in the best interest of the patient. Yet they are protected from antitrust scrutiny and liability.

As Dr. Bruce Yaffe told the *Times,* under managed care American medicine was being transformed from doctor and patient vs. disease to doctor vs. patient vs. insurance company.

Once again, the administration was as interested in packaging as in its product. Recovering the semiotic advantage lost during the first months of its tenure, it thoroughly iconized its proposed health-care policy, forcing anyone who wished to challenge it to deal not only with an exotically complex proposal but with the carefully massaged image of the president's wife. Since the promoted image was that of an intelligent, charming feminist paragon, it became difficult to suggest that Mrs. Clinton might be involved in one of America's largest economic giveaways. Or that much of her defense of the program came down to uncredible versions of "trust us" or "excellent question, Senator" or "we will be sensitive to that" or "we share your concern." Or that the plan would primarily benefit a few large American corporations. Or that the administration's cost accounting assumed a level of accuracy never before seen in Washington fiscal projections, let alone in any of Clinton's number-crunching to date. Or that the plan would, to varying degrees, replace medical decisions in health care with fiscal ones, supplant the traditional doctor-patient relationship with a highly institutionalized system, reduce greatly a patient's choice, and generally remake medicine along corporate lines.

With considerable assistance from the media, the canonization of Mrs. Clinton began in earnest late in the spring of 1993 as the health-care task force was trying to complete its work. Reported the *New York Times* on May 7: "Suddenly Hillary Rodham Clinton is back dominating the newsstands, from *Family Circle* to the cover of *People,* from *Time* to the *Washington Post.* Her aides insist that the timing is all coincidental, but some political professionals see it as a useful exercise in image-burnishing for the release of the Administration's long-awaited proposal for health-care reform."

Typical of the fawning coverage was a *Washington Post* article headlined: HILLARY CLINTON'S INNER POLITICS: AS THE FIRST LADY GROWS COMFORTABLE IN HER ROLES, SHE IS LOOKING BEYOND POLICY TO A MORAL AGENDA.

The *Times* quoted Democratic poll taker Geoffrey Garin, who said: "This is going to be a very complicated plan, and in those circumstances people's faith in the author will be pretty important. If you don't know exactly know what a 'health alliance' is all about, at least you know whether you trust Hillary Clinton."

It worked. A study of the first six months of the Clinton administration found that 79 percent of Mrs. Clinton's network TV coverage was favorable, as opposed to only a third of her husband's.

The Hillary hype escalated as Mrs. Clinton spent several days on Capitol Hill at the end of September fielding softball questions from members of Congress. Gone was all memory of an attorney who had once represented a failing S&L before an agency of her husband's government. Absent was any sense of the irony over a lawyer for corporate interests being used as a national role model. Even conservatives were cowed, and feminist leaders, who had long demanded control of their own bodies, smiled or applauded as Mrs. Clinton proposed turning the bodies of all Americans over to the care of a handful of huge corporations.

It would be one thing if managed competition's advocates could cite some empirical basis for their arguments, but managed competition had been promoted largely by conservative theorists. As the *Left Business Observer* put it, "Managed competition comes from an economist's mind, not human experience." Meanwhile, single-payer advocates argued that:

• The private insurance industry now spends at least 33 cents in order to provide $1 worth of health care. Comparable costs for Medicare are 2.5 cents, and for the Canadian single-payer system only 2 cents.
• It takes 6,682 workers to administer 2.7 million Blue Cross policies in Massachusetts, more than the total number of employees needed in the Canadian system, which serves 25 million.
• The private insurance companies have left some 81 million Americans with medical problems facing either higher premiums, excluded coverage, or denial of all coverage.
• Between 1980 and 1989 the average per-employee cost of a typical group Blue Cross/Blue Shield major medical plan quadrupled.
• Health insurers engage in redlining by both geography and occupation.
• Part of Clinton's original cost-accounting assumed an incredible 50 percent decline in the annual increase of funds spent on health care between 1996 and 1997. The plan also assumed a $239 billion cost savings in Medicare and Medicaid between 1996 and 2000. How would these savings be achieved? Most likely by cutbacks in service. Further, Medicaid has a current overhead of 3 to 4 percent. Under the Clinton plan it would be run through the private insurance system with an overhead of 13 percent, an increase in costs that would have to come from somewhere, presumably from the Medicaid program itself.

- Despite the administration's reliance on competition to keep costs down, medical costs were 26 percent higher for hospitals in highly competitive areas than they were in non-competitive communities, according to a study by University of California researchers James Robison and Harold Luft.

Nonetheless, during the long months of Mrs. Clinton's task force, there was little talk in Washington of the single-payer, Canadian-type system that a majority of the American public had said in polls that it would like. As with the budget, the media gave short shrift to some very basic facts. Thus the *Washington Post* played down on page 5 a study by the Congressional Budget Office reporting that a single-payer system could save the country $114 billion on its present annual health-care costs.[33]

When the issue was raised, opponents argued—borrowing from the propaganda of the health industry—that Canada's system would mean long waits for surgery and other horrors. In fact, Canadians, like other citizens in countries with real national health insurance, are decidedly more satisfied with their health care than are Americans. Asked if they would prefer the American system, only 3 percent of Canadians said yes.

In one of the best summaries of the health-care situation, the September 1992 *Consumer Reports* concluded:

> A single-payer system that draws its inspiration from Canada's is not the best solution for those doctors who are mainly concerned about their own pockets, or for hospitals with ambitions to become major medical centers. It certainly isn't a good solution for health insurance companies; many of them would go out of business. But it is the best solution for the growing number of consumers shut out of the private-insurance market and the even larger number who have reason to fear their coverage might disappear at any time.

As for managed competition, Rep. Stark said, "When you get it down to sea level, it doesn't do anything, which is why everybody likes it. There's no new taxes needed, it provides universal access, and if you believe all that, that's somewhere between the tooth fairy and the chuckling oyster." At the end of Clinton's first year, Stark (whose subcommittee would review the legislation) said the measure was still at ground zero: "We're going to have to negotiate a sentence at a time."

The Corporative State

Throughout such Clinton programs as health care there is persistent attention to the needs of big business. This is not surprising; in a little state like Arkansas, large corporations have a lot of say, and politicians, if they wish to stay such, listen closely. At the local level this can lead to considerable corruption, but applied to a whole nation it does far more than pervert or cheat the system, it starts to transform it. When one adds up the administration's approach to NAFTA, health care, research and development, and technology, it is clear that Clinton has reversed the traditional Democratic idea that the poor need help and the corporations need regulation.

There is, for example, the new economic council, modeled, significantly, on the national security council. There is the extraordinary (for a Democrat) obeisance to the concerns of big business in health care and trade. There is the shaky assumption that the government may intervene at will in the marketplace, the better to help those in the corporate world who deserve to be helped.

The idea of turning technology centers into a sort of agricultural extension service for industrialists is a case in point. The potential for scandal and waste in this proposal seems virtually limitless, presenting, for example, the opportunity to emulate the situation in Clark County, Nevada, where there are forty farmers and thirteen federal agricultural agents.

Clinton's argument that such centers are needed to increase American productivity wavers on a number of grounds. First, the idea that the government is an efficient incubator of ideas and innovations lacks evidence. Second, these centers have the potential of becoming the equivalent of military bases; God help the politician who tries to close one.

Third, economist Robert L. Samuelson has noted in *Newsweek* that business investment, as a percentage of gross domestic product, was higher in the 1980s than in the 1970s, and nearly 30 percent higher than in the 1950s. Samuelson also said that research and development—which Clinton wants to subsidize heavily—jumped dramatically in the 1980s, up 52 percent compared to the 12 percent gain in the previous decade.

Fourth, despite Clinton's oft-expressed concerns about productivity, the truth is that since 1980 productivity has outstripped real wages. In 1991–92, in fact, real wages went up only .6 percent annually, while productivity increased 2.7 percent. Economist Tony Riley told *Fortune* that the trend would continue through the nineties and that "a weak labor market makes it easy for employers to keep the fruits of productivity growth for themselves."[34]

Finally, the McKinsey Global Institute pointed out in a report written by a number of long-time Democrats that the average U.S. factory worker already produces 25 percent more per hour than a worker in Japan or Germany. And according to Peter Drucker, American workers produce fifty times more per hour than they did eighty years ago. In fact, American productivity is one of the main reasons for our chronic unemployment, a problem much more likely to be solved by a shorter workweek than by creating 170 government-funded feeding troughs for corporate America.

The pattern for such ideas comes from the defense industry. While this industry is often attacked for waste and fraud, it is in one sense immensely efficient: it has made itself the major welfare recipient of the United States government. As described by Pentagon whistleblower Ernest Fitzgerald in *The Pentagonists:*

> The privileged Pentagon contracting corporations took for granted they would give to their government customer in accordance with their ability, or their mood of the moment. The grateful government would see to it that the ever-malleable contracts

were changed to conform to the giants' actual products. And the big corporations would be compensated in accordance with their need, as documented by their actual spending.[35]

As early as the seventies the Pentagon-industry buddy system began having spin-off effects. Jimmy Carter established an Executive Interchange Program—under which industry officials would be seconded to the government in an example of what Fitzgerald called "institutionalized conflict of interest." Carter put it like this: "Through this effort, both the public and the private sectors jointly contribute to great sensitivity and responsiveness in the interest of all Americans. . . . Boundary lines between government and business are blurring. The activities of both have become increasingly similar."

The long-standing sweetheart deal between government and the defense industry was soon to be threatened by the end of the Cold War. Something had to be done. On October 19, 1987, the *New York Times* reported that a Defense Department advisory board had recommended that the Pentagon take "a more assertive role in setting economic policy to head off an increasing loss of technological leadership to both our allies and adversaries." As the *Times* euphemistically put it, "The plan would inject the military into unfamiliar policy arenas."

The plan of the Defense Science Board, a collection of defense contractors in industry and academia headed by Robert A. Fuhrman, president of Lockheed, called for the creation of an "industrial policy council" which would be headed by the president's national security advisor. This body, according to the *Times,* "would recommend policies to bolster industries that support the military." The defense secretary would also become a member of this civilian economic policy council.

The *Times* also noted other thinking along these lines: "The Pentagon is beginning to argue for broad industrial policies that would benefit high-technology industries as a whole, hoping that the rewards would reach sectors of the economy that directly serve the military."

Interestingly, the report was released only a few weeks before Margaret Thatcher declared the end of the Cold War, a view then at least partially shared by Reagan and Bush. The industrial policy report offered hope to a military establishment that saw the raison d'être of an evil empire being swept out by glasnost. We now needed to maintain a strong defense to protect ourselves not only against our adversaries but against our allies as well.

The report came at the end of an administration that had beatified the "free market economy." To those who read the Reaganites' dicta instead of their lips, however, it was clear that what Reagan was talking about was anything but a free market economy. And Reagan was not alone. There was broad acceptance in boardrooms and in Washington that capitalism needed to be better organized.

Reagan was not the first national leader to move in such a direction. In a speech in 1920 Benito Mussolini had said it was time "to deprive the State of all the functions which render it dropsical and vulnerable, reducing it to . . . that of the soldier, the policeman, the tax-collector and the judge." Yet while Mussolini started out a pure Reaganite, he ended up running a state that controlled most of its own industries, after a zigzag, often inconsistent, course pursued in the name of nationalism, defense, efficiency, and protection from foreign competition.

As Fitzgerald points out: "By setting up special parastate agencies or 'corporations' to replace failing or inadequate private enterprises, [Mussolini] was able to control the important economic sectors. Elitists everywhere found that laudable." Italians called it the *estato corporativo:* the corporative state.

Fitzgerald quotes two British academics who in the mid-seventies foresaw the dangers of such a state coming in the guise of industrial policy. Writing in *Economic Affairs,* R. E. Pahl and J. T. Winkler described corporatism (the British term for industrial policy) as a system under which government guides privately owned businesses toward order, unity, nationalism, and success. They were quite clear as to what this system amounted to: "Let us not mince words. Corporatism is fascism with a human face. . . .

An acceptable face of fascism, indeed, a masked version of it, because so far the more repugnant political and social aspects of the German and Italian regimes are absent or only present in diluted forms."

Thus, although the model generally cited in defense of organized capitalism is that of the contemporary Japanese, the original practitioners of a corporative economy were the Italians. Unlike today's Japanese economy, but like that of contemporary America, Italy's economy was a war economy. Several years before Kristallnacht, Mussolini's minister for the national economy, Giuseppe Belluzzo, was advocating commitment to technical achievement, state intervention in corporate affairs, and, in the words of Mussolini biographer Adrian Lyttelton, "consideration of Italian industry from the point of view of planning for defence needs." Belluzzo was particularly interested in promoting new science-based industries.

Lyttelton, describing the rise of Italian fascism in *The Seizure of Power,* writes:

> A good example of Mussolini's new views is provided by his inaugural speech to the National Exports Institute on 8 July 1926. . . . Industry was ordered to form "a common front" in dealing with foreigners, to avoid "ruinous competition," and to eliminate inefficient enterprises. . . . The values of competition were to be replaced by those of organization: Italian industry would be reshaped and modernized by the cartel and trust. . . .
>
> There was a new philosophy here of state intervention for the technical modernization of the economy serving the ultimate political objectives of military strength and self-sufficiency; it was a return to the authoritarian and interventionist war economy.[36]

Lyttelton writes that "fascism can be viewed as a product of the transition from the market capitalism of the independent producer to the organized capitalism of the oligopoly." It was a point that Orwell had noted when he described fascism as being but an extension of capitalism. Lyttelton quoted Nationalist theorist

Affredo Rocco: "The Fascist economy is . . . an organized economy. It is organized by the producers themselves, under the supreme direction and control of the State."

The Germans had their own word for it: *wehrwirtschaft*. It was not an entirely new idea there. As William Shirer points out in *The Rise and the Fall of the Third Reich,* eighteenth- and nineteenth-century Prussia had devoted some five-sevenths of its revenue to the army, and "that nation's whole economy was always regarded as primarily an instrument not of the people's welfare but of military policy."[37]

With the rise of the U.S. military-industrial complex, American attitudes concerning the proper relationship between the corporation and the state underwent fundamental changes. In the forty years since Dwight Eisenhower warned the country of the danger at hand, we have moved to a point where even former free-marketers like Reagan and Clinton see the country's salvation increasingly in a manipulation of the capitalistic system to serve the political and military goals of the state, in return for which the government serves the interest of its largest private firms. A sort of Arkansas writ large, only with multinationals rather than chicken producers calling the shots.

The potential pitfalls are enormous. Once a corporation's interest becomes indivisible from that of the state, it becomes a matter of state security to protect that corporation. We have already experienced this phenomenon in the nuclear power and defense industries, which are granted many of the immunities and protections of a military institution.

At the present time, government employees cannot strike; at what point in the development of an industrial policy will it be considered a national threat to strike against a corporation considered key to our success in "global economic competition"? At what point does it become our patriotic duty to support the interests of multinational corporations?

This is far from a theoretical question. In September 1993, in a major departure from both principles of the free market and anti-trust laws, the government and the big three auto makers announced a joint venture to develop a fuel-efficient car. Said Vice-President Gore: "We have a strategic interest as a nation in meeting the goal we've set in this program. It's an act of patriotism."[38]

Gore is not alone. In a *New York Times* review of a new book by Edward Luttwak, director of the Center of International and Strategic Studies, Jeffrey Garten says that Luttwak "calls for a mobilization of economic assets in the same way we once mobilized the military to fight wars. Consumer spending must give way to saving and the nurturing of our productive industries. The support of technologically advanced industries must be seen not just in terms of jobs or higher standards of living, but as an instrument of state power."

The corporative state has arrived. The argument—once considered a joke—that what's good for GM is good for America is now government policy.

If Clinton were a highly effective leader, there would be much more reason for concern in some of the foregoing, for he has honed his manipulative skills but not his democratic instincts. Few of his policies would revitalize democracy or significantly increase the average citizens' ability to deal with the private and public forces arrayed against them. He doesn't seem to actually oppose such programs so much as he just never gets around to thinking about them.

But it may not matter that much. Perhaps John O'Sullivan in the *National Review* was right in suggesting that we have not seen the beginning of the Clinton administration, but rather the midpoint of the Bush-Clinton years, a great mushy interlude in our history.

On the other hand, shortly before Clinton took office, Greg Guna suggested an eerie parallel with Mikhail Gorbachev:

> A faltering superpower gets a new leader who calls for change, promising an end to political stagnation and economic decline. He is younger by decades than his recent predecessors.

. . . His wife, a stylish dresser and savvy political force in her own right, is a source of controversy.

Critical of traditional politics—and yet very much its product—the nation's new leader wants to focus attention on domestic renewal. . . . Hard-liners warn that he promises too much, trying to be all things to all people.[39]

But it may also be true that Clinton is like no one so much as our collective selves, that once again the American political system has done exactly what it set out to do and given us the president we wanted, if not exactly needed.

If Clinton is erratic and indecisive while simultaneously boastful and smug, these qualities are not much at odds, for example, with what you find today at the top of major corporations, universities, and school systems. Much of America's leadership is involved in the gargantuan self-deception that it still controls the systems under its charge, that the god of progress still smiles upon us, and that the massive strains in our society are but mechanical malfunctions of a basically sound machine.

If we really wanted to help South-Central L.A. instead of assigning a few college students to go there and signify our concern, we have had plenty of time to make it known politically.

If we are sliding toward an authoritarian corporative state, controlled, as Connecticut teacher Charles Wiggins puts it, by "automated distrust," Clinton is only catching the wave. He is merely the greatest current symbol and not the cause of our descent from democracy and freedom.

If we are not yet ready to pay for our teachers, care for our poor, cease punishing the addicted for their illness, give purpose to our young, dismantle our overarching military economy, revive our liberties, and recover our democracy, then Clinton and the rest of Washington's powerful have heard us clearly. And our silence has brought with it the reassurance that in the nation's capital things can stay pretty much as they are.

The Club

Whatever defects Clinton and his crew brought to Washington quickly found company. Early in the republic the capital discovered the seven deadly sins, soon grew weary of them, and has spent the subsequent decades developing variations. Congress has often set the pace.

Its favorite vice is not that of the White House, namely the usurpation of democracy, but rather its neglect. The days of legislative tyranny by a Sam Rayburn or a Lyndon Johnson are long gone. Jim Wright was but a meek shadow of his mentors as he gave up the House speakership, asking his colleagues: "Have I been too partisan? Too insistent? Too abrasive? Too determined to have my way? Perhaps. Maybe so." In his place came bland Tom

Foley, who said, "Heightening tension is just another technique and it is not one I find particularly congenial."[1]

The consensus politics of Foley and Senate Majority Leader George Mitchell has been neither institutionally successful nor particularly popular with the voters. In fact, despite all the problems that Clinton faced in his first months in office, Congress remained far the larger target of public ire. In July 1993, when 51 percent of Americans had a favorable impression of Clinton, only 24 percent felt that way about Congress.[2]

This was in many ways a bum rap, since the worst that Congress had often done was to reflect the real divisions of a very divided country. Where Congress split with the new president—most notably on the budget issue—it did so for politically sound, if not notably courageous, reasons. Thus Congress got in trouble for doing what it was supposed to do—which is to listen to the people. One poll displayed the inconsistency remarkably: although the public was not happy with the president's economic program, a Democratic member of Congress who failed to support it would drop 15 percentage points.

The phenomenon of public impatience over the inefficiency and boisterousness of democracy is not new to the Congress, nor to legislative councils generally. There is an excessive expectation of legislative deportment usually achievable only in the most undemocratic, corrupt, or autocratic bodies. This public intolerance of what is often nothing more than healthy confrontation and necessary debate creates a covert bias toward autocracy—not for any ideological reason but simply because it seems more orderly and polite. Since a tightly run executive can stifle internal debate and present a dignified front to the public, whereas Congress is always brushing up against anarchy and confusion, the White House often finds itself with a sizable advantage over the legislature. The president, for example, is in a position to present a "comprehensive" health plan to the Congress; but that plan will have to be reviewed by several separate and potentially contentious Hill committees.

There are other serious handicaps the Congress faces, not the least of which is the growing territorial aggression of modern administrations and Congress's limited skill in counteracting it. A particularly striking example is Congress's acceptance of the so-called "black budget" consisting of funding for intelligence agencies, the specifics of which (in violation of the Constitution) are unknown to most of the members.

Despite creation of its own technological and budget oversight agencies, Congress is still outgunned by the massive complexities of the executive branch. It suffers from the transformation of tripartite government into a form of mediarchy with the president as celebrity-king. It persists in arcane, pompous, and pointless procedures, many faithfully transmitted to the public by C-SPAN. The Senate readily consents, but rarely exercises its constitutional power to advise the president on treaties and appointments. Congress weakens itself by the corruption it tolerates and the potential this creates for blackmail by the White House and federal police agencies.* It has largely given up its budget powers to the executive. It has drifted into an almost feudal dependency on the White House for the largesse of federal facilities and programs—forty-seven states, for example, were on the take for the supercollider program, and four hundred congressional districts got a piece of the B-1 bomber. Further, Congress has long suffered from leadership that is not only politically weak but stunningly uncharismatic. From constitutional powers to soundbites, Congress comes up short.

Not the least of Congress's problems is that the cohesiveness formerly provided by congressional bosses, their role secured by rigid seniority, was never replaced by anything else, not, for example, by the enforced loyalty of a parliamentary system nor by the greater party emphasis of proportional representation. Congress has become retail politics at its most complex.

Even such labels as conservative, liberal, and moderate over-

---

* In the first 110 years of the republic, reports *U.S. News & World Report*, members of Congress faced criminal charges about once every twenty-seven years. Between 1900 and 1970 this increased to once every two years. Since 1970, the law has been booking U.S. legislators at a rate of once every five months.

simplify and distort matters. As one example, Jeremy and Carol Grunewald Rifkin noted in *Voting Green* that green legislators do not conform to traditional geographic or ideological groupings. For example, the Rifkins found that 77 percent of the representatives receiving an A for their environmental record came from either the East or the Pacific Coast. Of those receiving an F, 81 percent were from the South, the Midwest, and the non-coastal West. Five out of the eleven highest-ranking green members of the House were black and three were women, far out of proportion to their presence in the House.

On the other hand, only four of the top eleven House greens rate a 100 percent score in the rankings of the liberal Americans for Democratic Action; on the Senate side only one of the top ten greens made a similar score in the ADA list. Meanwhile, the top greens in Congress all enjoy a lifetime AFL-CIO voting record of 80 percent or better.[3]

With the breakdown of the political parties and congressional autocracy, individual members of Congress have clearly gained independence, but they lack a concomitant growth in power. The condition can be described by analogy: if you go to a cathedral you are expected to keep the silence; if you go to a baseball stadium you may scream at will. In neither place, however, will your personal views attract much attention.

Although the media presents Washington as a city grappling with the major issues of our time, much of the town's workday is absorbed by highly specific concerns. The president is worried about the spin to give a statement or appearance. The lobbyist is obsessed with a very particular amendment to a very particular bill. The size of the capital's bureaucracy is necessitated in no small part by the number and specificity of regulations it must administer. And woe to the member of Congress who lets larger concerns surpass the parochial needs of the district.

Thus Washington is awash in the politics of particulars. Much of the time expended by the Clinton task force on health legislation had to do not with deciding upon principles but with tackling the innumerable exceptions to them. Go to a congressional hearing concerning something you consider a good idea and you are likely to be startled by the number of people and interests this benign concept will allegedly injure.

One of the best descriptions of how Washington really operates can be found in Thurman Arnold's *Folklore of Capitalism*. Arnold imagines applying the principles of a contemporary debate to the attempted rescue of Amelia Earhart:

> First, plans would have been made for the use of the best planes to search the ocean. Then, when this extravagance was attacked publicly, cheaper planes would have been used. By the time that this device had received condemnation for inefficiency, the rescue would have been changed from a practical, efficient endeavor to a public debate about general principles. Everyone would have agreed that people in distress must be rescued. They would have insisted, however, that the problem was intimately tied up with balancing the national budget, improving the character of people lost at sea, stopping the foolhardy from adventuring and at the same time encouraging the great spirit of adventure and initiatives and so on *ad infinitum*. They would have ended perhaps by creating a commission to study the matter statistically, take a census of those lost at sea, examine the practices in other countries. What was saved in airplane fuel would be spent on research so that the problem could be permanently solved.[4]

The town's most common skill, its trade of choice, is finding what is wrong with something. For the bureaucrat, this eliminates the need for action. For the politician, it lessens risk. For the lobbyist, it means points with the client. For the public interest group, democracy and justice are at stake. And for the lawyer and reporter, it is just instinctual. All day long, Washington hums with people trying to stop other people from doing something, and with considerable frequency they are successful. At times Washington seems a series of endless loop videos in which policies are debated, lobbied, and almost acted upon before the tape repeats itself once more. This is the city that first heard a president call for national health insurance in the 1940s, and it is where HUD Secretary Henry Cisneros spoke of President Clinton's commitment to the homeless only to be told by another administration aide, "Oh, he comes from Arkansas. It's a small state. After he's here for a while he'll get used to it."[5]

In an interview with *Time*'s Ann Blackman, Cisneros described the Washington he had found:

> We'll spend hours talking through a strategy of meeting all the objections to try and move our homeless initiative through the Office of Management and Budget and through congressional committees. We'll spend hours talking about how to please this or that person. Meanwhile, it's dusk. And people are starting to bed down for the night—for one more night in the park outside the window. And we could go on for days talking and never get one step closer to the people who are using cardboard for beds in the nation's capital.

There is no law or corrupt practice that makes it thus but rather something deeper: a primal urge to maintain the equilibrium of the capital. The imperative of the parochial rises to the top, club before country. There is no need for conspiracies; it is simply a part of the culture of a city that often reminds one of the ditty:

> *One cannot hope to bribe or twist,*
> *Thank God, the British journalist.*
> *But seeing what the man will do,*
> *Unbribed, there is no reason to.*

Which is one reason you didn't find too many unhappy lobbyists around Washington in the first months of the Clinton administration. While the Clinton rhetoric resonated with disgust over influence peddling, it soon became obvious that this was mostly rhetoric, that which wasn't rhetoric was not about to be enacted, and, in any case, Clinton was proposing enough new laws and regulations to provide a major jobs stimulus package for Washington lawyer-lobbyists over the next four years.

A few lobbyists and corporate lawyers did take major pay cuts. They were the ones hired by Clinton for his administration. Here are some examples:

- Bruce Babbitt, Secretary of Interior: His firm represented a Mexican industry coalition pushing for the North American Free Trade Agreement.
- Samuel Berger, Deputy National Security Advisor: Was a lobbyist for Caterpillar, Berg Steel Pipe, Poland, Timex, May Department Stores, and Toyota's U.S. subsidiary.
- Ron Brown, Secretary of Commerce: Represented foreign auto makers, American Express, Japan Airlines, Oman, Zaire, Baby Doc Duvalier, Gabon, and a coalition of twenty-one Japanese electronics producers. His firm has represented New York Life Insurance, Mutual Life Insurance, scores of Japanese firms and American multinationals, BCCI, and Guatemala.
- Hillary Rodham Clinton, White House aides Vincent Foster, William Kennedy III, and Webster Hubell, Associate Attorney General: Their firm has represented Tyson's Food, Beverly Enterprises, TCBY, and the country's largest parking meter manufacturer.
- Warren Christopher, Secretary of State: Was on the board of Lockheed and the parent company of Southern California Edison. His law firm has represented Southern California Edison, Bankers Trust, Lockheed, IBM, United Airlines, Occidental Petroleum, Fuji Bank, the Mexican government, Mitsubishi, as well as Exxon in suits related to the pollution of Prince William Sound.
- Mickey Kantor, U.S. Trade Representative: Has represented Occidental Petroleum, Martin Marietta, and Atlantic Richfield. His firm has represented Philip Morris, GE, United Airlines, and NEC.
- Bruce Lindsey, Personnel Director: Represented Drexel Burnham Lambert.
- Hazel O'Leary, Secretary of Energy: Was chief lobbyist for Northern States Power of Minnesota.
- Bernard Nussbaum, White House counsel: His firm has

represented Time Warner, Sears, Citicorp Real Estate, Goldman Sachs, and Salomon Brothers.

- Howard G. Paster, legislative assistant to the president: Former PR executive whose firm represented Anheuser-Bush, Union Pacific, the Healthcare Leadership Council, and the Pharmaceutical Manufacturers Association. With his former law firm, he had clients such as Chrysler, Northrop, and the National Rifle Association.

- Richard Riley, Secretary of Education: Represented the German firm of ThermalKEM. His firm has represented Honda, Mercedes, Philip Morris, and BMW.

- Robert Sussman, Deputy Administrator of the Environmental Protection Agency: former legal counsel for the Chemical Manufacturing Association.

- Togo West, Army Secretary: Was chief lobbyist for Northrop.

- R. James Woolsey, CIA Director: Sat on the board of British Aerospace Inc. and Martin Marietta. Represented the Swiss company Société Générale de Surveillance, McDonnell Douglas Corporation, and General Dynamics.[6]

Beyond such appointees was a gaggle of lobbyists who had played key roles in the Clinton campaign but for various reasons— including the wish not to be questioned closely about their affairs during a confirmation hearing—did not join the administration.

To one not immersed in the mores of the capital, such selections might seem odd, especially for a president who had promised major change in the way Washington does its business. It might even startle that 77 percent of Clinton's initial cabinet were millionaires, beating out both Reagan and Bush in this category. But in D.C., the Clinton choices barely raised an eyebrow. Clinton's cabinet may not have looked like America, but it certainly looked like establishment Washington. It required no corruption or conspiracy for the city's journalists to ignore it; everything was just too normal.

To be sure, a few questions were raised. Early in the administration, the new national economic advisor, Robert E. Rubin, wrote numerous clients of his former firm, Goldman Sachs, inviting them to stay in touch. Rubin, who had been one of Wall Street's "four horsemen" of leveraged takeover arbitrage, and who would shortly submit a financial disclosure form listing an estimated income in 1992 of $26.5 million from his GS partnership, wrote: "I hope I can continue to rely on your interest and support as I move from Broad Street in New York to Pennsylvania Avenue in Washington, D.C., and would be grateful for whatever suggestions you would offer."[7]

The story appeared on the front page of the *New York Times*. The *Times* quoted a federal lawyer who declared: "It doesn't strike me that there's anything there that would raise any kind of specter of a violation of law or regulation." A former Bush administration ethics official, while insisting on anonymity, told the *Times:* "Assuming severance of all financial ties, there is no legal prohibition to dealing with former clients and employers, but we always tried to negotiate a grace period of a year or so" before resuming contact. By Washington standards the exculpatory quotes of the anonymous federal and Bush administration officials had cleared Rubin, and the story died.

Thus do the sometimes disparate segments of official Washington come together to protect themselves from the outside critic, the populist insurgency, or the reformers' zeal. One may, for example, easily test the true range of opinion within the foreign affairs establishment by proposing some commonsensical (but to the experts grossly repugnant) idea such as ending all military aid to dictators and those countries inclined to bully their neighbors. In such an instance, the so-called "policy debate" suddenly disappears, and a deep commonality among those who control the country's foreign activities will become apparent.

Similarly, extraordinarily close relationships exist between certain committees of Congress, the agencies they fund, and concerned lobbies. In such political *ménages à trois,* the public interest is simply left out of the discussion.

Even the media knows when, in the Washington common interest, to look the other way. For example, the Senate Judiciary Committee's reaction to its embarrassment over the Clarence Thomas nomination has been to announce that henceforth derogatory personal information concerning Supreme Court nominees would be discussed in secret. While the Senate will have access to the transcript, release of information contained in it would subject a senator to expulsion. The media declined to raise the alarm over this remarkable affront to open government.

All but a few reporters were similarly indifferent when, during the Iran-Contra hearings, Rep. Jack Brooks asked Oliver North a question about administration contingency plans to suspend the Constitution under certain ill-defined circumstances. Committee chair Daniel Inouye responded that the issue would be discussed in executive session. As outlined by Alfonzo Chardy in the *Miami Herald,* the plan involved turning state and local government over to the military and the national government over to the Federal Emergency Management Agency under circumstances so broad they included domestic protest against U.S. military adventures. Thus, perhaps the most important question of the entire hearings never got a public answer.[8]

The blurring of lines in Washington is a daily occurrence. Lobbyists, reporters, and members of both parties get drunk together at black-tie functions like the Gridiron Dinner. There is only mild head shaking when a purportedly Democratic president promises not to campaign against Republicans who support his proposed trade agreement with Mexico. Little attention is paid when David Gergen invites John Ehrlichman to lunch at the White House mess.

Understanding such phenomena helps to explain why the major influx of new Congress members after the 1992 election had so little effect. What Washington does wrong is often not the result of individual avarice, malevolence, or even incompetence. The city has its own permanent style, its own rhythm, its own self-protective values—and it takes more than a handful of freshman legislators, eager reporters, or bright young White House aides to change it.

In fact, the crop of new representatives who hit the Hill in the wake of the House check-bouncing scandals proved little more resistant to tradition than its predecessors. According to Common Cause, the 110 newest House members raised nearly half of their campaign money from political action committees in the first six months of office.

And what of those replaced by the fresh political winds of 1992? According to a study by the Public Interest Research Group, 101 out of 319 people leaving the executive or legislative branches in January 1993 went into direct lobbying, and another 79 joined law firms that also do lobbying.

Although Americans are apt to inveigh against lobbies and "special interests" as much as they do against Congress, the former are just as much a part of the American system. Alan Taylor, writing in the *Journal of American History* about 1790s politics in upstate New York, notes that "interests" developed even before political parties:

> An interest collected together individuals of compatible desires out to advance their self-interests, but an interest was unequal and hierarchical. It coalesced around a leading man who could influence others and reward his supporters. The lesser partners reaped small favors from the more powerful in recognition of their support—a support that preserved the authority of the man at the top. In New York during the 1790s, commentators occasionally referred to "the agricultural interest," "the manufacturing interest," and "the mercantile interest," but these were abstractions that rarely seemed to have any concrete power; it was more common for "interest" to refer to the personal following that a leading man or a prominent family could influence, as in "the Livingston interest" or "the Van Rensselaer interest."[9]

Almost precisely two hundred years before Robert Rubin's epistle to his former clients, John Talbot wrote John Porteous in November 1792: "If you can find a freedom to give me your vote and influence, it will lay me under an obligation which I shall always be happy to make returns."

A few years later Ebenezer Foote advised congressional candidate Peter Van Gaasbeck, "Every Person wants a letter particularly addressed to himself or he supposes his importance is not duly noted."

The custom of "making interest" preceded significant party-building in most of the rural U.S. prior to 1800. Parties spread, says Taylor, from the seaport cities to the mid-Atlantic states, New England, and "last (if at all) to the South." Taylor quotes historian Harry Watson as saying of North Carolina, "A complex mixture of voluntary deference and coercion marked relations between political leaders and followers. . . . The use of party structures . . . was almost nonexistent."

Given the weakness of today's two major but amorphous parties, it may therefore not be surprising that such interest politics is once again thriving. Livingston and Van Rensselaer have been replaced by Perot and Limbaugh. And David Walls, writing in *The Activist's Almanac,* suggests that "the role once played by minor parties of injecting new political ideas and programs into the public arena has been largely superseded by the rise of nonprofit advocacy organizations and think tanks."[10]

Interest groups do often function as surrogate political parties, which helps to create an intricate political mosaic as indecipherable in its own way as the traditional two-party mush. Some of these interests are extraordinarily potent and broad-based. The American Association of Retired Persons has some 33 million members. For comparison, Dukakis received 41 million votes.

Each day some 8,000 new members join AARP; half of all Americans over the age of sixty-five belong. With 400,000 active volunteers and member services ranging from insurance to credit cards, the AARP rivals the two parties in terms of effective organizing and potential for political mobilization.[11]

Other lobbies are simply potent, such as the corporate and financial interests that turn up on the Hill at tax and budget times. These lobbies are important not just because of the campaign

money they generate but because they are frequently better prepared with legislative language and supporting arguments than the
legislators themselves.

The same is true of lobbying federal agencies. Although the
public often thinks of interest politics as something primarily occurring in the halls of Congress, the explosion of federal regulatory law and the huge purchasing decisions of the executive
branch make this no longer true. William Greider in *Who Will Tell
the People?* quotes an Environmental Protection Agency administrator as saying that in his arguments with the Carter White House,
three out of every four of the White House comments on EPA-
proposed rule-making "were cribbed right from industry briefs."

No one knows how many lobbyists there are in town. In 1981
Robert Reich, then a Harvard professor, estimated the Washington
regulatory "community" to consist of 92,500 people, including
lawyers, lobbyists and their employees, trade journalists, corporate
representatives, public affairs specialists, and consultants.[12] The
count is complicated by the fact that many lobbyists escape registration requirements. Says Charles Lewis of the Center for Public
Integrity, "No one in Washington ever admits they lobby."[13]

Whether the number of actual lobbyists is 10,000 or 30,000
seems to make little difference when you consider that, even at
the lower figure, every lobbyist meeting just once with each member of Congress would result in more than 5 million lobbying
contacts.

There was a time when lobbying was more of an art than a
profession. A Washington regular recalls an early job with one of
the most powerful lobbyists in town. Together they set out to visit
a southern senator. Once in the Hill office, the lobbyist and the
senator discussed nothing but hunting and fishing for forty-five
minutes. When it was time to leave, the pair walked out of the
suite, the senator's arm draped over the lobbyist's shoulder. As
they crossed the threshold, the lobbyist casually pulled out an
envelope and handed it to the senator, remarking, "Here's something you might like to look at." It was a request for assistance on
a certain legislative matter.

The lobbyist and his aide returned to their office, and the former immediately sat down to write a thank you note which he attached to backup material on his legislative request. The aide was then dispatched back to the Hill with the envelope to complete the courtly negotiation.

A radical change in lobbying occurred in the 1970s. Business executives who had previously regarded lobbying as something not quite respectable became worried by the success of Ralph Nader. They formed the Business Roundtable, a group limited to the CEOs of Fortune 500 companies and devoted to using the immense assets of these corporations—including their customers and employees—to affect political decisions in Washington. Greider reports that in 1970 only a handful of Fortune 500 companies had public affairs offices in Washington; by 1980, 80 percent did.[14]

Still, as late as 1979, according to Tip O'Neill, a businessman as savvy as Lee Iacocca would need basic lobbying advice. George Steinbrenner had set up a meeting between the Speaker and the boss of the then failing car company. The session did not go well, and the next day Steinbrenner told O'Neill, "Lee called me and said you were the coldest bastard he ever met."

Replied O'Neill: "What did he expect? He came in with a whole damn army. Do you think I'm going to tell him how to get the job done in front of all those lawyers and lobbyists? They'll just take credit for my ideas. Tell Iacocca to come back and see me, just the two of us, head on head, and I'll tell him what to do."

Iacocca returned and O'Neill asked him, "Tell me, how many people in my district work for Chrysler or one of its suppliers?"

Iacocca had no idea, so O'Neill told him to find out and to do the same for every congressional district in the country: "Make up a list, and have your employees and dealers in each district call and write letters to their own member of Congress."[15]

What O'Neill suggested is now practiced by many lobbies—corporate and public interest—on a daily basis. In the endless pseudo-referendum sponsored by these lobbies, the fact that the phone calls and letters are less than spontaneous matters little. Regardless of motivation, one such message is believed by various specialists to represent the views of 200–400 voters. Thus even a hundred letters or phone calls favoring a certain position can cause a member of Congress to pay attention.

Some firms have taken lobbying into cyberspace, moving so to speak from the grassroots to astroturf. One operation uses a sophisticated phone bank aimed at voters in a relatively few key congressional districts. It is operated, says an activist who has worked there, by "whatever policy wonks are out of work. Last year it was Democratic wonks; this year it's Republican wonks." The callers are looking for, say, one hundred constituents and ten community leaders in each district friendly to its client's legislative issue. When one is found, the caller keeps talking, drilling in the policy. Then the telemarketer asks if the voter minds being connected directly to his or her Congress member. Patched into the legislative office, the well-rehearsed constituent delivers the packaged message. The marketer then follows up by calling back the voter and offering to send a confirmatory mailgram (written, of course, by the firm).

A recent variation on this theme invites TV viewers to dial a toll-free number should they agree with the thrust of a lobby's commercial. When they call, they are quickly transferred to their own member of Congress.[16]

Such methods are not only extremely effective; many are beyond the scope of present lobbying laws, which anachronistically assume that lobbying pressure will be on government officials rather than upon their constituents.

There are other techniques. One is the increased use of fax banks by trade associations to organize their own membership for action. And in 1991, when Congress was considering legislation of critical concern to the regional phone companies, a dozen or so lobbyists from the Baby Bells stood outside the Senate floor. As David Corn reported in *The Nation:* "Each held a cellular telephone by which to relay every suggested change in the legislation to headquarters. There teams of lawyers and analysts scoured the proposed language and determined whether the bill would bring their companies new profits."[17]

Less high-tech but just as effective is what has been called "grasstop" lobbying. Here a pressure group simply hires close friends of targeted legislators whose sole job is to pressure their elected buddies. Michael Pertschuk, co-director of the Advocacy Institute, pointed out in a 1992 speech that Philip Morris's lobbying report to the House clerk in 1990 showed payments of $11,800 just to lobby Congressman Bill Richardson of New Mexico. And Senator Bob Dole, who has led the fight against various tobacco control measures, had his own grasstop lobbyist, who was paid $36,000 to pressure his buddy, the senator.

Pertschuk's information came from internal Philip Morris documents uncovered by anti-tobacco activist Alan Blum. In them, a senior lobbyist offers insights into the culture of pressure politics:

> With these people, you get just as much political clout by sponsoring a hunting or fishing trip rather than taking them to NYC. And it's cheaper and less hassle. This group really loves to hunt. The same guys I took to the racetrack in Oklahoma and hunting last year were the very ones that helped us hold the leadership firm on no cigarette taxes. . . .
>
> Last year, we gave out about $11,000 to Kansas legislators. It may not sound like much, but that's the most we could give without sticking out like a sore thumb. . . .
>
> If the current media flap over legislators' trips dissolves, we are planning on taking four trips [to NYC] with honoraria involved. Two Senate trips with three members and spouses on each trip. . . .
>
> We continue to give to the various caucuses and they will continue to be of service to us. . . . This type of contribution does buy political clout. . . .
>
> John M. has done a great job with his first session as our lobbyist. He is best friends with the Speaker and used major personal clout to kill our cigarette tax.

None of this sophisticated manipulation means that lobbying is immune from normal Washington inefficiencies. As one lobbyist put it, "There is lots of locomotion masquerading as cerebration." There are, for example, the long lunches at restaurants such as the Palm, Prime Rib, and Mr. K, during which lobbyists and government officials balance drinks in one hand and the legal niceties of pressure politics in the other. And there are the briefings provided by trade associations that allow corporate field representatives to report to the home office that they had "breakfast with Senator Jones and he let it drop that . . ."—never mentioning that the meal was in the company of ninety-five other lobbyists.

Sometimes the reason for the lobbying can be a bit obscure, as when a campaign for year-round daylight savings time was covertly inspired by a manufacturer of charcoal seeking to expand the grilling season. And much legislation is so complex that only a lobbyist and a member of Congress could love it. A corporate summary of the 1993 Senate and House tax bills, for example, consumed forty-two pages even in highly abbreviated tabular form. The result is that many issues of principle become extraordinarily convoluted and arcane as they proceed through Congress. Not surprisingly, public advocacy groups have taken to responding to the establishment's legalisms with more of their own.

Go back to the sixties and Ralph Nader was about the only public-interest lawyer in town who wore a suit, and his wasn't pressed. Today, many advocacy groups have drifted into the lawyerly style and pace of the establishment they are supposedly trying to change. They have, in their own way, become capital institutions, part of the ritualized, status-conscious, and very safe trench warfare of the city.

A case in point is Americans for Democratic Action, a multi-issue labor-oriented organization once powerful enough to attract vehement right-wing assaults, but now a sort of liberal Leisure World. Some years back, I joined ADA in the hope that it might once again become a potent progressive force. Many considered it no longer relevant to Washington politics, yet it had an annual budget of nearly three-quarters of a million dollars and some

20,000 members. At the very least it was sucking money and energy from the progressive cause; at best it could be reborn. I eventually became an executive vice-president, but simultaneously became increasingly frustrated. It seemed that many in the organization were not unlike Charles Hodge, who taught at the Princeton Seminary in the early nineteenth century and bragged that in his fifty-year career he had never broached a new idea. The leadership deeply resented attempts to evolve an alternative to the war on drugs, to democratize policy-making, and to increase chapter and youth influence. When several of us formed a "progressive caucus," the leadership appreciated neither the effort nor the irony of its name, and within a year the leaders—including the past treasurer, the current chair of the Chicago chapter, the former chair of ADA's youth organization, and I—had been purged from our official positions.

I had naively assumed that ADA wanted to change, and that the debate would only be over the direction. After all, the organization clearly had lost most of its influence and was sitting on the political landscape, in the words of Disraeli, like a range of exhausted volcanoes.

But the organization's leadership wanted nothing of the sort. What it really wanted was to retain its status as the traditional voice of liberals in Washington, even if this status had the limited élan, say, of being an alleged Russian count in Manhattan. To have challenged liberal orthodoxy would have been to lose caste with its orthodox liberal allies in Congress and to lose funding from its orthodox labor backers. In short, ADA could not regain its former political stature without risking its social position, and it preferred the latter.

Nothing tested a progressive organization's relative interest in politics and status more than the arrival of the Clinton administration. There seemed a broad assumption that under Clinton many of these groups would function in much the same sort of influential manner as, say, the Heritage Foundation had under Reagan. This led to numerous acts of encouragement, support, and obsequiousness during the campaign and immediately thereafter. The Sierra Club turned its considerable grassroots network loose. Gay groups raised at least $3.5 million.[18] And ADA, two months before the convention, moved to switch its endorsement from Tom Harkin to Clinton without making a single demand, clearly motivated more by a desire to curry favor than to create influence.

When it developed that much of the love for Clinton would be unrequited, activists became more feisty and critical. But there were still a considerable number who could be found enjoying whatever power can be squeezed out of an occasional phone call from the White House or a feel-good briefing at the Executive Office Building. As one environmental activist said of some of his peers, "They love to go to the White House; they love to go to the meetings. They're very susceptible to any attention."

Even among more realistic activists, the first year of the new administration meant considerable adjustments. One told me, "The environmental movement played by the rules. The Sierra Club worked its ass off during the campaign. Now you just don't get much to show for it." Others, despite problems with Clinton, felt grateful for progress, no matter how small, and to have at least an occasional inside line to the administration through Vice-President Al Gore.

Of all the groups that cast their lot with Clinton, the environmentalists seem to have experienced the broadest range of reactions. This is not that surprising, given that environmentalists are a far more varied lot than is often supposed, ranging from archconservative conservationists to radical tree-spikers.

Environmentalists have long and sophisticated experience working the Washington scene. According to Kirkpatrick Sale in *The Nation,* they also have "at least 12,000 grassroot groups, some 150 major nationwide organizations, a total budget of perhaps $600 million a year, an estimated membership of 14 million Americans, the support, according to various polls, of some 75 percent of the population, and considerable political clout at all levels."[19] Some might say that the environmentalists prove that citizen lobbying can produce change in Washington, but such stats also indicate the massive force it takes to make the capital budge.

Consider, for example, gays and lesbians who, despite their considerable contribution to the Clinton campaign coffers, took a major beating on the issue of gays in the military. With no power-house like Gore on the inside, without a strong grassroots strat-egy, opposed by the Pentagon (the largest lobby in the country), and with the antipathy of much of the nation, the gay movement would find itself ending up in some ways more beleaguered than before Clinton had come to its aid. As *New York Times* journalist Jeffrey Schmalz wrote shortly before he died of AIDS: "Bogged down early on in a battle over homosexuals in the military, Clinton has grown wary of anything that the public might perceive as a gay issue."

Thus the infinitely more critical AIDS crisis suffered, leading Bob Hattoy, the gay aide eased from the White House to the In-terior Department, to say of Clinton's political advisers: "I don't think they'll address AIDS until the Perot voters start getting it."[20]

The dilemma gays and lesbians initially faced was not unlike that of other progressives. Said Tanya Domi of the National Gay and Lesbian Task Force early in the term, "For the first time, we have an administration with a more positive attitude toward us, and we don't know the best ways to relate to that, whether from the inside or the outside."[21] As late as mid-April a poll found 88 percent of gays and lesbians approving of Clinton's handling of the presidency, and 74 percent believing that he was keeping his campaign promises.[22]

As the gay ban issue was heating up, though, Beth Donovan of *Congressional Quarterly* wrote that colleagues were coming up to gay Congress member Barney Frank "to complain that they were hearing only from opponents. That, Mr. Frank says, elevated the fear of a backlash against members who support lifting the ban. 'House members needed to hear from gays and their parents and friends and relatives,' he says."

To someone living in a city like Washington, where significant gay participation in politics is not only taken for granted but actively solicited by politicians of all stripes, the gay ban debate seemed somewhat anachronistic. Even as the joint chiefs were trembling over gays in their midst, a candidate for D.C. city council chair (and former Clinton campaign co-chair) was accused of stacking the endorsement meeting of the Gertrude Stein Democratic Club in an attempt to ensure the gay group's endorsement. In much of urban America, candidates long ago discovered that homosexuals register to vote in extraordinarily high numbers (93 percent for gays, 90 percent for lesbians) and have unusually high average household incomes (nearly $52,000 for gays, almost $43,000 for lesbians), much of which is categorized as disposable. In fact, for Washington's economy, the 1993 national gay and lesbian march turned out to be even better than the Clinton inauguration. According to the D.C. Convention and Visitors Association, the weekend event brought in $177 million to the city, compared with only $65 million from the inaugural.

Says gay journalist Frank Browning of Pacific News Service and National Public Radio: "As political and economic creatures, our utility to the larger society exists for two reasons: we spend money disproportionately to our numbers . . . and we vote more aggressively than other Americans. It is for similar reasons that American Jews have had disproportionately more influence politically and economically than their numbers would suggest."[23]

Yet as political scientist Larry Sabato told CQ's Donovan, gays fighting the military ban failed to follow up on the opening their contributions had provided: "Money may open the door, but votes and mail and phone calls make the sale."[24]

Besides, the $3.5 million raised by gays sounds like a lot until you consider that the real-estate industry raised $11 million to influence the parties and congressional races in 1991–92; the medical-industrial complex coughed up $20 million; and even the restaurant and bar industry gave almost as much as the gays. The ante for the Washington influence game has become enormous. Ask the Mexican government. Since 1989, that country has spent $30 million to persuade Americans of the need for a North American Free Trade Agreement. That was more than the three largest previous foreign lobbying campaigns—South Korean, Japan, and Kuwait—combined.[25]

The ill effects of Washington influence peddling present one of the strongest arguments for devolving power from the capital to the fifty states and their localities. While corporate lobbyists function at all levels, it is often easier and cheaper for citizen action groups to fight them locally than it is to take them on nationally. Even the environmental movement, with its major presence in Washington, has benefited enormously from the impact of local action and pressure. In 1992 alone, for example, the one hundred largest localities pursued an estimated seventeen hundred environmental crime prosecutions, more than twice the number of such cases brought by the federal government between 1983 and 1991.[26]

Another example has been the drive against smoking. While the tobacco lobby ties up Washington, 750 cities and communities have passed indoor smoking laws. And then there is the Brady Bill. By the time the federal government got around to acting on it, half the states had passed similar measures.

So powerful is the potential for decentralized action that pressure groups sometimes demand that federal or state laws prevent lower levels of government from imposing their own restrictions. In one case, the North Carolina legislature passed anti-smoking legislation that, under tobacco industry pressure, preempted local action on the matter. The bill, however, had a six-month delay before it took effect; during this interim some thirty communities passed their own laws.

Richard Klemp, vice-president for corporate affairs for the Miller Brewing Company—that is to say their chief lobbyist—laid out the stats of the problem in a 1993 speech. Klemp noted that the firm had to deal with 7,600 state legislators, 535 members of Congress, 50 governors, one president, hundreds of regulatory officials, and thousands of mayors and city councils. "At each biennium," he said, "there are more than 200,000 bills introduced in the state legislatures and 12,000 bills introduced in Congress, any one of which could have a limiting or potentially devastating effect on the brewing industry. . . . In 1991, we tracked 1,200 bills that were relevant to our bottom line. Out of these, 48 were enacted into law, and of those, 41 were supported by Miller."

Klemp, successful lobbyist that he is, is unfazed by such an overwhelming prospect:

> At Miller, lobbying is coordinated by our Corporate Affairs Department. Working together as a team, Corporate Affairs conveys our heritage and dynamism and communicates the key message that "beer belongs." I like to compare us to the Superbowl champions. Our team is on the field, and no matter what the other side, whether it's a competitor, a hostile congressman, or anti-alcohol group—no matter what they throw at us, we're ready to make that play and win for our side.[27]

One of the greatest checks on influence politics is a press that considers it news. Today this is only intermittently the case. That the press has the power to focus public attention and outrage has been repeatedly demonstrated, but the choice of targets often appears random. Thus the House check-bouncing affair assumed immense importance, but the fact that ex-lobbyist Ron Brown, the new secretary of commerce, had promised to recuse himself for only twelve months on issues affecting former clients and not at all in matters affecting his law firm, passed virtually without notice.

The relationship between the Washington media and the national government has always been ambivalent. On the day after the House approved the First Amendment, a member accused the press of "throwing over the whole proceedings a thick veil of misrepresentation and error."[28] At the other extreme, George Will quietly helped Ronald Reagan prepare for his debates, and when Pat Buchanan, former right-wing White House official turned columnist, ran for the presidency, he was replaced on a TV show by former right-wing White House official turned TV commentator John Sununu.

Similarly, as media personality David Gergen was being hired by the White House, former Pentagon flack Pete Williams was being transformed from Pentagon publicist to NBC correspondent. Wrote *Newsday*'s Marvin Kitman:

> Williams was one of the architects of the most reprehensible press censorship policies we've ever had. . . . Williams broke new ground in disinformation, Orwellian double-talk and obfuscations like "some collateral damage." . . . The oddest thing is that nobody batted an eyelash at the hiring announcement . . . nobody protests, or even cares. The barbarians are in the gate, for Pete's sake.

No less than Washington's politicians and lobbyists, Washington's journalists are creatures of the capital's culture. The status of their subculture has improved measurably in recent decades, aided in no small part by the growing tendency of journalists to write about each other—a tool of upward mobility unavailable to other trades and professions.

This is not to say that most reporters are overpaid. The stories one hears about media stars—such as the network hotshots and those who appear on talk shows engaging in an activity known as "talking out their ass"—are the exceptions. Many print reporters especially pay a lifetime penalty for being excessively literate and insufficiently good-looking or garrulous. Further, like many hardworking government workers, they have little voice in the decisions of the system they serve. They remain trapped in a purgatory between the disdain of the public and ineffectualness within their own bureaucracy.

Yet while the changing status of journalism has made its ordinary practitioners neither content nor rich, it has nonetheless tended to widen the gap between reporters and those they write about. By education and social standing, if not by salary, journalists have joined the ruling class. And they like to act the part.

Thus 11,000 journalists showed up in Tokyo for the glamorous but unilluminating gathering of world leaders at the G7 summit, while, until it was over, the disastrous flooding in the Midwest had to take journalistic second place.[29] In a more subtle example, the Washington media consistently adopts the current jargon of the capital no matter how misleading it may be to the average reader. For example, a budget cut in Washingtonese may not be a cut at all but rather (a) an increase less than inflation, (b) an increase less than an earlier projection, or (c) a congressionally approved increase less than the president's request. To the lay citizen such language may seem deceitful; to the politicians and the press it is a shared tongue.

Where the compatibility between the coverers and the covered becomes far more serious, however, is when the former ignore, distort, or mislead to press their cause. Perhaps the most egregious example during the Clinton administration has been the coverage of health-care reform and NAFTA.

In the first six months after the election, the *New York Times* ran sixty-two stories that mentioned "managed competition," but only five referring to "single-payer," with none of these being more than a single-sentence reference.

Even before the election, the *Times* had editorialized that "the debate over health care reform is over. Managed competition has won," an outcome that the paper found "delicious" and "wondrous."

According to *Extra!,* the media watchdog magazine,

> The justification media managers give for the imbalance of attention is that while managed competition is supported by the Clinton administration, a singlepayer system is not "politically viable." What this means is that news judgments are based on elite preferences, not on popular opinion: The *New York Times'* own polling since 1990 has consistently found majorities—ranging from 54 percent to 66 percent—in favor of tax financed national health insurance.[30]

Extra! also noted a similar twisting of the story on the *MacNeil/ Lehrer Newshour.* Single-payer advocate Dr. Steffie Woolhandler

appeared with three government officials who were mostly supporting managed competition. Ignoring the fact that it was his own
staff that had determined the participants, Robin MacNeil made
such comments as "Dr. Woolhandler, that's three against one on
the cost reduction thing," or "since you're in the minority." Mac-
Neil also asked Woolhandler: "If this [program] that has a political
consensus and the other one that you advocate is considered impossible politically at the moment, why are you then against the
one that is viable and would produce a large amount of reform?"

In 1992 there were fourteen hundred news conferences at the
National Press Club alone.[31] The average American reporter, one
study tells us, now works in a newsroom with forty-five other
people, typically for a publication owned by a chain. Some of
these chains are Fortune 500 companies; some are subsidiaries of
such companies. Covering the story is no longer just a journalistic
matter, it is a bureaucratic problem. It requires not only news
sense, but corporate sensitivity. Journalism is no longer the trade it
once was, nor the profession it pretended to be, but a very big
business. When you add corporate caution to social climbing and
the inoffensive product favored by much of the media, a huge
news hole develops in Washington.

To an extent not generally realized, this hole is partially filled
by an ad hoc mixture of freelance journalists, activist congressional aides, government whistleblowers, class-action litigants,
and public interest groups that function as a cross between a form
of alternative media and a people's Government Accounting
Office. This odd assortment also includes reporters and producers
from a number of major television programs such as *60 Minutes,*
Frontline, and *20/20,* who are among the best and most committed journalists covering Washington.

Within this subculture you will find people like Pentagon
whistleblower Ernest Fitzgerald and lawyer Jack Blum, who kept
the BCCI story alive as a Senate aide when most of the city's media
could not have been less interested. There are people like Louis
Clark and Tom Devine of the Government Accountability Project,

who have had an extraordinary record of assisting government whistleblowers, publicizing their stories, fighting their cases in court, and protecting them against almost inevitable retaliation. There is the many-tentacled Public Citizen with interests ranging from unsafe foods to nuclear power. There is the National Security Archives, a repository of data on governmental deeds and misdeeds, and the Project on Government Oversight, which discovered the famed $600 Air Force toilet seats. There is the Advocacy Institute that teaches organizations how to lobby without money and counsels public interest groups. And there are individual staffers from congressional offices as diverse as that of black liberal John Conyers and white conservative Charles Grassley.[32]

While it is comforting, and sometimes entertaining, to observe efforts to exorcise the city's darker side, many of these unfortunately tend to be short-lived. A few years ago, for example, the Project on Government Oversight exposed a major congressional junket that had occurred under the patronage of various large lobbies. The lobbies were assisted by free transportation from the Air Force and by Air Force bagmen, a term of art for Pentagon officer-lobbyists always ready to carry a Congress member's luggage or provide a wide range of other services. ABC News featured footage of corpulent congressmen cavorting on a Barbados beach with their corporate sponsors and of the embarrassed attempts by the participants to explain the whole thing.

In the wake of this disclosure, Keith Rutter of PGO estimates that some five similar junkets were canceled. The Democrats moved their annual schmoozefest from the luxurious resort at Greenbriar to the more serious surroundings of Williamsburg, with one aide saying that the party "didn't want another Barbados on their hands."[33]

The problem, Rutter admits, is that while such efforts can have definite short-term impact, long-term they may just make people behave more cautiously. Indeed, a Public Citizen study found that during 1991–92, corporations, trade groups, and educational institutions paid for at least 680 senatorial junkets.[34]

Still, the fact that these groups and individuals manage to accomplish what they do with so little institutional or financial super-structure suggests that the problem of covering Washington well is as much a function of will as of mechanics. The media, like much of the rest of Washington, has become too large, comfortable, and complacent to do well the job it was sent to the capital to do.

The easiest way for the media to give the impression of inde-pendent analysis is to call upon "experts" at the various think tanks around town. Many of these experts are, in fact, former government officials biding their time until recalled to the inner sanctums of power or are currently serving as consultants to those in office. While think tanks can sometimes be productive—the libertarian Cato Institute is an example—and occasionally provide a haven for truly original thinkers, they primarily function as the Catholic Church of conventional politics, their priests propagating the faith, blessing the faithful, redirecting the errant, and showing up at fundraising dinners to add a little class and offer the benedic-tion. And their collection plates are regularly filled by large corpo-rations with some distinctly non-academic goals in mind.

In fact, it is questionable how much cogitation actually occurs at a Washington think tank. Says Jonathan Rowe of those in the Heritage Foundation's tank, they "don't think, they justify."

Public television is particularly susceptible to these political benchwarmers, whose biases are gracefully concealed by their ac-ademic or quasi-academic cover. Thus the *Washington Post* re-ported that conservative think-tanker Ben Wattenberg was looking for corporate and foundation funding for a public television show that would feature "intellectuals" debating the issues of the day. On Wattenberg's list: Robert Bork, Jeane Kirkpatrick, William Kris-tol, Roger Wilkins, James Q. Wilson—mostly intensely partisan conservative activists, with Wilkins being the only liberal in the crowd.[35]

It works the other way as well. The bestowal by establishment institutions of memberships or fellowships upon members of the media can have a remarkably taming effect on the latter. Usually this is done discreetly, but in the October 30, 1993, issue of the

Washington Post, Richard Harwood frankly described journalistic participation in the Council on Foreign Relations, "whose members are the nearest thing to a ruling establishment in America."

The officials who are members—including the president, six cabinet members, and David Gergen—would hardly surprise one familiar with this citadel of conventional wisdom. Nor the fact that two out of three members live in either Washington or New York. Nor that ex-presidents, corporate CEOs, university presidents, and the like pad the list.

What is a bit startling, however, is that more than 10 percent of the membership of this ideological cavalry for establishment foreign policy are journalists. Included as directors over the past fifteen years have been names like Heldey Donovan and Strobe Talbott of *Time,* Elizabeth Drew of the *New Yorker,* and Philip Geyelin of the *Washington Post.* Members include Dan Rather, Tom Brokaw, Jim Lehrer, Charles Krauthammer, William Buckley, and George Will. According to Harwood, seven editors of the *Washington Post* as well as Katherine Graham belong, as do three editors of the *New York Times.*

One might suppose that given the media's discouragement of gay, women, and minority journalists from participating in marches and demonstrations, Harwood's piece was intended as a self-critical exposé. Far from it. He writes approvingly: "The membership of these journalists . . . is an acknowledgment of their active and important role in public affairs and of their ascension into the American ruling class. They do not merely analyze and interpret foreign policy for the United States; they help make it."

While institutions such as the Council on Foreign Relations, Brookings, and the American Enterprise Institute have long added theoretical underpinnings to political policy, Clinton's arrival has forced such institutions of the New York–Washington axis to take seats behind the Cambridge-headquartered John F. Kennedy School of Government. In fact, the Clinton administration seems practically a subsidiary of this academy of wonkdom. Half of Clinton's cabinet has ties to the school either as students, officials, fellows, or faculty: Les Aspin, Bruce Babbitt, Ron Brown, Henry Cisneros, Robert Reich, Richard Riley, and Donna Shalala.

The Kennedy School is to government what Harvard's business school was to corporations in the 1980. There is a similar emphasis on technical skills—decision trees, case studies, and so forth—and little interest in ethics or philosophical or humanistic principles. Not surprisingly, a lot of the money for the school comes from large corporations who are more than happy to have their tax-deductible contributions used to teach public officials the Kennedy School way of governing.

This bureaucratic boot camp did once consider creating a "chair in poverty" to study "who has been poor for a long time and why," but according to the *Washington Post,* then dean Graham Allison (now in Clinton's Pentagon) was unable to come up with the money. It didn't really surprise him since, after all, most donors are "wealthy people, not poor people." The conservative nature of this institution can be gauged by the fact that flaming moderate Robert Reich was considered its left wing, a flank that apparently did not qualify him for tenure.

Executive dean Hale Champion told the *Post,* "If there isn't a lot of traffic between here and Washington, then we're not in touch with what's going on."[36] A Kennedy School graduate student in an interview with Andrew Ferguson of the *Washingtonian* put it more succinctly:

> The vast majority of people [at the school] are idealists. They want to change the world. But it's more than that. To be honest, we feel that we're entitled to change the world. . . .
> You think that's arrogant. Maybe it is. But look around you. What you've got here are some of the brightest people in this country. If the country needs to change, let's face it, we're the ones to change it.[37]

It's not the first time that Harvard has felt entitled to such a role in Washington. In the 1960s Harvard theorists applied their paradigms to Southeast Asia with disastrous results. The 1980s were propelled in part by dubious management theses emanating from its business school. In the 1990s we find not only the Kennedy School rising to power, but former members of the Soviet bloc coming under the sway of Harvard B-School professor Jeffrey Sachs, whose plans for weaning these emerging republics from communism appear an economic version of General Sherman's approach to weaning Georgia from the Confederacy.

While it is true that our two most recent presidents have been Yale men, the correlation between this fact and the problems of the nation seem without provable causation. This may be because Yalies have tended to prefer money while Harvard graduates (although not eschewing lucre) show a greater interest in influence and power. Thus the excesses of Yale tend to manifest themselves individually, while those of Harvard confront us institutionally.*

This certainly is the case in Washington, where Harvard grads permeate the upper level not only of politics, but also of the media, the law, and the think tanks, carrying with them an aura of what songwriter Allen Jay Lerner called Harvard's "indubitable, irrefutable, inimitable, indomitable, incalculable superiority."

This Harvard old (still mostly) boy network is a significant—yet because of its discretion underrated—influence on the city's values and policies, reflecting, in the words of the historian and reluctant Harvard grad V. L. Parrington, the "smug Tory culture which we were fed on as undergraduates." Writing for his twenty-fifth reunion report in the early part of this century, Parrington said:

> Harvard is only a dim memory to me. Very likely I am wrong in my judgment, yet from what little information comes through to me I have set the school down as a liability rather than an asset to the cause of democracy. It seems to me the apologist and advo-

---

* A partial exception to this rule occurred during the Clarence Thomas hearings when it appeared that most of the protagonists were connected to Yale: Thomas, his nominator, his accuser, his accuser's corroborators, his accuser's attackers, and some of his accuser's interrogators. Still, the issue remained intensely personal, and hardly within the scope of typical geopolitical discourse.

cate of capitalistic exploitation—as witness the sweet-smelling list of nominees set out yearly for the Board of Overseers.

Seventy-five years later, this smug Tory culture quietly thrives in Washington. Not the least indication of this is the fact that products of Harvard and/or Yale constitute one-third of the top positions in an administration that said it was going to look like America.*

Admittedly, Harvard and Yale do not provide the city's only adult fraternities. The capital is crisscrossed with networks of those both inside and out of government sharing a common state political history, an alma mater, or even a branch of military service. Novelist (and former managing editor of the UCLA newspaper) Clancy Sigal even revealed an old boy sidebar to the Watergate affair. Wrote Sigal of schoolmates Bob Haldeman, John Erhlichman, and Alex Butterfield:

> The political really is personal. We validate our strongest beliefs not on a soapbox but in social relationships. Bob, a Beta, and his fiancee, Jo, double-dated with a Delta Gamma, who later married John, a Kappa Sig. Bob's sister was in the same sorority as Alex's wife-to-be. In short, the political relationships of almost all the top Watergate conspirators were originally mediated through their sorority dates: Watergate was a function of Greek Row networking.[38]

The number-crunchers form another important Washington subculture, led by the uncritically accepted shamans of economics. The latter's success with *ex cathedra* calculations has encouraged much of Washington to speak so confidently about numbers

---

* Your author went to Harvard, but graduated *magna cum probation* and belongs to that line of Harvard dissidents that goes all the way back to Henry Thoreau, who had little truck with the place after he was through; to the abolitionist Wendell Phillips, who left Harvard a list of social causes to which it had contributed nothing; and to Ralph Waldo Emerson, who said the college's graduates come out "with a bag of wind, a memory of words—and do not know a thing."

that one almost forgets how many of them were once only English majors.

The effect of numbers on the city has been profound. At times it seems that there is no government anymore, only a budget office. The idea of a budget bureau at the federal level goes back only to Warren Harding. As late as 1975, Austin Kiplinger could write that the president's budget officials were outnumbered by those of the various departments and thus "have to be especially sharp" and make up in clout what they lack in numbers. Today, few feel sorry for the White House budget squad, which has replaced not only many of the functions of departmental financial officials but those of the departments themselves.[39]

As the numerologists rose in power, programs increasingly became transformed into line items. Numbers began serving as adjectives, ideas were reduced to figures, and policy became a matter of where one placed the decimal point. Thus, what should be a debate about programs becomes one about arithmetic, witness the media's dissection of the numerical arguments made by both sides in the Gore-Perot NAFTA debate or the arithmetic anarchy that quickly developed around the health-care issue. It is an emphasis that can produce bizarre results, such as the attempt cited by William Greider of various federal agencies to develop a cost-benefit factor for human life. The FAA figures it at $650,000 for the purpose of airplane crashes; the Labor Department thinks a dead construction worker is worth about $3.5 million, while OMB disagrees, putting the value of a hard hat at only $1 million.[40]

Every day in Washington, many of the best and the brightest occupy themselves computing such figures, defending them before Congress, citing them before a trade association, or recalling them on C-SPAN. Adding and subtracting are among Washington's favorite activities, often providing a digital shield against discussing what the figures actually represent. Few speak of numbers with the clarity of Charles Dickens in *David Copperfield:* "Annual income twenty pounds, annual expenditure, nineteen nineteen six, result happiness. Annual income twenty pounds, annual expenditure twenty pound ought and six, result misery."

Not all number-crunchers push policy and vice versa, but digits and decimal places often lend specificity to the otherwise mushy art of the policy wonk. Central to their work is the ability to project certitude. One banker acquaintance of George Bush's recalls delivering the then president a prescient warning about the pending S&L crisis, only to have it summarily dismissed by Bush's aide Richard Darman, who convincingly and swiftly ticked off the reasons why the banker was wrong.

Little can puncture the self-assurance that inflates the world of the Washington expert. In office, a critical mass of them can create such documents as the Clinton health-care package. Defending its complexity, Clinton advisor Ira Magaziner offered a revealing explanation: the Clinton team didn't want to leave questions for some health policy board to decide in the future. In other words, the Clinton people knew more than anyone else, not only in the present but for the indefinite future.

Even more significant to the city has been the rise of lawyers. Our current obsession with the lawyerly view of the world, exemplified by Clinton's over-attorneyed cabinet, is not native to American culture. While nearly half the signers of the Declaration of Independence and the Constitution were lawyers, it was some decades after the republic's founding that attorneys got to the point that they would be attacked as "unanointed rulers" of the land. The establishment of the profession had been hindered by several factors, not the least of which was hostility to what some perceived as the monarchical residue of English common law.

Even more important, however, was the conflict between law and nature. Perry Miller, in his *Life of the Mind in America,* depicts this with the example of Natty Bumppo, the James Fenimore Cooper character.

In *The Prairie,* the old scout Bumppo has violated game laws and then pointed his rifle at a constable. Judge Temple orders his arrest and at the trial warns his counsel, "Would any society be tolerable, young man, where the ministers of justice are to be opposed by men armed with rifles? Is it for this that I have tamed the wilderness?"

To which Bumppo's advocate replies: "He's simple, unlettered, even ignorant; prejudiced, perhaps, though I feel that his opinion of the world is too true; but he has a heart, Judge Temple, that would atone for a thousand faults; he knows his friends, and never deserts them, even if it be his dog."[41]

Here, says Miller, was the great legal issue of the nineteenth century: "the never-ending case of Heart vs. Head"—the natural goodness and wisdom of the American citizen vs. the exotic, syllogistic acrobatics of the law. Wrote Miller: "It was not that the American people were positively resolved on becoming lawless, in the manner of cinema badmen, but they did profoundly believe that the mystery of the law was a gigantic conspiracy of the learned against their helpless integrity."[42]

Although de Tocqueville would soon find that people no longer seemed to distrust lawyers, this to his mind was not good. He considered lawyers, who "form the highest political class and the most cultivated portion of society," a "counterpoise" to democratic government: "They constantly endeavor to turn it away from its real direction by means that are foreign to its nature."

It was about this time that one justice declared, "It is the unenvied province of the Court to be directed by the head and not the heart. . . . No latitude is left for the exercise of feeling."

By the end of the century, Thorstein Veblen found the lawyer "exclusively occupied with the details of predatory fraud, either in achieving or in checkmating chicanery, and success in the profession is therefore accepted as marking a large endowment of the barbarian astuteness which has always commanded men's respect and fear."[43]

Throughout the twentieth century, popular and political culture has been marked by distrust of lawyers. Jim Hightower likes to tell of the Texas trial lawyer who stole from the rich and gave approximately half to the poor. And H. L. Mencken once suggested that since behind every bad law was a lawyer, they should all be executed and their bones sold to a mahjong factory.

Yet despite this substantial provenance of skepticism, the past few decades have seen an explosion of lawyerly influence on American life and politics perhaps rivaling that of the early nineteenth century. As one small indication, the number of employees in private legal services in Washington, D.C.—excluding those in the D.C. and federal government—rose 33 percent between 1985 and 1990 to nearly 30,000, to about one out of every ten working-age adults.[44]

What such numbers do not tell is the parallel rise in the influence of the lawyer's perspective. The technology of torts, with its tyranny of precedents and its infatuation with retribution over resolution, has, in the words of the country and western song, walked across our heart like it was Texas. No politics, no ideology, no culture has been immune. All of American life has been hauled into court. Thus we find in our path not only the endless droppings of corporate attorneys, but civil rights advocates who insist that the law will lead us to love each other, feminist counselors who believe that the world's oldest conflict can be settled on appeal, colleges that publish what amounts to a lawyer's guide to correct sex, and public-interest activists trying to run a revolution out of the courthouse.

Obviously the law has had a crucial role in such matters as civil rights and bringing the megacorporation to heel. But such achievements hardly justify an exclusive contract to direct the course of social change. If today's lawyer-leaders had come to the fore thirty years ago, the sixties would have been just a lawsuit, not a cultural and political revolution. There would have been no music, no madness, no drama, and without them, probably not much change as well. There are things you just can't do with a lawsuit. Martin Luther King, as usual, put it well: "Something must happen so as to touch the hearts and souls of men that they will come together, not because the law says it, but because it is natural and right."

In November 1992 we sent to the White House a man and a woman who represented the Washington professional ideal—he an unreconstructed student of law, numbers, and policy options, and she a dutiful advocate for corporations. No small amount of the conflict that has occurred since may be traced to an inchoate resentment of what the Clintons and their often incomprehensible policies represent: a new level of control of American culture by a mandarin class against which average citizens can array only a helpless integrity.

Natty Bumppo is back, only now he is fighting trade agreements. Here was the hidden issue in NAFTA, the sleeper problem with the Clinton health-care plan. The 2,000-page NAFTA agreement and the 1,300-page health legislation could have been envisioned only by a lawyer. After all, as Perot pointed out, if you just wanted free trade with Mexico, all you had to do was plug some zeros into existing tariff agreements. If you only wanted universal health care, you could take the Medicare law and strike the words "over 65" from it. The path from such admittedly oversimplified solutions to the engorged legislation of the Clintons led past too many hidden agendas, too many unidentified bank accounts, too many unspecified bottom lines. Many American heads could not sort it out, but many American hearts knew it was wrong.

After all, even NAFTA's supporters admitted it was far more than a trade agreement; it was part of the new world order. Late, perhaps too late, many had come to sense that this new order was not for them; that it was part of some strange and massive alteration in how things are run and who runs them, a hidden revolution against the sovereignty and ground rules of their country.

It was, in the end, another step in the replacement of politics, laws, and culture by a Darwinian international marketplace mediated, if at all, by secret trade tribunals rather than public debate, one more step in the substitution of corporate law for constitutional democracy.

The 1960s, the civil rights movement, feminism, and environmentalism all brought the country social as well as political change. Federal Washington has absorbed the latter, but to a remarkable degree has remained unaffected by the former. The city has observed these phenomena not by changing its heart but by changing the federal code.

This is why, perhaps, Clinton can have such a good record of appointing minorities in high places and do so little to help those in low places. Blacks, women, Latinos, even gays, are welcome into the most powerful offices of the city, provided they play by the rules of the club. It is the city's political and social culture—not one's own ethnic and sexual characteristics—that ultimately defines those who inhabit power.

Federal Washington is similarly unaffected by the contrasting culture of a local city that has lived with the twin indignities of racial segregation and political subservience, overcoming the former but still struggling with the latter. Despite the lessons to be learned there, local Washington is regarded as terra incognita, a place of danger, and, in the truest sense, a colony.

Federal Washington is a culture in which much seems to happen but little gets accomplished. It is a culture in which neither the battles nor the words about them are necessarily real, in which the interests of the federal enclave too often precede those of the country, and in which speaking of something is considered the moral equivalent of actually doing it.

It is a culture that can admit neither to itself nor to the larger world the degree to which its various systems are out of control. Nor can it admit that when it defines corruption only by its most precise legal limits, it exempts itself from any broader decency.

It is finally a culture that has been remarkably successful at isolating itself from the reality it is attempting to govern. The abstract, soulless security of the capital protects it from the pain it causes, the suffering it neglects, and the concerns it can quantify but not ameliorate. Here statistics substitute for tears, data for anger, and mechanically modulated voices recounting promises never to be fulfilled serve as a placebo for real hope and joy.

It is, in the end, the place described in Tennessee Williams's *Camino Real:* "Turn back, traveler, for the spring of humanity has gone dry in this place and there are no birds in the country except wild birds that are tamed and kept in cages."[45]

Signs along the Highway

CAN MORE WORDS SAVE US? INFORMATION
HIGHWAYS VS. DATA LANDFILLS. THE
WORD ACCORDING TO OSBORNE AND
GAEBLER. THE WORD ACCORDING TO US.
WHEN WORDS FAIL US: OUR RESPONSE TO
THE DECLINE OF ALMOST EVERYTHING.
DISCOVERING THE INNER FRONTIER. DO
TANKS VS. THINK TANKS. AMERICA GETS
ANOTHER CHANCE.

- A commercial for General Electric displays seventy-seven distinct images in sixty seconds.
- The head of a West Coast management systems firm reports that some clients receive up to thirty voice-mail messages a day—that's one phone call every sixteen minutes.
- In 1962 there were 2,801 appeals to the Supreme Court. In 1992 there were 7,245. The number of signed opinions by the court has remained roughly the same—about 110 a year.[1]

From couch potato to CEO to Supreme Court justice, Americans stagger under too much information. No longer, it seems, does truth set us free; rather, it leaves us catatonic—burying us in its details and imprisoning us in its walls of noise and glare.

If we are an ordinary television viewer, we may react by accepting the medium's primary message that life is a vicarious experience. We may adopt the role that television has proposed for us, that of spectator, and come to believe that we have no more control over the events on CNN or the 11 P.M. news than we do over the third base coach's signals on ESPN.

If one is a Supreme Court justice or president of the United States, the sense of overload and ultimate ineffectiveness may be even more acute, but this sense will be suppressed, remaining a sort of trade secret. Few politicians or judges will say, even euphemistically, "I am helpless." As long as they choose to hold office, they must remain unindicted co-conspirators in the myth of their efficacy.

Thus it is not surprising to find the Clinton administration buoyantly proposing to manage the glut of information by making it possible for more of it to flow faster to more places. The poet might suggest a sanitary landfill for the redundant, false, and destructive data of our time, or argue that we need more rest stops— or even more roadkill—rather than more routes; our president has called instead for a system of superhighways.

In its broadest shape, it is not a malignant idea. One can argue that much of the damage of the information revolution has already happened. I am struck, for example, by how tepid the image of cyberspace seems in comparison to my previous futures. Being linked directly to my travel agent is hardly on a par with a box that would tape-record anything on TV while I'm out or those *Collier* illustrations of what a rocket to the moon would look like. Being able to play Jeopardy with my cousin in Seattle falls far short of the *Popular Mechanics* projections of my childhood, in which cars would fly and we would all have Dick Tracy two-way radios on our wrists. In fact, of the eleven consumer potentials for the new information technology listed in a 1993 *Newsweek* story, more than half are already available to some degree on computer and several on television.

But then the American establishment's enthusiasm for information highways is based on far more than just satisfying consumer fantasies or even meeting data-flow demands of corporate America. What is evolving is not so much innovation as inundation, and not just new systems of relaying information but new systems of controlling and selling it.

There is, for example, apparently a large after-market in network shows like *20/20.* One industry expert hypothesized that just 5 percent of viewers willing to pay one buck to call up a single *20/20* program that they missed could result in a $2 million annual gross from this one edition of one show—potentially a $2 *billion* a year business just in personalized network reruns.

The pending record merger between Bell Atlantic and TCI is the most prominent example of what's happening; its scope unravels even the greatly weakened anti-trust principles of the last decade. And there are other ominous noises, such as the attempt by the Clinton administration to control the coding of computer signals in order to ease eavesdropping by the FBI and NSA.

Beyond such economic and civil liberties questions, however, is a more profound one: what's the point? Writing in the *New York Times,* Bill McKibben noted: "I suspect our saturation with information we don't need, with noise that increasingly rattles us, will begin to pall, that we will come ever more to resent the time it steals from our lives. Very few people anymore want a real superhighway through their neighborhoods, and perhaps it will someday be the same with megatube."

There is already a huge business devoted to blocking information. Caller ID helps you to determine the data stream to your home, channel controls protect your children from violent images, and if I can guess the length of a commercial break, my zapper will allow me to surf elsewhere until it is over.

There is also a huge non-business in unregulated information highways such as Internet, described by James Gleick as an "amorphous unruly, impolite and anarchistic" data network run by millions of users rather than by a corporation or a government.

These developments are encouraging and remind us how much easier it is to predict the hazards of a new technology than it is to imagine how humans might learn to cope with or even sub-

vert it. The computer, once considered primarily a tool of orthodoxy, has now become a major weapon against authoritarianism.
The highly effective campus anti-apartheid protests were organized with the help of a computer bulletin board that advised new-
comers how to plan demonstrations and deal with the media. In
the last days of the Soviet Union, the relative security of computer
information provided dissidents a means of communications with
each other and with the outside world. More recently, computers
have established the first strong link among environmentalists
working to save Lake Baikal in Siberia. The lake is the earth's
oldest and deepest, containing one-fifth of the earth's fresh water
and isolated from those who might help it. Irina Glazyrina wrote
from Chita, Siberia, to two staff members of the Sacred Earth Network who had helped establish the system: "I think we'll start
implementation of our program very soon. Without doubt we
could not have made all these arrangements so fast without e-mail.
Sometimes it seems to me that Chita is close to the center of the
Universe. Almost every day I receive interesting information, a lot
of best regards and kisses from my friends. Life has changed.
That's great!"[2]

And thousands of miles away, in the Silicon Valley community
of Sunnydale California, a city councilman was elected with 60
percent of the vote after campaigning almost exclusively on the
Internet computer network.

Computer bulletin boards like Peacenet, despite their considerable temptation to waste money and time, tilt both the sense and
the reality of power toward the user. To be able to read the accounts of real Russians at the height of the anti-Yeltsin uprising—
with the potential of responding to them—is to move into a relationship with events that not even CNN can hope to emulate. So
successful, in fact, has the Internet network become that the Clinton
White House uploads to it news releases, statements, and speeches
and plans to expand the link to include thirteen hundred Social
Security offices and all three thousand county extension offices.

Cable television can also have unexpectedly democratic side

effects, as when a New England small town's broadcast of a council meeting so infuriated one viewer that he leaped out of bed and rushed to the session to make his protest—still in his pajamas. In its more conventional moments cable has provided a substantial forum to ethnic and political minorities and is an accessible reminder of both the diversity and the marvelous eccentricity still abroad in the land—sometimes combined in one program, as in a program devoted to gospel aerobics.

Yet the very anarchistic nature of our new sources of data—including computer services, cable channels, special interest magazines, and the archives of our video store—also means that we may have less information in common. At a time when communications and transportation make it ever simpler to cross geographic and cultural borders, we increasingly seem to make the trip alone. We see far more than we understand or are understood. Louis Farrakhan and the Anti-Defamation League have the same technology available to them, but they are checking in at different bulletin boards.

This is our conundrum: an excess of information and a shortage of comprehension. In Washington it leads to indecipherable 1,300-page bills on health care and 2,000-page trade agreements with Mexico; in Crown Heights and L.A. it can lead to cruelty and death.

But an excess of information is not new. Walk in the woods on a pleasant fall day and try to count the images and information that surround you. Even the suggestion seems stupid because without ever thinking about it, we have learned to both aggregate and filter our experience, blending the colors into one coherent picture even as we are drawn toward the details of an unusual plant or stone.

It is harder in the city since many of its signs must be learned, but to the urban dweller these complex and subtle signals guide one to a likely store or a pleasant bar—and away from potential danger. They also help us create our own village—an implicit community defined by the routes we take, the places we go, and the people we see and know.

Likewise, the dedicated sports fan has little trouble blending information and emotion. Even such computer-aided excesses as the ability to determine who stole the most bases in the American League on cloudy third Wednesdays in July does not deter enthusiasm. In sports, data and passion happily exist side by side.

In our politics, however, information has become increasingly distant from experience, faith ever more separated from fact, and numbers removed from our feelings. Listen to the average Washington expert on the radio or on C-SPAN—not just to the content but to the scratchy, antiseptic tone—and one can easily forget that the subject may, in fact, be the pain, hope, or death of real people: "Welcome. The White House has announced that the end of the world will occur at approximately 3 P.M. today. To discuss this development and its implications for the economy and for minorities, we have invited several experts from the Apocalyptic Institute to join us for a discussion . . . ."

Once you remove from political information the mediating influence of memory, of place, of passion, of individuals with all their stories and peculiarities, you no longer have a politics of communities but one of sterile systems. And the primary goal of any system, once it gets large enough, is just to keep itself alive.

This is one of the things this book has been about: a fable about a system and a politics that has come to expend so much of its energy keeping itself alive that it finally has too little left to do what it is supposed to do. About a system that has been absorbed so long with keeping itself alive that it has, in fact, *forgotten* what it is supposed to do. About disorder and decay and the state that the politicians and press call gridlock. About a system run by "symbolic analysts" who spend their days distributing data that in endless and degrading reiteration creates unreadable fifth-generation photocopies of reality and meaning.

If the federal government were a city, it would be the third-largest in the country—bigger than Chicago. It takes a lot of energy to run Chicago, but then that's Chicago's business. It takes a lot of energy to run the federal government, but the federal government is supposed to be doing something other than just running itself. Nonetheless, in that government every decision of every day must be weighed against two often uncomplementary sets of requirements—those of America and those of the system that runs it, the de facto third-largest city in the land. Even in the best of times, the system may come first; in the worst of times, its demands become obsessive as it struggles to maintain itself.

Much as Mikhail Gorbachev was chosen by the Soviet leadership to rescue the Communist system, so this country's establishment has dispatched Bill Clinton on a similar mission on behalf of the late-twentieth-century American system. If you listen carefully to the messages, there is a great deal of fear: "global competition," crime, immigration, drugs, disorder, low test scores, racial tension, declining values, "runaway" health costs. Managed competition advocate Lynn Etheridge warned a group in Washington, "If the private sector screws up, they're going to be out of business." He was talking about health care, but it might have well been the official warning label of the Clinton administration, a reminder to its political allies that both time and energy are running out.

That's why the Clintonites were so grateful for *Reinventing Government*. This book by David Osborne and Ted Gaebler has become a Clinton administration bible.

Written in the pentecostal managerial style common to the self-help shelves of airport bookstores, the book finds that Total Quality Management—a favorite of the bureaucratic born-agains—falls short because it has only five principles instead of Osborne and Gaebler's ten. There are thirty-six alternatives to standard service delivery, five advantages to mission-driven government, four approaches to budgeting, sixteen ways to the customer's heart, and eight things to measure and monitor.

What this book is about is best expressed by Bill Clinton himself in the cover blurb: "Should be read by every *elected official* in America. This book gives *us* the blueprint" (emphasis added). *Re-*

inventing Government at its core is a guide to saving the existing system; it tells government managers and politicians how to improve it and how to reduce complaints about it. To this end it provides some useful, some dubious, and some tediously obvious suggestions.

The book may in fact lead to improvements in the details and mechanics of government—particularly, we learn from Al Gore, efficiencies in the purchase of government ashtrays. Trying to save money clearly has merit at a time when the Postal Service, suffering a $1.3 billion deficit and having laid off 30,000 workers, pays $7 million to create a new logo and paste it on everything it owns—a decision defended by its "director of corporate identity," who says: "We are a viable communications agency and it's critical that we prepare for the 21st century by updating our image with a 21st century look."[3]

But what this book does not do is tell citizens how to regain control of their government, revive democracy, save the planet from the scourge of ecological excess or mediate among the various cultures and ideologies they may find in their communities. Government is reduced to a matter of management. The book is written with an unexamined self-assurance, an abstract quantification of human experience, and an indifference to real politics. It reminds one of repeatedly unsuccessful remedies proposed by urban planners of the sixties and seventies or of the plastic, mechanistic schemes for regional government that crop up from time to time. There is no philosophy here other than good business. Even what some might consider an environmental issue—the reduction of water use in Tucson's toilets—becomes a matter of "demand management." And, inevitably, entrepreneurial spirit, privatization, market-driven forces, and similar clichés from the corporate cookbook spring to the aid of the beleaguered government official.

There is, to be sure, the required talk of "empowerment," and the example of Kimi Gray, every conservative's favorite public housing resident, but more revealing are the authors' thoughts on what it takes to be a public leader these days:

> It is not enough that a leader has a vision of change, he or she must get other community leaders to buy into that vision. . . . A shared vision is not the same thing as a consensus. Entrepreneurial leaders rally their communities to their visions, rather than accepting a least common denominator consensus. This does not eliminate conflict; it simply assures that enough of the community shares the leaders' vision to overcome the opposition.[4]

In other words: if a mayor and the board of trade and local developers have the shared vision that a new convention center would be nifty, this can overcome the least common denominator consensus that the city is going to hell in a handbasket—in part because the mayor is a tool of the board of trade and local developers. Such a dynamic helps to explain why we have so many new convention centers and so many old urban problems at the same time.

In part, what Osborne and Gaebler have done is to catalog existing examples of the growing intrusion of corporate culture into politics. The trend owes a debt to Dwight D. Eisenhower, who iconized the chief of staff system and made Nixon the nation's first corporate vice-president. Out of this dubious heritage of Sherman Adams and Richard Nixon, we find ourselves finally in 1993 with a president in love with corporate culture and a Congress apologizing in boardroom babble for even thinking about exercising its constitutional powers over Somalia. Said Senator Robert Byrd: "The president of the United States is our commander-in-chief and I do not believe that we should attempt to micro-manage military operations here in Congress."

Senator Dole agreed: "I don't want to micro-manage foreign policy."

This from a Congress that hadn't actually declared a war since 1941.

But also in this book so admired by Clinton, one finds that the concept of citizenship simply disappears. The voter is transformed into a mere customer, an alteration of which the authors seem quite proud. Even that Peter Drucker of an earlier age, the ever entrepreneurial Benjamin Franklin, knew the difference between being a citizen and being a customer. Gordon Woods notes in *The Radicalism of the American Revolution*: "Government, wrote Benjamin Franklin, resembled a business company, and rulers were just 'directors' hired by the owners to carry out their wishes. These 'directors' are the servants, not the masters [and] the power they have is from the members and returns to them."[5]

Or, as Ross Perot more bluntly told an anti-NAFTA rally: "You own this country."

Customer is not the only word being used to change the nature of citizenship. David Kemmis, the mayor of Missoula, Montana, points out in *Parabola: The Magazine of Myth and Tradition* that the word *taxpayer* "now regularly holds the place which in a true democracy would be occupied by 'citizen' ":

> Taxpayers bear a dual relationship to government, neither half of which has anything at all to do with democracy. Taxpayers pay tribute to the government and they receive services from it. So does every subject of a totalitarian regime. What taxpayers do not do, and what people who call themselves taxpayers have long since stopped even imagining themselves doing, is governing.[6]

The question of whether we should give up our citizenship in favor of customerhood or being a taxpayer has never made it to the ballot. It doesn't have to. Like much political change these days, the idea has grown more by osmosis than by choice, the product of a "shared vision" among the elite, dutifully disseminated by a media that has lost much of its capacity for skepticism.

It is by such seemingly mild alterations that democracy and our communal identity start to slip away. William O. Douglas put it well: "As nightfall does not come at once, neither does oppression. In both instances, there is a twilight when everything remains seemingly unchanged. And it is in such twilight that we must be most aware of change in the air—however slight—lest we become unwitting victims of the darkness."[7]

An autocracy you can have through simple sloth or indifference; a democracy takes constant tending. Asked whether the new government would be a monarchy or a republic, Benjamin Franklin replied, "A republic, if you can keep it." Tanks are not necessary to undo it; our own carelessness with words and thoughts can lead us to surrender without struggle what we once thought central to our cause. Our own absorption with contemporary scenes and symbols flashing across the screen can lead us to forget—if we ever knew—what went before and why those who went before once thought it mattered.

So let's turn off the set for a moment, stop thinking about new information, and consider that already passing through our lives— the words and phrases we hear every day, words and phrases used to define our country and ourselves. What lies between these words and reality, between what we say we are, what we really are, and what we once were, is a wilderness of myth and self-deception through which we must backtrack in order to find our way home again.

Here, like stolen highway markers in a freshman dorm room, are a few of the signs that tell us where we would like to be but which no longer place us there:

Democracy

The democratic franchise, while greatly broadened from a time when only propertied white males could vote, has lost its depth. We have, in effect, more people sharing less power. Take, for example, the New England town meeting, often cited as a model of direct democracy, in which each enfranchised resident had a voice and a vote in the proceedings of the community. By the 1990s the term's meaning had been completely turned on its head: now it is a meeting, perhaps nationally televised, in which citizens of a remote, impermeable government listen to, and are cynically manipulated by, an official or candidate. All three key elements of the original town meeting—community, decentralized power, and direct democracy—have decayed and disappeared.

Other traditional signs of a vibrant democracy have been either distorted or enfeebled. We are apathetic in our voting, removed from our representatives, regularly deceived in our discussions, and ineffectual in our efforts to change our conditions. As historian Michael Zuckerman has written:

> We confront, then, a crisis if not an essential collapse of the classical conception of citizenship. We confront a citizenry that cannot inform itself because its government operates so substantially by stealth and deliberate deception, and we confront a citizenry that does not care or dare to inform itself because it is preoccupied with private fulfillment. In the days of the Framers, civic participation was an assumptive attribute of the man of virtue, just as virtue was almost inconceivable apart from political engagement. In our own day, as Robert Bellah has observed, sustained involvement in public affairs is so exceptional that we scarcely have a term for it. We call men and women "good citizens" if they merely cast a ballot every year or two, since most Americans no longer do even that much. The eagerness of the electorate to give up its civic entitlements and obligations is mirrored in the keenness of the Congress to avert its attention from executive usurpations, and that keenness in turn heartens the executive to attempt further usurpations.[8]

Market Forces

Encomiums to the wonders of market forces fill speeches and media reports. One National Public Radio reporter even went so far as to describe a form of government called *market democracy,* apparently a blend of the Bill of Rights and the *Wall Street Journal* editorial page.

In fact, most free workers in this country were self-employed well into the nineteenth century. They were thus economic as well as political citizens.

Further, until the last decades of the nineteenth century, Americans believed in a degree of fair distribution of wealth that would shock many today. James L. Huston writes in the *American Histor-*

ical Review: "Americans believed that if property were concentrated in the hands of a few in a republic, those few would use their wealth to control other citizens, seize political power, and warp the republic into an oligarchy. Thus to avoid descent into despotism or oligarchy, republics had to possess an equitable distribution of wealth."[9]

Such a distribution, in theory at least, came from enjoying the "fruits of one's labor," but no more. Businesses that sprang up didn't flourish on competition because there generally wasn't any, and besides, cooperation worked better. You didn't need two banks or two drugstores in the average town. Prices and business ethics were not regulated by the marketplace but by a complicated cultural code and the fact that the banker went to church with his depositors. Although the practice was centuries old, the term *capitalism*—and thus the religion—didn't even exist until the middle of the nineteenth century.

Americans were intensely commercial, but this spirit was propelled not by Reaganesque fantasies about competition but by the freedom that engaging in business provided from the hierarchical social and economic system of the monarchy. Business, including the exchange as well as the making of goods, was seen as a natural state allowing a community and individuals to get ahead and to prosper without the blessing of nobility.

In the beginning, if you wanted to form a corporation you needed a state charter and had to prove it was in the public interest, convenience, and necessity. During the entire colonial period only about a half-dozen business corporations were chartered; between the end of the Revolution and 1795 this number rose to about 150. Jefferson to the end opposed liberal grants of corporate charters and argued that states should be allowed to intervene in corporate matters or take back a charter if necessary.[10]

With the pressure for more commerce and indications that corporate grants were becoming a form of patronage, states began passing free incorporation laws, and before long Massachusetts had thirty times as many corporations as there were in all of Europe.

Still, it wasn't until after the Civil War that economic conditions turned sharply in favor of the large corporation. These corporations, says Huston,

> killed the republican theory of the distribution of wealth and probably ended whatever was left of the political theory of republicanism as well. . . . [The] corporation brought about a new form of dependency. Instead of industry, frugality, and initiatives producing fruits, underlings in the corporate hierarchy had to be aware of style, manners, office politics, and choice of patrons—very reminiscent of the Old Whig corruption in England at the time of the revolution—what is today called "corporate culture."

Concludes Huston: "The rise of Big Business generated the most important transformation of American life that North America has ever experienced."

By the end of the last century, the Supreme Court had declared corporations to be persons under the 14th Amendment, entitled to the same protections as human beings. As Morton Mintz pointed out in the *National Law Journal,* this 1886 case ignored the fact that "the only 'person' Congress had in mind when it adopted the 14th Amendment in 1866 was the newly freed slave." Justice Black observed in the 1930s that in the first fifty years following the adoption of the 14th Amendment, "less than one-half of 1 percent [of Supreme Court cases] invoked it in protection of the Negro race, and more than 50 percent asked that its benefits be extended to corporations." During this period the courts moved to limit democratic power in other ways as well. For example, the Supreme Court restricted the common-law right of juries to nullify a wrongful law; other courts erected barriers against third parties such as banning fusion slates.

It was during this same time that the myth of competitive virtue sprouted, helping to justify one of the great rapacious periods of American business. It was a time when J. P. Morgan would come to own half the railroad mileage in the country—the same J. P. Morgan who got his start during the Civil War by buying defective rifles for $3.50 each from an army arsenal and then selling them to a general in the field for $22 apiece. The founding principles of what we now proudly call the "American free market system" flowered in an era of enormous bribes, massive legislative corruption, and the creation of great anti-competitive cartels. It was a time when the government, in a precursor to industrial policy, gave two railroad companies 21 million acres of free land.[11]

And it was also the time that American workers, who had once used commerce to free themselves from the economic and social straitjacket of the monarchy, found themselves servants of a new rigid hierarchy, that of the modern corporation.

The political movement of populism, which Jonathan Rowe calls the "last spasm of economic freedom in an American context," did battle with the new corporations but lost, as did the Eurocentric socialists who followed. Save during the Depression, generations of Americans would come to accept the myth of free enterprise. After all, even if it was far from free, it was providing jobs and rising incomes. Now, however, the myth is cracking. The signs are all around:

• Downsizing cost America 2 million jobs in two years.[12] There has been a drastic cutback in company-funded pensions. Labor unions have been in retreat in terms of both membership and power. Average real wages are at their lowest in thirty years. Two of every five jobs in the U.S. are now temporary or part-time, most without health or similar benefits.[13]

• Even American elites have stopped using the adjective *free* so much. Now they more frequently refer to simply a *market economy.*

• Economist Gary Schilling estimates that the unemployment rate for new college grads during the nineties will be 10 percent, and the Labor Department suggests another 25 to 50 percent will be underemployed at jobs below their skill level.[14] In 1950 black and white teenage unemployment were the same. Today black teenagers are twice as likely to be unemployed.[15] During 1968–70, real unemployment among central-city blacks with less than a high-school education in the Northeast was 19 percent; for central-city whites it was 15 percent. Today, the figure is 57 percent for blacks and 38 percent for whites.[16] The median real income of young families headed by a parent under thirty fell 32 percent between 1970 and 1990.[17]

Beyond such statistics is the point raised by historian Zucker-man: "Amid the vast combines of contemporary technological society, the personal independence that was prerequisite to civic virtue for the Founding Fathers becomes precarious if not impossible."[18]

Peace

• In 1784, the Continental Congress declared that "standing armies in time of peace are inconsistent with the principles of republican government, dangerous to the liberties of free people and generally converted into destructive engines for establishing despotism." In 1953 President Eisenhower said, "Every gun that is made, every warship launched, every rocket fired signifies—in the final sense—a theft from those who hunger and are not fed, those who are cold and are not clothed. This is not a way of life at all, in any true sense. . . . It is humanity hanging from a cross of iron."

• Now, the Clinton administration proposes to spend less than 2 percent of the defense budget on military conversion over the next five years.[19]

• In 1993, a Harris poll found that confidence in the military was at a twenty-seven-year high. The percentage of those having positive feelings about the military was more than double that of the next best regarded American institution, the Supreme Court. Support in every other category save the White House (e.g., the press, Wall Street, and medicine) had dropped. Meanwhile Clinton was maintaining the military budget at average Cold War levels, and General Colin Powell was being prominently mentioned as a candidate for the presidency, rating in a Wirthlin survey far above other public officials, including both Clintons.

Entrepreneurship

In 1903, Milton Kronheim, age fourteen, decided to go into business. He had been working at his cousin's liquor store on D.C.'s M Street. The cousin suggested he quit high school and run a branch of the company for six dollars a week. Milton asked for eight dollars, was rejected, and went off to start his own firm, which grew to be one of the most successful liquor operations in the Washington area. Said Kronheim: "In those days it didn't require a lot of capital to open a store. I didn't buy expensive fixtures. All I needed was some shelving."[20]

In 1993, the city of Washington, D.C., required the following of a non-profit organization that wanted to serve liquor at a three-hour benefit: an application filed in person ten working days prior to the event; proof of age of the applicant; a letter from "the true and actual owner or designated agent of the premises where the event is to be held authorizing the sale or consumption of alcoholic beverages on subject premises"; a copy of the certificate of occupancy and/or public hall license; two completed and notarized copies of form BRA-70, which is a stipulation that the city may check the applicant's FBI file; a criminal records check by the local police; an ABC manager's permit; fundraising and/or other licenses from the Business Service Division; the reading, signing, and retaining of the notice regarding the "District of Columbia Legal Drinking Amendment Emergency Act of 1986"; a $200 permit fee; and, should someone other than the applicant wish to pick up the license, a written statement for the file to this effect.[21]

Efficiency

Then: Franklin Roosevelt managed to fight the Depression with a White House staff smaller than that now allotted Mrs. Clinton. He fought World War II with less staff than Al Gore.

Now: Wrote Lars-Erick Nelson in the *New York Daily News,* "On Friday, February 5, at ten o'clock in the morning, I telephoned the Pentagon press office and told the colonel who answered the phone that I needed information on duplication in the armed forces. He replied: 'You want the other press office'."[22]

Then: In late summer of 1933, when it appeared that the National Recovery Administration would not be able to provide adequate employment, FDR aide Harry Hopkins began laying the groundwork for a huge jobs program. Hopkins—who had pledged to himself to put 4 million people to work within four weeks—fell somewhat short. In the first four weeks only 2.8 million workers were put on the government payroll. Hopkins didn't reach the 4 million goal until January.[23]

Now: Congress in 1993 approved a jobs stimulus bill only four and a half times the size of the annual budget for the nation's military bands.

Justice

•   America has the highest percentage of its population in prison of any country. The fastest-growing public housing program in America is prison construction. Meanwhile, federal funds for fighting white-collar crime are insufficient to pay law enforcement officials to even read—let alone examine thoroughly—bank reports of large cash transactions.

•   According to Dan Baum in *The Nation,* more Americans are in federal prison today for drug crimes than were in federal prison for all crimes when Ronald Reagan took office. The number of prisoners in California increased 1,000 percent between 1980 and 1990. Eighty percent of them had a drug problem, but only 10 percent were receiving treatment.[24]

•   According to the *New York Times,* "prosecutors acknowledge that in tens of thousands of cases property is taken from individuals who are never charged or convicted of crimes." The federal government is currently seizing about $2 billion worth of private property annually under civil forfeiture laws without due process. Included are some 17,000 cars taken from people suspected of smuggling illegal immigrants.

•   In the late 1960s there were two federal agencies enforcing the drug laws on a budget of less than $10 million. Today there are fifty-four agencies splitting a $13 billion budget.[25]

• Speaking before the 1991 National Guard Association Conference, Lt. Gen. John B. Conway, Chief of the National Guard Bureau, said: "Our commander in chief has declared war on drugs. Our mission as America's National Guard in this war is clear: make America drug-free in as short a time as possible using any means necessary no matter what the cost." So between January and August of 1992, the National Guard made nearly 20,000 arrests, searched 120,000 cars, and searched more than 1,200 buildings. Said one National Guard official quoted by the newsletter *Justica,* "The National Guard is America's legally feasible attitude-change agent." The regular Army, however, would still like to get in on the act. Lt. Gen. J. H. Bindford Peay III, the chief of staff for operations and plans, said in an Army publication, "We can look forward to the day when our Congress . . . allows the Army to lend its full strength towards making America drug-free."[26]

• A few years ago, Robert Dupont, a former high government drug official turned professor of psychiatry at Georgetown University, proposed in the *Washington Post* that there be mandatory drug tests for attending school or getting a driver's license. Those who failed drug tests repeatedly would be incarcerated in "large, temporary health shelters." There would be some invasion of privacy and civil rights, said the doctor, but "this is a price we would need to pay for life in a modern, interdependent community."

• There is a video game called "Robocop," subtitled "The Future of Law Enforcement," in which the officer on the screen kills a score of people just waiting for someone to insert a quarter.

A Nation of Laws

• *From rules promulgated by Antioch College regarding "interactions" of a sexual nature:* "All sexual contact and conduct between any two people must be consensual; consent must be obtained verbally before there is any sexual contact or conduct; if the level of sexual intimacy increases during an interaction (i.e., if two people move from kissing while fully clothed—which is one level—to undressing for direct physical contact, which is another level), the people involved need to express their clear verbal consent before moving to that new level; if one person wants to initiate moving to a higher level of sexual intimacy in an interaction, that person is responsible for getting the verbal consent of the other person(s) involved before moving to that level; if you have had a particular level of sexual intimacy before with someone, you must still ask each and every time. . . . Asking 'Do you want to have sex with me?' is not enough. The request for consent must be specific to each act."

• *From a column by Steve Twomey in the* Washington Post: "Alexandria [Va.] says every block party must be covered against $1 million in claims, though it might grant some waivers. . . . It wants protection, though it does acknowledge it has never been sued over anything that has happened at any block party in the recorded history of Alexandria, Va. . . . A man in Arlington sued a management company because he got struck by lightning while sitting in a metal lawn chair on the roof of a building, where he had gone expressly to watch a thunderstorm."[27]

• *One sentence from President Clinton's Health Security Act:* "In the case of an individual enrolled under a health plan under a family class of enrollment (as defined in section 1011(c)(2)(A)), the family out-of-pocket limit on cost sharing in the cost sharing schedule offered by the plan represents the amount of expenses that members of the individual's family, in the aggregate, may be required to incur under the plan in a year because of general deductible, separate deductibles, copayments, and coinsurance before the plan may no longer impose any cost sharing with respect to items or services covered by the comprehensive benefit package that are provided to any member of the individual's family, except as provided in subsections (d)(2)(D) and (e)(2)(D) of section 1115."[28]

Land of Opportunity

• A study by the Department of Transportation found that 87 percent of some 100 cities with taxi service restrict entry into the business in some way. Chip Mellor of the Institute for Justice notes that Denver has denied every application for a new taxicab company since 1947. Chicago and L.A. are also closed. Boston's permits cost $60,000 and New York's $140,000.

• Starting something in Washington has become so difficult that some firms pay the overtime of fire inspectors to ensure a required visit. Complained one frustrated permit seeker to the *Washington Post:* "I don't understand. You would think that there would at least be some corrupt way of getting it going."

• Many people and firms get things going by simply ignoring the law. Accountants reviewing applications for aid in South-Central L.A. reported that 40 percent of the firms lacked proper records, including tax filings.

• The simple act of hiring one part-time worker in America today requires the completion of a W2, W3, W4, the local equivalent of each of these, a quarterly unemployment form, an annual unemployment form, a withholding tax form, a quarterly Social Security and Medicare form, and a workers' compensation insurance form.

Productivity

• The cost of cleaning up the *Exxon Valdez* oil spill was included as part of our gross national product for those years. Al Gore points out in *Earth in Balance* that when calculating GNP, natural resources are not depreciated, nor is the topsoil that washes down the Mississippi River.

• The nation's garbage has increased 200 percent since 1960 just because of greater packaging.

• According to the *Oakland Tribune,* an item of food travels about thirteen hundred miles before it is eaten. A carrot has to go two thousand miles.

- The average American's auto mileage has gone up 300 percent since 1950.[29]

- The *Washington Post* reports that Americans spend 37 billion hours annually just standing in line. According to Environmentalists for Sustainable Transportation, Los Angeleans waste 100,000 hours each day while caught in traffic jams.

- To such quantifiable waste must be added the more amorphous variety caused by corporate lawyers, lobbyists, marketing consultants, CEO benefits, advertising agencies, leadership seminars, human resource supervisors, strategic planners, regional conventions, national conventions, international conventions, facilitating, supervising, planning, processing, analyzing, tax advising, marketing, consulting, as well as litigating what might be done if we had time to do it. We have come to the point where many now believe that having a "process" is the same thing as creating a product. Others think calling something a "product" makes it so. A checking account becomes a product, so does a life insurance policy, and so forth. Thus, as the nation makes relatively fewer real products, those in business talk about them more, as though attempting through semantics to recreate our manufacturing base.

Similarly, as what could reasonably be described as service declines, the use of the term increases. "To provide you with better service," the sign at the site of my former ATM read, the device had been moved ten blocks away. And an operator at the telephone company opened our conversation with: "This is Robert. How can I be of excellent service to you today?"

Urban Revitalization

The problems of the 80 percent of Americans who live on about 2 percent of the land have been a favorite topic of the media and politicians for a quarter of a century. We have had urban planning, urban policies, urban empowerment, and urban revitalization.

What we have not had is urban progress. In 1970 there were

about 3,400 poverty census tracts in the 100 largest cities, constituting about 27 percent of all these cities' tracts. By 1990 there were 5,600 poverty tracts, constituting 39 percent of the total.[30]

What is startling about this failure is the amount of money that has been blown to avoid it. Big-city mayors have spent billions of dollars on freeways, urban renewal, new stadiums, airports, and convention centers, and matters have simply become worse.

On the other hand, direct federal urban aid for normal functions, as a percentage of cities' own revenues, is where it was in 1969—roughly 6.5 percent, as opposed to 25 percent just before Reagan took over.[31]

Meanwhile, in a D.C. public school, a girl who has been raped brings a news clipping about the attack to her teacher and asks that it be posted on the bulletin board. For once, someone has noticed her.

Honesty

Much as urban reality has ignored urban rhetoric, our increasing emphasis on honesty in government not only has failed to bring us relief but has been met by ever-blossoming evidence of political corruption.

The problem, in part, is that we are attempting to achieve by law what formerly was accomplished by habit, an effort easily susceptible to failure. But it is also the case that the very complexity of our system encourages corruption, creating ever more crevices into which slime can seep. Beyond this is the enormous internationalization of crime. The BCCI scandal, for example, involved not only hundreds of ordinary drug dealers and other criminals from various countries but the intelligence services of five nations and at least one government, Pakistan, which was seeking to finance its nuclear weapons development.

Attorney Jack Blum, who helped keep the spotlight on the BCCI scandal, says that "no really major crime is domestically limited anymore." This leads to a massive problem of getting law enforcement officials in different countries to cooperate and establish common rules. As it is, the sixth-largest holder of bank assets in the world today is Grand Cayman, which has a population of 18,000, 570 commercial banks, one bank regulator, and a bank secrecy law.

Closer to home, we find government constantly transforming itself to stay ahead of the reformers. Sometimes it's just a matter of words: politicians don't take bribes anymore, they only have an "appearance of a conflict of interest."

Sometimes it's a matter of increasingly fine legal distinctions. Consider, for example, the variety of standards invoked by Clinton appointees for avoiding conflicts of interest. While one cabinet appointee said he would build a "Chinese wall" between himself and his formerly highly remunerative interests, another nominee limited her recusal to matters having a "direct and predictable effect" on her prior employers. Ron Brown set himself an even more lax standard by refusing to recuse himself in matters affecting his law firm.

The Washington media still tends to regard political corruption as a sporadic matter disconnected to patterns of culture or behavior. When a major scandal brews, many Washington journalists find themselves with an awkward problem. The person (or persons) they have spent so much effort courting as a news source is now charged with wrongdoing. To move too early into an adversarial relationship risks both the journalist's sources and caste. It is far safer to let some other journalist pursue the story. If it turns out to be a dry hole, the friendly reporter retains the confidence of the source, perhaps even gaining stature by refusing to join the chase. If, on the other hand, the source turns out to be a crook, the friendly journalist can move with appropriate editorial sorrow into an adversarial camp before anyone notices that he or she has been conned.

Some of the media have also been compromised by their association with intelligence agencies, a relationship that can easily cloud journalistic vision. A deputy director of the CIA boasted that as late as the 1970s, "you could get a journalist cheaper than a call girl."

But covert ties are hardly necessary to affect coverage. The tendency of Washington journalists to judge success by access to the powerful makes them, on the most mundane and daily level, hostage to those about whom they write.

In such a culture, important truths can go untold, such as the fact that on numerous occasions over the past thirty years, the course of the nation's politics has been dramatically altered by criminal activity. From assassinations to illegal wars, from perjury to stolen briefing books, from soybean contracts to the yuppie manipulations of Wall Street, the story of recent American politics has also been the story of crime. We have repeatedly moved, shocked and enthralled, from scandal to scandal, in each case operating on the assumption that with investigation, exposure, and punishment, wrongs would be set right and the ship of state would once again regain its graceful course. We are presented each act as a random event, shunning evidence that suggests it may be but a small part of a pattern, that we may be dealing with serial corruption of the democratic system rather than isolated and atypical perversions.

The mainstream media says that there is no pattern, that each event stands by itself, and that those who draw connections between incidents are "conspiracy theorists," "flakes," and "paranoids." On a few occasions, when a conviction is handed down, it proudly proclaims that "the system works," but more often the affair simply drifts into oblivion with perpetrators unapprehended, crimes unsolved, and critical questions unanswered. Once the media has wrung all the public titillation out of a scandal, it moves on as though the past never happened.

The truth of major elections, prominent assassinations, curious murders, suspicious accidents, Watergate, Iran-Contra, and Iraqgate is consigned to America's archives as old news. And the pattern is never mentioned, unless to disparage someone who would ask the questions one more time.

This is not, however, how the media covers more mundane forms of criminal activity. We never hear journalists claim that the Mafia is the figment of paranoid minds. At the local level we are far more able to conceive of loose conspiracies with overlapping interests and agendas, at times working in tandem, at others bitterly opposed. We do not dismiss the existence of a mob simply because we have been unable to find its bylaws or determine the exact nature of its leadership.

Much as gangs flourished during Prohibition (or today in the wake of the breakdown of the American city), mob politics has flourished in the context of national political disintegration. One doesn't need a conspiracy for this to occur, only a propitious environment. The big difference is that during Prohibition (and with traditional corruption), politics was used to provide money and power; in the political racketeering of recent decades, money and power have been used to control politics.

Education

• According to the author of a computer-based study on the difficulty of school textbooks, a twelfth-grade honors English course in Ithaca, New York, is "no more difficult than eighth-grade books were before World War II." First-grade readers are at about "the level at which a farmer talks to his cows."[32]

• Percentage of likely 1992 voters who could identify the Bushes' dog Millie: 86 percent. Percentage who knew that both Bush and Clinton supported the death penalty: 15 percent.[33]

• Percentage of Ivy League students who could not identify both their U.S. senators: 50 percent.

World Class

The UN Development Report for 1993 found that the U.S. ranked sixth in overall quality of life among the nations of the world. If white Americans were considered alone, their quality of life would rank first. On the other hand, if African Americans were considered alone, their quality of life would rank thirty-first. American Latinos would rank thirty-fifth.[34]

Life in the Breakdown Lane

As we try to close the gap between the words we hear and the reality we find, we can come to feel a little desperate, confused, and incoherent. We know something dramatic has happened, something terribly wrong, yet the politicians keep saying it's all right, that they "feel your pain" and that it will all work out.

Under this great disingenuous blanket of comforting noise, much is just plain lost. Consider, for example, a few matters *not* discussed during the 1992 campaign:

An annual loss of energy equivalent to the Pentagon budget due to our failure to adopt sound conservation measures. The bipartisan involvement of the Washington establishment in the BCCI and S&L scandals. The tens of billions of dollars lifted from the Star Wars program and the fact that the damn thing never worked anyway. The incredible waste of a whole generation of young black males that we would rather lock up than employ productively. Prisons that serve as incubators for AIDS.

It seems sometimes that if the atrophy of the American imagination, skill, and will is not halted, we may wake up one morning and find that no one in this country knows how to make anything anymore. We may discover our dearest friends and relatives in a catatonic state before the TV and the device won't even be on. When we call for help, we may find that 911 has become an endless-loop voice mail system from which one can never disconnect. We may even, some day, elect a hologram as president—and we'll have become too dumb to notice.

Okay, that's hyperbole, but this isn't: The mayors of at least fifteen large cities decided in 1993 not to seek reelection. The *Washington Post* said that many did so because they have "become weary of fiscal crises, rampant drug related crime, homelessness, AIDS and other social problems that have worsened since they first sought office."[35]

Scale is an important factor in the breakdown of America's systems such as these cities. The larger the system, the more time and money it must spend keeping itself alive rather than accomplishing what it is supposed to do. For example, in January 1992, the sheriff of Bristol, Virginia, committed suicide after a grand jury began investigating him for embezzlement. According to the *Washington Post,* the sheriff had been sent prisoners by the federal and D.C. government along with payments to cover costs. The reimbursements, however, were based on federal and D.C. standards. In D.C. it costs more to house a prisoner for a year than it would to send him to Harvard. But what cost $55 a day in D.C. required only $6 a day in Bristol, Virginia, where the sheriff ran not only a jail but a vegetable garden as well. The sheriff allegedly pocketed the difference—what might be called the float on the inefficiency of scale. It turned out to be close to a half-million dollars in D.C. funds alone.

But the breakdown of America affects small systems as well. For example, Al Thompson is director of public works in Freeport, Maine. The town manager says he has seen Thompson work forty-eight hours at a stretch: "We're lucky if we can get him to take two weeks off a year. We literally have to force him to take time off." In 1992 one of his ditches won third place in a statewide ditch competition. He has been known to haggle even with low bidders on a contract, his department has had no turnover in years, and when the town went through a budget crisis, the employees offered to adjust their schedules to avoid overtime costs.

The *Maine Sunday Telegram* quoted the town manager as saying, "Unfortunately, the Al Thompsons of the world are an endangered species." Explained the paper: "College-educated administrators, trained in the increasingly technical aspects of municipal infrastructure are taking over."

Al Thompson will retire soon. Then a man who can dig the third-best ditch in the state of Maine will be replaced by someone "trained in the increasingly technical aspects of municipal infrastructure."[36]

We are in trouble. We shouldn't be afraid to say it, as if pretending not to notice the collapse of America's cultural, economic, and political systems will somehow slow the disintegration.

Jefferson saw it coming and was not afraid to say so. He knew that governments fail us, even the one he helped design. Writing of the need to establish the rights of citizens, he said:

> From the conclusion of this war we shall be going downhill. It will not then be necessary to resort every moment to the people for support. They will be forgotten, therefore, and their rights disregarded. They will forget themselves but in the sole faculty of making money, and will never think of uniting to effect a due respect for their rights. The shackles, therefore, . . . will be made heavier and heavier, till our rights shall revive or expire in a convulsion.[37]

Across ethnic groups, ages, regions, religions, and politics, we share a feeling that something has gone wrong, that somehow we missed a turn, that the future, once our greatest frontier, is closing. The reactions to this cultural and political breakdown have varied markedly. In the presidency, for example, we have experienced three different responses in a dozen years. Ronald Reagan argued that we could go back to the way we were. George Bush said we could keep things the way they are. And Clinton said we were going to have to change, but skipped the details. As the American electorate has progressed from appealing but futile nostalgia to the acceptance of inevitable if uncertain alteration, our presidential choices have traced our movement. It is a course that is far from complete, and in a curious way the indecisiveness and confusion of the Clinton administration reflects, and in some way suits, this incompleteness.

Could it be, a Washington psychiatrist suggested to me, that Clinton is functioning not as a leader but as a therapist, with the American dysfunctional family as his patient? It is an appealing image that in some ways evokes what seems to be happening.

Or perhaps it's just what Clinton wants to seem to be happening. There are so many shifts. After only nine months in office, David Gergen announced that the president had already undergone an "evolution." Another aide told the Associated Press that

Clinton "doesn't want to be the mechanic-in-chief, he doesn't want to be actuary-in-chief on health care questions. He's looking at [providing] more of a vision of where we're trying to go, how society should evolve."

It was an odd description of a man who a few months earlier had planned to cure the nation in a hundred days and who had just released a 239-page briefing book on health care. On the other hand, this was also the man who had recently indicated that American policy would be—serially or simultaneously?—to arrest and/or negotiate with Somalian General Aidid.

Policies flowed through the Clinton White House like generations of fruit flies in a science lab. Yet amid the fluidity of his own values and opinions, the rampant uncertainty of the times, and the painful impermanence of his constituents' lives, Clinton was clearly searching for someplace firm and safe to stand. Somewhere to stop and say to the American people, "If that is the way you wish to go, I will lead you."

For much of the corporate world, the end of American empire seems to have inspired (along with demands for more governmental assistance to the "free" marketplace) a search for comfortable clichés. Thus the phenomenal rise of the need to "meet the challenge of global competition in the first half of the twenty-first century," a phrase that can justify anything from moving the plant to Mexico to adding another $10 million to the CEO's bonus. The phrase is implicitly exculpatory; a business cannot be blamed for new competition, only for failing to beat it. The Japanese have thus provided a handy distraction from having to ponder why American business has gotten into the mess it has, reflection that would raise such issues as corporate indifference to worker participation, conditions, and satisfaction; declining product quality and innovation; and misguided management principles promulgated by an excess of managers being paid too much for doing too little.

In fact, while some of America's largest corporations engage in massive layoffs, "reinvent" themselves, and, with creaky ostentation, announce amazing discoveries such as the importance of the customer, many smaller firms have slipped into the new economy smoothly and easily. These are the firms that create jobs. In the 1980s, for example, American small businesses added some 14 million new jobs, more than twice as many as were created in either Western Europe or Japan. Many of these businesses were very small: Between 1984 and 1990, businesses with fewer than twenty employees created 7.1 million jobs. Meanwhile during the eighties, Fortune 500 companies cut back employment at a rate of about 400,000 jobs a year.

Why the difference? Writing in the *New York Times,* brokerage firm president Muriel Siebert offered one explanation: "Unlike monolithic Fortune 500 companies, small businesses behave like families. [A study] indicated that one reason for the durability of businesses owned by women is the value they place on their workers. It showed that small businesses hold on to workers through periods when revenues decline. Rather than eliminate workers, they tend to cut other expenses, including their own salaries."

Yet another reaction to America's decline and disorientation is anger and blame. It shows up in racial assaults and sexual violence, in 20 million dittoheads listening to Rush Limbaugh, in a growing incapacity to empathize with citizens who are suffering the most, and in the revived popularity of the death penalty.

But you also see it in more respectable corners. Here is Donna Shalala on workfare: "I don't think we should subsidize poor mothers to stay out of the work force when working-class mothers are going into the work force."[38]

A few years ago only a conservative Republican politician would so glibly ignore the lack of jobs and the need to care for one's young as major reasons for poor mothers not being in the labor pool. Now this sort of posturing has become part of what E. J. Dionne Jr. of the *Washington Post* has called Kojak liberalism.

It has become part of our mythology that such phenomena as racial hatred, sexual violence, violent crime, and now even poverty, must be attacked as isolated pathologies with our success primarily dependent upon our toughnesss.

We have been tough on welfare cheats, illegal immigrants and their employers, drunk drivers, druggies, pornographers, repeat offenders, terrorists, white-collar criminals, Sister Souljah, and Howard Stern.

We have demanded a return to basics in education and have gotten tough on those who fall below our standards. Some are advocating a new school year, longer and tougher than the old.

We have so toughened our stand against murder that death row stories have become commonplace.

We have learned the principle of "tough love" in dealing with our children.

We have taken a tough-minded approach toward government expenditures. We have gotten tough on our doctors, our journalists, and each other, suing for sums unheard of a few years back.

Our movies and our television are revoltingly tough.

It has become almost impossible to find a politician who has not recommended a tough new law to deal with something or other.

We have made ourselves tougher by finding ever more drastic tests of our fitness, progressing, as it were, from jogging to marathons to triathlons.

We have hung tough, stayed tough, and gotten going when the going got tough.

We have increasingly approached major problems as wars: a war on drugs, a war on AIDS, a war on obscenity. War is tough.

Those issues that do not rate full battle dress are handled in a manner not aimed at cajoling or encouraging us into the ways of righteousness but designed to shock us into goodness. Thus the television ads showing the cocaine addict floundering in the toilet stall, and the posters plastered with the protruded bare stomach of the pregnant girl ("If you think a pimple is bad") or of tortured animals. And in one corner of Washington's Mall there is a new Holocaust museum, designed to leave its visitors appalled and shamed for their species. It is also an unintended monument to the times: the capital's first tough museum.

The problem with all this toughness has been twofold. First, it turns out we are not all that tough, and second, trying to be doesn't work particularly well.

To cite just a few examples, consider that during the era of toughness our children have become more obese, television holy men have turned out to be charlatans, anti-Semitism has increased, role models in business and politics have gone to jail for assorted weaknesses in astonishing numbers, and sports heroes have been uncovered as junkies or drugstore behemoths. Above all, it is hard to recall a time when America was so afraid of so many things.

The most common campaign pledge is, "Trust me to be tough." and hardly any on the national scene have the courage to suggest that at least part of our problem may be our preoccupation with being so. What presidential candidate would dare tell Americans what Edmund Burke told his tough British compatriots about the American colonies? Burke warned, "If you do not succeed, you are without recourse; for, conciliation failing, force remains; but, force failing, no further hope of conciliation is left."

And here is where we find ourselves after all our toughness: Our force has failed us and there seems little possibility to reconcile our people, our problems, or our national accounts. Increasingly we speak in terms of inevitability: the permanent underclass, the irrevocably criminal, the irreversible damage to the ozone layer, the invincible national debt. We demand toughness yet expect failure, much as in our cities more and more children have learned a toughness that is synonymous with death.

H. Ross Perot's initial approach to America's problems—when he wasn't plugging tough ideas like door-to-door searches for drugs—was to pinch pennies. If Clinton offered false hope, Perot offered little but unrelenting fiscal responsibility. John White, the Harvard economist who helped to write the Perot campaign's economic plan, told *USA Today* in the fall of 1993: "Perot has served a certain value as a kind of national scold on some of this stuff. But over time, it gets to wear a bit thin. At some point you have to say, 'We understand what you're against, but what are you for?' "

Yet Perot's influence extended far beyond his standing in the polls or among Washington columnists. He had set off a movement that gained a life of its own. It appeared that many of his supporters valued his independence as much as his ideas and saw in Perot's undiluted rhetoric and unmassaged opinions a model of what American politics should be about. Like a majority of the American people, Perot's backers were ready to remake national politics, including the creation of a new party. And it was no accident that many small business owners so empathized with Perot that they risked alienating customers by hanging his posters in their shops; Perot's words spoke to what remained of American individual initiative.

The media, however, focused on Perot's tightwad politics and was quick to publicize efforts of a similar direction, especially among the young. Although there was no particular evidence that these youthful disciples of castor oil economics were typical, we found *Time* giving two pages to the young new right, barely mentioning its conservative ties and funding. Included was the Third Millennium, one of whose founders is Douglas Kennedy, a son of Robert Kennedy. Said Kennedy modestly: "We've put our finger on the tone of who we are as a generation." Among this generation's supposed goals, as outlined in the "Third Millennium Declaration," was to raise the retirement age, declaring that "social security is a generational scam." It also fretted that, "like Wile E. Coyote waiting for a 20-ton Acme anvil to fall on his head, our generation labors in the expanding shadow of a monstrous national debt."[39]

There were other groups such as Lead or Leave, which has received money from both Perot and GOP conservative financier Pete Peterson. There were nicknames—Generation X—and books such as *13 Gen: Abort, Retry, Ignore, Fail?* Andrew Cohen of *The Nation* noted that this "*Zeitgeist* industry" had a certain incestuous quality, with crossovers of activists and sources of funding. "Unaware of this cross-pollination," wrote Cohen, "the media generated dozens of stories supported by only one or two sources, all fixed on the notion of deficit-busting and all passing it off, incredibly, as a preoccupation of people in their 20s."

The generation was much more complicated than that. Beyond the self-promoting generational warriors of Lead or Leave, for example, was a great mass of apolitical young. Then there was the quasi-nihilist strain of black rappers, white skinheads, and their followers. And the woman described in the quarterly *Who Cares* who denied her parents' suspicion that she worships Satan by saying, "I'm not stupid enough to believe in anything."[40]

There was even a revival and transformation of the beat culture of the fifties. The transformation, admittedly, was considerable. In an article on the new beats, *New York* magazine noted that MTV was inserting thirty-second poetry slots between videos. Said writer Rebecca Mead, "30 seconds will buy you about four lines of *Howl* or perhaps eleven of *The Waste Land*." A poet who rambled on for thirty-two seconds was told to speed it up.

At the same time there were still echoes of what Jack Kerouac had called a "generation of furtives with an inner knowledge . . . a kind of beatness . . . and a weariness with all the forms, all the conventions of the world."[41]

It's back again. You sense it, just as you sense the waiting. That, in part, was what the poems and the guitars and the coffee shops had been about: words and music and places to wait until something really happened, until the inner knowledge could be turned from the lonely existentialism of the fifties into the collective action of the sixties. You sense it now in the voluntary simplicity; the indifference to form; the quietness of the rebellion; the patience.

But then, if you follow the right trail, you will also notice something quite different, quite unlike the 1950s and even more unlike the 1980s. You will notice how the frustration and the discouragement sometimes flows not into anger or cynicism or fatalism but into a just, kind, and imaginative engagement with the causes of the pain.

You will find Americans who are reacting to what is and is not happening by simply doing what needs to be done. Not just by volunteering, but by imagining and creating, not just by critiques but by action, not by merely serving but by giving birth and regenerating, not by rejecting but by redeeming.

It doesn't always start where or how one might think. Buried in the news following the L.A. riots were details of a $3.6 billion recovery plan offered by two of the city's most notorious gangs, the Bloods and the Crips. Here, included among larger proposals, are a few of their ideas:

> All pavements/sidewalks in Los Angeles are in dire need of resurfacing . . . .
>
> We want a well-lit neighborhood. All alleys shall be painted white or yellow . . . .
>
> All trees will be properly trimmed and maintained. We want all weeded/shrubbed areas to be cleaned up and properly nurtured. New trees will be planted to increase the beauty of our neighborhoods.
>
> All schools shall have new landscaping and more plants and trees around the schools; completely upgrade the bathrooms, making them more modern, provide a bathroom monitor to each bathroom which will provide freshen-up toiletries at a minimum cost to the students. . . .

At a time when white America—and even much of black America—was wallowing in a post-apocalyptic vision of the city fostered by movies and the evening news, at least some at ground zero were envisioning a place of beauty—a community.

Similarly, at a time when much of America, including its political leaders, was giving up on the city, a gang truce movement sprouted. At one meeting, 164 current and former gang leaders and members from twenty-six cities, together with some fifty observers (mostly from churches), gathered in Kansas City. The mainstream media was excluded, but Jim Wallis of *Sojourners* magazine came as an invited observer and advisor. He wrote: "The initiative . . . came from the young people themselves in the ghet-

tos and barrios. Expressing disappointment in the established political, civil rights, and church leadership, they decided to act on
their own."

The text for the closing sermon by the Reverend Mac Charles
Jones—"I ran some streets myself. . . . I've had the FBI after
me"—was the story of the prodigal son, a story of redemption. At
the end of the summit, Wallis watched as summit co-chair Fred
Williams helped some Kansas City Crips and Bloods work out
their differences:

> Fred could have spent the rest of the day talking with national
> and international media. Instead, he spent these last several hours
> with these local young men. . . . That's the way the hope of the
> gang summit will spread—kid by kid, gang by gang, city by city. It
> will grow by patience, perseverance, exhausting work, and unde-
> niable love. It won't be effectively spread through the media, but
> through hundreds of grassroots efforts and organizations.

David Milner is white, but he, too, has rejected the post-
apocalyptic urban vision. An economics major at Middlebury, he
postponed entering the University of Chicago Business School after winning a utility company grant for his social service scheme.

Milner's plan was to organize a community using college
scholarships as a hook. He established Funds for the Community's
Future in the belief that by uniting to help its youth, a community
could help itself. The program—started at Washington's McKinley
High School but quickly spreading—linked students, school, community, the larger city, and businesses. At the community level,
moneys were raised through community service projects and
fundraisers. These efforts were matched by FCF and its supporters.
Scholarship winners, screened by community, school, and FCF
committees, were expected to remain active in their community.

Milner, who is in his mid-twenties, had the students do market
research on their classmates and then approach the school's most
popular retailers for funds. Students have been given professional
SAT preparatory courses, sometimes with startling results. Six new

community organizations have sprung up around McKinley. Courses were given in public speaking and fundraising for both students and residents, and a student-run business has been established. Says Bernice Lewis, president of the Brookland Public Housing Tenant Association and a member of an FCF advisory committee, "I've never seen something so marvelous in all my life. And the best thing is that the government is not involved."

Milner tapped as volunteers any of his classmates or friends who might have a few months to spare while looking for a job or waiting for grad school. He got one of the best law firms in town to give FCF free legal services and another to give it free space. And he brought in older and more jaded types such as myself to sit on an advisory committee and watch one of the best shows in town. In a city where bullets are sometimes randomly fired at public swimming pools, FCF is making a few of the pieces work again. David Milner says we don't need more think tanks, what we need is more do tanks.

I got the same sort of lift shortly after the Clinton inauguration when I attended a conference on new politics, in this case largely of the green variety. Although the green philosophy of decentralized democracy and ecological wisdom is the most important new political paradigm since the social welfare state, the story has been largely missed by the media. This is partly because the phenomenon is so invasive and so human that it does not need a central hierarchy, armies, or mass media to take hold. More than either a movement or a politics, it is an idea—which, like the idea of democracy, spreads in the manner of a benign virus rather than like an empire.

The greens are, of course, concerned about environmental matters, but there is far more to their politics than that. Beyond ecological wisdom, their core values include equality, non-violence, and social justice. They have taken traditional left issues and blended them with a humanistic perspective that leaves them—as they like to say—neither left nor right but ahead. One green candidate in Missouri ran on the perfect platform for the 1990s: Common Sense and Common Decency.

Even before the greens got on five state ballots, the green idea was having a profound effect on American politics, so much so that Clinton, in choosing a vice-presidential candidate, elected to give himself a green glow rather than seeking traditional geographical diversity.

Not only have green issues floated to the top of conventional campaigns, but in a little more than a decade green politics have grown from being a German eccentricity to the point where there are now green parties in at least seventy-three countries, including seventeen in Africa; a pan-European green federation that includes countries of the former Soviet bloc; and a global green steering committee.

Nothing like this has ever happened in politics: the autonomous, undirected budding of scores of compatible parties around the globe, joined by a passion to save the planet, devolve power, and inject decency into governmental affairs—linked primarily by computer bulletin boards and occasional conferences. The global village exists, and it is very green.

Of course, such politics takes a lot of time. Sometimes you can't wait. As when during the last recession, the lease on a certain restaurant in Great Barrington, Massachusetts, expired. The local bank wouldn't lend restaurateur Frank Tortrello money to move across the street. So Frank decided to print his own. He called them Deli Dollars. Each sold for $9 and could be redeemed for $10 worth of food after six months. Not only did the idea provide Frank with enough money to make his move, but it spread throughout the community. A local farm issued notes with the slogan "In Farms We Trust," featuring the head of a cabbage instead of the head of a president. New restaurants followed with their own currency, and the local bills started showing up everywhere, including in church collection plates.

Others are also reinventing money. Alternative currency has cropped up in Ithaca, New York, and is being used by seven hundred individuals and business. In Seattle, some have devised cardboard money. In another town, wooden coins.[42]

Then there's Daisy Alexander, a retiree from Montclair, New

Jersey, and Pepe, a recent immigrant from Havana, Cuba. They both live in a low-income senior housing development section of Miami, Florida. At first glance, Daisy and Pepe seem to have little in common. But they are bound to each other—in friendship and through the common bonds of a new economic system called time dollars or service credits.

Time dollars, described in the book *Time Dollars: A Currency for the 90's* by Edgar Cahn and Jonathan Rowe, operate like a blood bank. People help others in their community and get credits in a computer data base that they can draw upon in times of need. Cahn and Rowe describe how time dollars have transformed more than a hundred communities and how grassroots groups built the new currency.

Here's how it works for Daisy and Pepe: Daisy volunteers three days a week tutoring first-graders at the elementary school across the street from her home. Every week Pepe comes to her house and takes her grocery shopping. An amputee with a cane, Daisy is dependent on Pepe to provide this service for her. But no money changes hands. Daisy simply "cashes in" the time dollars she earns tutoring to "pay" for Pepe's shopping help. In turn Pepe earns time dollars to buy services he needs. But Daisy and Pepe gain in other ways as well. Both are renewed and enthused about the opportunity for helping, and inspired by the social activities that the sense of community has produced.

"The potential benefits of the time dollars concept are limitless. It can touch every life in every community, ranging from an apartment complex to an entire nation, every facility, from a nursing home to a university campus," says author Cahn. "It fosters a sense of financial independence, camaraderie, community spirit, harmony among age groups, races, religions, income levels, and even political adversaries."

In each of these cases, citizens have come to understand that money is just a way that we translate the value of products and services. Just because one may not have money does not mean there is no value to be exchanged. It is simply a matter of coming up with a way to keep track of it without the services of the Federal Reserve.

Our final stop on this side trip to hope is the Righteous Men's Commission, which has sprung up not far from the White House. The RMC aims to return the streets of besieged neighborhoods to the community—not through vigilantism but through a firm presence and such ideas as getting a council of "elders" now in prison to urge a truce among the young brothers. Says commission leader Rahim Jenkins, there are two seats of government in D.C.: city hall and the central facility of Lorton Reformatory.

Jenkins describes watching a drug deal go down, calling the dealer over, and explaining to him—Jenkins's tone is not threatening so much as inexorable—that he can't be dealing drugs while "these babies are going back and forth" to school. The dealer leaves. One of Jenkins's younger colleagues asks a truck driver to stop blasting the sound. At some times in some places in D.C., such an appeal might result in one being silenced forever, but this time the truck driver complied.

"That's what it's going to take—reclaiming this city block by block," says Jenkins.

And maybe the country as well. Over and over you hear a variation of the phrases "block by block," "kid by kid," "one by one." From Rahim Jenkins and Jim Wallis, yes, but also on September 5, 1990:

"Block by block, school by school, child by child, we will take back the streets."

That was George Bush. And on November 21, 1993:

"We have to take our communities back. Community by community, block by block, child by child."[43]

That was Bill Clinton.

To be sure, Bush and Clinton were talking; Wallis and Jenkins are walking. But sometimes it has to work like that, sometimes it takes a lot of talking before anything happens in politics. And sometimes just the sound of the words foretells a shift in the wind.

In these efforts, there is a clear circumference. Certainly FCF will not end poverty, nor the greens eradicate all pollution, nor time dollars replace all money, nor the Righteous Men's Commission eliminate all drug abuse. The Bloods and the Crips may not get toiletries in the high-school bathrooms, and some of these programs may slip on their own promise and become far less than—or even betray—their dream.

But at least those now involved have stopped waiting for someone else—Bill Clinton or some other someone else—to do it for them. They have stopped the blaming and complaining and explaining. They have adopted the notion of personal witness, the faith that individual commitment is the only decent and just power any of us have. It is the sine qua non of a functioning community, the necessary harbinger of change.

It is not perfect, but there is no other guarantee, nothing else that really seems to work. And one of the things that make these people very different from Bill Clinton and the rest of federal Washington is that they insist—even at the price of their own influence—on living within a community rather than inside a system.

They understand that the revival of our rights, the recovery of our heritage of common sense and decency, and the resuscitation of our collective spirit will not come as a result of denial or of management techniques. It will not be found on an airport bookshelf, or in cutting the deficit, or in "rising above ideology," or along information highways, or by being tough, or in "market forces," or in a thousand pages of legislation.

Their ideas seem at one level revolutionary and at another totally futile. To some it may appear that personal witness can create change only when it massively aggregates itself, as it did with King in the American south and Gandhi in India. Anthropologist Margaret Mead thought otherwise: "I never doubt that a small group of thoughtful, committed people can change the world. Indeed it is the only thing that has."

By the rules of establishment economics and political science, such thinking is naive. But Robert Axelrod, in his computer studies of approaches to the classic game problem known as the "Prisoner's Dilemma," found that reciprocation of another player's moves—i.e., a primitive form of cooperation he called "tit for tat"—was the best strategy. In fact, reciprocity and cooperation work so well they can resist the pressure of more aggressive concepts. Says Axelrod in *The Evolution of Cooperation,* "A population of nice rules is the hardest type to invade because nice rules do so well with each other."[44]

Axelrod began publishing his ideas in the early 1980s, at the start of an administration that couldn't have cared less. More recently, mathematically inclined biologists have been applying Axelrod's approach to discover the role that cooperation and altruism play in nature.

Reporting on this development, the *New York Times* of April 14, 1992, described some examples from the natural world:

> Rather than going it alone, individual cells of Myxobacteria, for example, hunt their prey in cooperative groups, hemming in a target much as a pride of lions corners a gazelle. Vampire bats returning from successful forays share foods with unrelated but needy vampire bats. Some fish deliberately assume unnecessary risk on behalf of their schools by scouting out the intentions of potential predators.

The *Times* cited two European scientists who had done further research on the prisoners' dilemma game and found that "a certain degree of 'generous' tolerance of an opponent's selfish betrayals gives players a statistical advantage, provided the same competitors play many matches."

Political scientists like to talk about *realpolitik;* economists find no room for altruism among their sainted market forces. But listen to Dr. James A. Shapiro of the University of Chicago, who studies the cooperative behavior of single-cell bacteria: "I don't know of any organism that really lives in isolation. . . . I think we are moving away from the reductionist explanations of animal behavior based on the behavior of single cells in isolation. Now we're looking at organisms, even bacteria, as parts of networks, in which single cells constantly interact with the higher organisms of which they are components."

For the moment, there is no prophet among those cooperative cells of humans attempting to revive their communities, only the strong hint that these Americans, with their acute sense of the realities in which their hopes must float, are doing something beyond the readily apparent scope of their endeavors. In these small places something more is happening. Energy is being restored. Life is being born. The inner frontier, the only one left to us, is opening. America is once again being given another chance.

Bringing Politics Home

POLITICAL MACHINES, OLD AND NEW.
HOW SYSTEMS FAIL US. WHY HUDGE AND
GUDGE WERE BOTH WRONG. REFRAMING
OUR STORY. THE IDEOLOGY OF SCALE. DE-
VOLVING POLITICS AND REVIVING OUR
RIGHTS.

This book has been about politics, but it has also been about home and the distance between the two.

The distance hasn't always been that far.

In 1816, Columbus, Ohio, had one city council member for every 100 residents. By 1840 there was one for every 1,000 residents. By 1872 the figure had dwindled to one to every 5,000. By 1974, there was one council member for every 55,000 people.[1]

The first U.S. congressional districts contained fewer than 40,000 people; my current city council member represents about twice that many. Today the average U.S. representative works for roughly 600,000 citizens. This is double the number for legislatures in Brazil and Japan, and more than five times as many as in Australia, Canada, France, Great Britain, Italy, and West Germany.[2]

It isn't just a matter of numbers. Back in the early days of television and the late days of the Daley era in Chicago, Jake Arvey was an important man in national Democratic politics. At Democratic conventions, Walter Cronkite and David Brinkley would ponder what Arvey was going to do; presidential candidates would seek his blessing.

Yet Arvey's power base was not a national organization nor telegenic charisma, but rather the 24th Ward of Chicago, from which he helped to run the city's Democratic machine.

Another Chicago politician described it this way: "Not a sparrow falls inside the boundaries of the 24th Ward without Arvey knowing of it. And even before it hits the ground there's already a personal history at headquarters, complete to the moment of its tumble."

There was plenty wrong with the Daley machine and others like it. One job seeker was asked at a ward headquarters who had sent him. "Nobody," he admitted. He was told, "We don't want nobody nobody sent."

Among those whom nobody sent were women and minorities. The old machines were prejudiced, feudal, and corrupt.

And so we eventually did away with them.

But reform breeds its own hubris, and so few noticed that as we destroyed the evils of machine politics we also were breaking the links between politics and the individual, politics and community, politics and social life. We were beginning to segregate politics from ourselves.

George Washington Plunkitt would not have been surprised. Plunkitt was a leader of Tammany Hall and was, by the standards of our times and his, undeniably corrupt. As his Boswell, newspaperman William Riordon, noted: "In 1870 through a strange combination of circumstances, he held the places of Assemblyman, Alderman, Police Magistrate and County Supervisor and drew three salaries at once—a record unexampled in New York politics." Facing three bidders at a city auction of 250,000 paving stones, he offered each 10,000 to 20,000 stones free, and having thus dispensed with competition bought the whole lot for $2.50.[3]

Tammany Hall was founded in 1854; its golden age lasted until the three-term La Guardia administration began in 1934. For only ten intervening years was Tammany out of office. We got rid of people like Plunkitt and machines like Tammany because we came to believe in something called good government. But in throwing out the machines, we also tossed out a philosophy and an art of politics. It is as though, in seeking to destroy the Mafia, we had determined that family values and personal loyalty were somehow by association criminal as well.

Plunkitt was not only corrupt but a hardworking, perceptive, and appealing politician who took care of his constituents, qualities one rarely finds in any plurality of combinations in politics these days. Even our corrupt politicians aren't what they used to be. Corruption once involved a complex, if feudal, set of quid pro quos; today our corrupt politicians rarely even tithe to the people.

Politics, Plunkitt said, "is as much a regular business as the grocery or the dry-goods or the drug business," and it was based on studying human nature. He claimed to know every person in his district, their likes and their dislikes:

> I reach them by approachin' at the right side. . . . For instance, here's how I gather in the young men. I hear of a young feller that's proud of his voice, thinks that he can sing fine. I ask him to come around to Washington Hall and join our Glee Club. He comes and sings, and he's a follower of Plunkitt for life. Another young feller gains a reputation as a baseball player in a vacant lot. I bring him into our baseball club. That fixes him. You'll find him workin' for my ticket at the polls next election day. . . . I rope them all in by givin' them opportunities to show themselves off. I don't trouble them with political arguments. I just study human nature and act accordin'.

Plunkitt also believed in sticking with his friends: "The politicians who make a lastin' success in politics are the men who are always loyal to their friends, even up to the gate of State prison, if necessary. . . . Richard Croker used to say that tellin' the truth and stickin' to his friends was the political leader's stock in trade." These principles had become largely inoperative by the time of Lani Guinier.

His prescription for becoming a statesman was to go out and get supporters. Even if it's only one man, "go to the district leader and say: 'I want to join the organization. I've got one man who'll follow me through thick and thin,'" and then you get his cousin and his cousin and so on until you have your own organization. It was a principle that worked well for Tammany Hall, which at its height early this century had 32,000 committeemen and was forced to use Madison Square Garden for its meetings. In contrast, when the Democratic National Committee decided to send a mailing to all its workers a few years ago, it found that no one had kept a list. The party had come to care only about its donors.

But most of all Plunkitt believed in taking care of his constituents. Nothing so dramatically illustrates this as a typical day for Plunkitt as recorded by Riordon:

Plunkitt was aroused at 2:00 A.M. to bail out a saloon keeper who had been arrested for tax law violations. At 6:00 he was again awakened, this time by fire engines. Tammany leaders were expected to show up at fires to give aid and comfort. Besides, notes Riordon, they were great vote-getters.

At 8:30 A.M. he was getting six drunk constituents released. At 9:00 he was in court on another case. At 11:00, upon returning home, he found four voters seeking assistance. At 3:00 he went to the funeral of an Italian, followed by one for a Jew.

At 7:00 P.M. he had a district captains' meeting. At 8:00 he went to a church fair. At 9:00 he was back at the party clubhouse listening to the complaints of a dozen pushcart peddlers. At 10:30 he went to a Jewish wedding, having "previously sent a handsome wedding present to the bride." He finally got to bed at midnight.

Concluded Riordon: "By these means the Tammany district leader reaches out into the homes of his district, keeps watch not only on the men, but also on the women and children, knows their needs, their likes and dislikes, their troubles and their hopes, and places himself in a position to use his knowledge for the benefit of his organization and himself. Is it any wonder that scandals do not permanently disable Tammany and that it speedily recovers from what seems to be crushing defeat?"

These glimpses are instructive because they contrast so markedly with the impersonal, abstract style of politics to which we have become accustomed. It was, to be sure, a mixture of the good and the bad, but you at least knew whom to thank and whom to blame. As late as the 1970s the tradition was still alive in Chicago, as 25th Ward leader Vito Marzullo told a *Chicago Sun-Times* columnist:

> I ain't got no axes to grind. You can take all your news media and all the do-gooders in town and move them into my 25th Ward, and do you know what would happen? On election day we'd beat you fifteen to one. The mayor don't run the 25th Ward. Neither does the news media or the do-gooders. Me, Vito Marzullo, that's who runs the 25th Ward, and on election day everybody does what Vito Marzullo tells them. . . .
>
> My home is open 24 hours a day. I want people to come in. As long as I have a breathing spell, I'll go to a wake, a wedding, whatever. I never ask for anything in return. On election day, I tell my people, "Let your conscience be your guide."[4]

In the world of Plunkitt and Marzullo, politics was not something handed down to the people through such intermediaries as Larry King. It was not the product of spin doctors, campaign hired guns, or phony town meetings. It welled up from the bottom, starting with one loyal follower, one ambitious ballplayer, twelve unhappy pushcart peddlers. What defined politics was an unbroken chain of human experience, memory, and gratitude.

Sure, it was corrupt. But we don't have much to be priggish about. The corruption of Watergate, Iran-Contra, or the S&Ls fed no widows, found no jobs for the needy, or, in the words of one Tammany leader, "grafted to the Republic" no newly arrived immigrants. At least Tammny's brand of corruption got down to the streets. Manipulation of the voter and corruption describe both

Tammany and contemporary politics. The big difference is that in the former the voter could with greater regularity count on something in return.

In fact, we didn't really do away with machines, we just replaced them. As Tammany Hall and the Crump and the Hague and the Daley organizations faded, new political machines appeared. Prime among them was television, but there were others such as the number-crunchers, policy-pushers, and lawyers running Washington, as well as a new breed of political professional, including campaign consultants, fundraisers, and pollsters.

The curious, and ultimately destructive, quality of some of these new machines—particularly the media and the political pros—was that they had such little interest in policies or democracy; rather, they were concerned with professional achievement or television ratings or making a buck. When one of the most skilled of the new pros, James Carville, was asked whether he would take a post in the Clinton administration, he admitted candidly that he knew only about winning elections; he didn't know about governing. And his Clinton campaign sidekick Paul Begala once remarked, "Someone says *issue;* I say *gesundheit.*"

Of course, some of the new machines were very much interested in politics. Whether in the guise of public interest groups, trade associations, or corporate PACs, these organizations became our surrogates in politics.

The political action committees, created (it is hard to believe) as a reform, helped to legalize and institutionalize corruption. And even those organizations professing the most noble causes often came to be run with all the democratic spirit of, say, the American Asbestos Promotion Council. Increasingly they began to emulate the operational style of their most detested opponents, seeing their own members largely as a source of funds and over time coming to accept the Beltway assumption that amending line 3 of Section 1 of Title 6 was the moral equivalent of progress.

For some the point of politics has gone. Said Geri Rothman-Serot as she pulled out of a race in Missouri:

> This year, as I once again pursued a Senate seat, I found myself, by all accounts, the front-runner for the Democratic nomination. During this process, my eyes have been opened to the frustrations of this profession. Our political system and the way it works makes it difficult to be successful and to maintain your principles. In the face of the new American politics, many conclude there is little place for them.

Teresa Heinz, the widow of Sen. John Heinz, could have been a strong contestant in the 1994 race for senator from Pennsylvania. Instead she announced: "I've decided to take my own path. . . . The best ideas for change no longer come from political campaigns. Today, political campaigns are the graveyard of real ideas and the birthplace of empty promises."[5]

The people of the country recognize the problem but are understandably confused as to what to do about it. It is, for example, hard to devise a plan of action if the media consistently shuts its eye to new ideas or programs not part of the existing system. To be noticed, an idea must first be successful, but to be successful it must first be noticed. The media tends to take a pass on this conundrum, accepting the notion that those things that are wrong must be corrected by and within the system. Yet it is somewhere in that assortment of readily dismissed new proposals, concepts, and schemes that the solutions to our crises inevitably lie.

Writer John Gall has said that "systems tend to oppose their proper functions." The ideal proper function of the American system is life, liberty, and the pursuit of happiness. Yet as it gropes its way through its third century, the system in reality increasingly endangers human life, denies personal liberty, and represses individual happiness.

It is not a particularly graceful or perceptive way in which to end our era of empire. We have no de Gaulle or Mountbatten to help ease the way from the imperial to the more mundane. Indeed, most of our leaders seem possessed of one or both of two notions: either that the system is working despite all contra-indications, or that history can be reversed by a few pieces of well-chosen legislation or by a cleverly designed propaganda campaign: *Just Say No to Facts.* Clinton has tried both approaches.

Unfortunately, complex failing systems have little capacity to save themselves. In part this is because the solutions come from the same source as the problem. The public rarely questions the common provenance; official Washington and the media honor it. Even a failure as miserable as that of Vietnam had little effect on the careers of its major protagonists, those men who not only were wrong but were wrong at the cost of 50,000 American lives. They continue to be quoted copiously, cited as experts and transmogri-fied into statesmen. Failure compounded with notoriety is worth still more. Thus, Henry Kissinger and Oliver North can count on much larger lecture fees than, say, Marion Wright Edelman or Bar-bara Jordan.

Complex systems usually try to save themselves by doing the same thing they have been doing badly all along—only harder. This is because the salvation of the system is implicitly considered far more important than the solution of any problems causing the system to fail. We have seen some dramatic examples of this phenomenon in recent times. The Vietnam War quickly became a battle to justify the decision to enter it. As it lost all other purpose, the system became incapable of facing either battlefield or politi-cal reality until confronted with a proto-revolution of the young.

In the Alaskan oil spill, we found ourselves relying upon the world's largest government and the world's largest corporation to repair the damage caused by *their* policies. We became angry when we discovered it wasn't working as well as it should, al-though there is no logical reason for these flawed systems to work better in crisis than they had in ordinary times.

And then there is the miserable, ineffective, and hypocritical "war on drugs." Armed with such mindless principles as "Just Say

No" and "Zero Tolerance," our drug policy has been driven by its military metaphor. The drug problem is really an outward and visible sign of a multitude of other crises. It is a symptom of the bored, underpaid, or unfulfilled worker; the teenager without hope; the parent alone and adrift; the city without community; the education without meaning; the graduate without moral vision; the culture without purpose.

That the situation might have more in common with a health epidemic than with a military engagement is hardly discussed. That we might never win, but only mitigate, is rarely considered. And to question whether the country should trash its constitution in order to prevent a small number of people from making fools of themselves is sometimes considered just short of drug trafficking itself.

Yet the war itself has been a failure. No one can prove otherwise. We are no longer fighting the war on drugs to save the lives of addicts or to protect citizens accidentally in its line of fire. We are certainly not fighting to cure the problems that fuel drug use.

If this were not so, we would at least notice the absurdity of building more prisons when, for example, 40 percent of the homicides in Washington result in no arrest, one-third of the arrestees have their charges dropped, and a third of those going to trial are acquitted.[6] We would note the hypocrisy of demanding a tougher approach to violent crime while jamming our court system with minor drug cases. We would be concerned that the number of gangs in L.A. has doubled since the war on drugs was revived in 1985, that we have effectively declared war against our inner cities, and that the chances of dying are greater for a young urban black male in his hometown than they were for blacks fighting in Vietnam. We would pay some attention to the resilience of hardcore drug use, the correlation between our efforts to eradicate it and urban murder rates, and the minimal sums we allocate to treating the disease of addiction.[7]

In truth, just as in Vietnam, we are fighting the war on drugs in order to justify the decision to have begun it in the first place. We are fighting to protect the jobs and the budgets of those who still insist, in the face of massive evidence, that it will work. We are not fighting *against* drugs; we are fighting *for* the drug war system.

The question we ought to be asking is not what a failing system should be doing but whether such a system can do anything except to make matters worse, all the more so by trying to do something about it. The problem is similar to that illustrated by President Eisenhower's bumbling agriculture secretary Ezra Taft Bensen. When Bensen announced that he would be working day and night on the farm problem, another politician wisely commented, "I wish he wouldn't. He was causing enough trouble when he was just working days."

Ironically, we have come to our present unhappy state in no small part because of our willingness to turn over individual and communal functions to the very systems we now ask to save us. Functions formerly performed by community, family, and church have now been assumed not only by government but to an increasing but unappreciated degree by the private corporation. Consider the modern shopping mall, a common contemporary replacement for a town business district. Although these complexes clearly serve a public function (and are often built with considerable public concessions), they are in fact controlled by a single corporation. This corporation may, without any consultation with the persons who use the mall, enact a wide variety of laws that will be enforced by the public police. There have been repeated cases where corporate owners have sought to deny the public its constitutional rights (such as those of the First Amendment) on the grounds that the petitioners were on private property. The village square has thus been privatized.

High-rise apartment buildings offer another example of corporate assumption of community functions. High-rise owners sometimes brag in their advertising of the wonderful "community" they have created for their tenants, but unlike in a traditional community, the rules for trash collection, control of pets and barbecue grills, and security are not decided by an elected council but by the corporate lord of the manor.

Meanwhile, both liberals and conservatives (although they consistently deny it) act repeatedly on behalf of state centralization, the difference being that conservatives tend to want the government to assume controlling functions while liberals and progressives want government to take over caring functions. Thus under conservatives we get more missiles and prisons, while under liberals we get more day-care centers and farm subsidies. Since few of these programs evaporate upon a change of administration, there is a growing bipartisan intervention of government in our social and cultural lives.

Government and corporations are poor surrogates for families and community. Since, however, much of their growing influence comes in the arguable name of progress, we seldom address the long-range effects of such change. As the system becomes more cumbersome, we happily embrace solutions that seem to offer individuals at least a fighting chance in their struggles with it. We willingly suspend seemingly abstract doubts in order to survive. We may, for example, wonder what children raised in corporate or government day-care centers will actually turn out to be like, but we do not wonder too long or too loudly because our economic system appears to offer little other alternative.

In fact, this is not really true. We can ask the how of what we do as well as the what; it is simply that the nature of our political conversation seldom seems to allow us the opportunity.

In 1910, G. K. Chesterton described two characters, Hudge and Gudge, whose thinking evolved in such a disparate manner that the one came to favor the building of large public tenements for the poor, while the other believed that these public projects were so awful that the slums whence they came were in fact preferable. Wrote Chesterton:

> Such is the lamentable history of Hudge and Gudge; which I merely introduced as a type of an endless and exasperating misunderstanding which is always occurring in modern England. To get men out of a rookery, men are put into a tenement; and at the beginning the healthy human soul loathes them both. A man's first

desire is to get away as far as possible from the rookery, even should his mad course lead him to a model dwelling. His second desire is, naturally, to get away from the model dwelling, even if it should lead a man back to the rookery. But I am neither Hudgian nor a Gudgian. . . . Neither Hudge nor Gudge had ever thought for an instant what sort of house a man might probably like for himself. In short, they did not begin with the ideal; and, therefore, were not practical politicians.[8]

Much of American politics follows the Hudge-Gudge model, producing failure for both conservatives and liberals—the former offering us an army of the homeless, and the latter presenting us finally with drug-infested housing projects.

To break this cycle, we must change not only our political policies but the very way we regard politics. Until we bring politics home—devolving its power, abdicating its phony expertise, and undermining its arrogance—we will remain trapped in a temple to a false god.

Bart Giamatti, long before he became baseball commissioner, wrote: "Baseball is about going home and how hard it is to get there and how driven is our need. It tells us how good home is. Its wisdom says you can go home again but that you cannot stay. The journey must always start once more, the bat and oar over the shoulder, until there is an end to all journeying."

True politics, in imitation of baseball, the great American metaphor, is also about going home. Members of Congress consider it the sine qua non of their routine. Presidential candidates engage in an elaborate if disingenuous ceremony of finding the American home during primary season. And in between, everyone in politics pays extraordinary attention to political shamans like Gallup and Roper whose magical powers center upon their understanding of what's happening "at home."

Yet as with so much in our national life, we are only going through the motions, paying ritualistic obeisance to a faith we no longer follow. In fact, we have lost our way home.

A few years back, I attended a planning session for a liberal conference that was to focus on the Bill of Rights. Several of us suggested that we might consider what the Bill of Rights left out and proposed a panel on the "natural rights" of Americans. The idea excited me because it offered an opportunity to examine what it meant to be a real live American human, not merely an American legal or economic entity. It might be the beginning, for liberals at least, of restoring the idea of the actual individual— rather than the aggregated individual—to the center of their thought and policies.

The idea was quickly shot down, in part because it was argued that the poor and the suffering did not have the luxury of such "New Age" concepts. Locke, Rousseau, and Madison were not exactly proto-hippies, and the Declaration of Independence was not written by Jerry Brown, but these traditional liberals simply could not see beyond the question of economic rights.

We had touched on the hidden debate of American politics. On one side stand the liberals, the conservatives, and the Marxists, and on the other the libertarians, the greens, and the decentralist progressives. What, we were really discussing, is politics about?

In one corner—the one preferred by capitalists, Marxists, and many liberals—are those who see the individual as possessing certain rights, but still being at heart primarily an economic creature.

In the other corner are those who see the human franchise extending far beyond matters of survival and fiscal equity to include the right of privacy, the right of the individual as inherently superior to that of a corporation, the right to follow one's own moral vision, the right to make one's own mistakes in peace, the right of a community to govern itself, and the right of a citizen to be served by the state and not be a servant of that state. Oh yes, there is also the oft-forgotten right to be happy.

Somehow it had seemed relevant that on the three-hundredth anniversary of what might be called liberalism's first position paper—in which John Locke argued that the state exists to preserve the natural rights of its citizens—we spend some time on humans as other than creatures of government. Three hundred years later, however, these leading American liberals couldn't understand what Locke was talking about.

Such issues may seem far removed from the drug wars of our cities. Yet the armed zombies wandering our streets are grim examples of what can be produced by a society that pretends they don't matter. By caring only marginally for the economic survival of our inner cities and not at all for their soul or culture, by denying individual dignity and worth to their residents, by refusing them money, power, or even adequate audience, the system has created the environment in which the drug wars have flourished.

Here is the payoff for not caring about the intangibles of human existence; for providing education, shelter, and social services on the cheap; and for excessive faith in a megasystem that cannot respond to a reality that stretches only a few blocks. Following the advice of Daniel Burnam, we have made no small plans, and thus we find ourselves, finally, with no solutions applicable to the small and real places in which each of us live.

We cannot hope to work our way out of this dilemma by more great plans and massive "wars." We must take the time to recreate what we have destroyed. Just as we are cleaning up the toxic wastes, the fouled rivers, and the noxious atmosphere that are our environmental legacy, so we must confront the ecological destruction of our political system. We must do this to have a reason for America to continue to exist. The conflict can no longer be the phony battle between liberals and conservatives that leaves us the Hudge-Gudge choice between control by huge corporations, huge government, or a conspiracy of the two. The question is whether we can restore the individual and the community to the center of American political life.

Given the glum evidence cited in this book and elsewhere, it certainly seems unlikely. The little icons of hope appear too trivial to matter. Not much on the evening news encourages us, and the growing number of Americans who describe themselves as victims suggests a nation determined not to recover from its various traumas.

On the other hand, what psychiatrist Steven Wolin and his wife, child development specialist Sybil Wolin, reported in their study of troubled families may work for communities, cities, and our country as well. Like many psychiatrists, Steven Wolin had originally adopted a damage model of human psychology. The Wolins, in their book *The Resilient Self,* describe this model as one in which troubled families "are seen as toxic agents, like bacteria or viruses, and survivors are regarded as victims of the parents' poisonous secretions. . . . The best survivors can do is to cope or contain the family's harmful influence at considerable cost to themselves."[9]

But as Steve Wolin deepened his work with troubled, and particularly alcoholic, families, he found a surprising number of adult children who had not repeated their parents' drinking patterns or become psychological disaster areas. They had developed an alternative, a model in which they were not unharmed but had used adversity to build a satisfying life, developing such compensating virtues as insight, independence, relationships, initiative, creativity, humor, and morality.

The Wolins continue:

> In the 1980s in this country, the Damage Model seeped down from the professional to our popular culture in a big way. The survivor-as-victim image became the rallying point for a recovery movement that is still growing today. As the movement has spread its influence, diseases, addictions and human frailties have occupied the limelight of our awareness, and resilience has fallen into the shadows. We are fast becoming a nation of emotional cripples, incapable of managing the expectable problems that life doles out every day.[10]

What the Wolins were saying went far beyond the problems of individuals or the profession of family therapy. The damage model is the same one we commonly use to describe America's communities and our politics.

Consider, for example, the L.A. riots. In the thousands of words pouring out after the L.A. uprising, you could easily search in vain for one sentence implying that anyone—victim, participant, or would-be reconstructionist—had any real hope for our inner cities other than partial salvation through moral conversion or partial recovery through endless subsidy. The reaction to South-Central L.A. brought to mind Gertrude Stein: "There ain't no answer. There ain't going to be any answer. There never has been an answer. That's the answer."

But what, if just for a moment, we had put aside our fatalism and asked ourselves a different sort of question: How could we turn South-Central L.A. into a good place to live?

Simply mouthing the words reframes the issue. It is a revolutionary question because, by asking it, we bring the people of South-Central L.A. out of the shadows of stereotypes, statistics, and sob stories. We begin to view their problems as we might that of a neighbor rather than that of an abstract crisis to whose amelioration we must dutifully but futilely tithe in the name of doing something.

The people living in a community like South-Central L.A. are mostly normal people in abnormal circumstances. To be sure, such communities have an excess of social deviants, but they are deviants of their own community's norms as well as those of America in general. It is one of the libels of our times to assert that the failure of these communities is a failure of morality or of courage. Walk down any inner-city street in America and you'll find more people with more courage, resilience, and integrity than you'll find in your average bank, college administration, or offices of the president of the United States. These are not folks living on the hidden welfare of old boy networks, sinecures granted by virtue of college degrees, or tenure achieved by election to public office, but people who every day have to face the most extraordinary strains on their dignity and self-respect.

Back in the 1960s, when I was editing a center-city newspaper,

I thought it would be interesting to list all the churches within our two-square-mile circulation area. It turned out there were over a hundred, ranging from a couple of Catholic parishes to the Revolutionary Church of What's Happenin' Now. Yet this same community was, we were told even then, in the grips of pathology.

The first, easiest, and cheapest positive step anyone thinking about America's cities can take is to eradicate words like *ghetto, pathology, at risk, culture of poverty,* and *permanent underclass* from their vocabulary. These words are powerfully self-fulfilling rhetoric and alibis for indifference. Until we see these communities as real places with real people entitled to the same pursuit of life, liberty, and happiness as any other American, we will continue to regard them as targets of triage rather than as an integral part of our society. We will see them as inevitable victims rather than probable survivors.

Our sense of victimization, our self-fulfilling description of failure, is not limited to central cities. Our political discourse has bogged down in its acute and debilitating understanding of what's wrong. The Wolins describe well an alternative:

> Our lives are a story. There are as many stories as there are lives, and each of our stories is many stories. As authors, we are free to script and cast ourselves as we choose. Out of our complicated and varied experiences, we each select the events that have meaning for us and interpret them to fit our inner picture of who we are. Then we arrange the details in a plot that defines us—our problems, our strengths and our possibilities. In turn, the story we write exercises a powerful influence on how we feel and behave. As we construct our story, it constructs us.[11]

The reframing that Dr. Wolin suggests to his patients can be applied as well to the national story or the story of our own community. To free ourselves from the political machines that overwhelm us, we must first free ourselves from their story.

The best politics, it seems to me, moves effortlessly from what we were to what we should be without denial, indifference, or denigration. As Arthur Schlesinger Jr. has noted, a community without a history is like an individual without a memory. Part of our reframed story must restore our memory of what it has meant to be an American. Recovering our past in both its rights and its wrongs is essential to a new politics.

We can also free ourselves from the orthodox version of events by such technological means as cable television and computer bulletin boards and such non-technological means as gathering in small groups and telling each other stories. *Utne Reader* has had considerable success encouraging the revival of salons where people come together just to socialize and share common interests. There are other models such as book clubs and Swedish-style study circles. On my list of untested personal projects is a living newspaper—a gathering of people who would tell the most important news of their week to each other. In one case, the story might be personal; in another, a snippet from a novel; in another, the president's health-care program. I strongly suspect that the random editing of this living newspaper would produce more interesting copy than the carefully compiled morning edition on our doorsteps. Finally, resting almost forgotten in our past is the notion of the political club, premised on the inseparability of politics from our culture, our friends, and our sense of fun. Nothing would so herald the regeneration of democracy in this country as the revival of political clubs.

Such ideas may seem puny, but only because we have come to accept the notion that the enormous institutions of government, media, industry, and academia are natural to the human condition. In fact, as ecological planner Ernest Callenbach has pointed out, "We are medium-sized animals who naturally live in small groups—perhaps 20 or so—as opposed to bees or antelopes who live in very large groups. When managers or generals or architects force us into large groups, we speedily try to break them down into sub-units of comfortable size."

Too often, however, we fail. Today, if you want to tell it to the boss, you may have to travel a couple of thousand miles just to get to the receptionist. All of our systems appear to be on steroids.

And, as with the drugged athlete, nature eventually pulls the plug. The institutions that have imposed a tyranny of size upon us not only fail to accomplish what they set out to do but are now themselves disintegrating.

The collapse of huge institutions is one of the primary characteristics of our times. The Soviet Union falls apart, and no sooner have we declared the Cold War won than a new American administration tells us it will not be able to carry out the normal functions of a government because—although not saying it quite so bluntly—it believes we are nearing bankruptcy. Corporate icons like Sears and IBM totter. The savings and loan industry hits the mat. Our city governments are in extraordinary disarray.

We see it and yet we don't. Our loyalty to our assumptions and ideologies as well as our natural difficulty in accepting mortality even in non-human systems leads us to underrate such changes, to keep trying to do things the old way one more time.

There is growing evidence that in the wake of this decay, traditional ideological conflicts such as those between left and right are becoming far less important. As writer Thomas Martin has noted, a new ideology is rising, the ideology of devolution—or decentralizing—demanding the transfer of power to lower levels of government.

Already this ideology of scale has swept through the Soviet Union and Eastern Europe. Its voice is heard in Spain, in Quebec, and in Northern Ireland. It is the voice of people attempting to regain control over societies that have become increasingly authoritarian, unresponsive, and insensitive, a revolt of ordinary humans against the excesses of the state, reflecting the global gap between the peoples of the world and their own governments.

America is not immune from these forces. All around us is evidence of the disintegration of effective government and a growing alienation of the people from that government as a result. Our systems of governance have become too big, too corrupt, too inflexible, and too remote from democratic concerns to respond equitably and rationally to the changing needs of the people.

There are far more engagements in this struggle of scale than the media would lead one to think. In fact, much of the positive change since the sixties has involved moving the idea of devolution out of the commune and into the community and the nation. The statist Marxists are fading; new progressives want the utility controlled by their city and not by a national administration.

The greens and the libertarians, whose emphasis on decentralization removes them from normal left-right characterization, are advance troops for human scale. Their work is backed by the practical ideas of community land trusters, co-housing groups, more than 30,000 cooperatives, students of human ecology, community school boards, neighborhood development corporations and community councils, supporters of civic enterprise (i.e., community ownership of utilities and businesses), and centers of devolutionary thought such as the E. F. Schumacher Institute. In black school districts in Chicago and white villages in New England, citizens are carrying out a quiet revolution against the inefficiencies and cruelties of bigness.

It will take time because we have come to make false assumptions about the benefits of large-scale economies (based on accounting that, among other things, ignores ecological costs), we are daily intimidated by the megasystems in which we work or under whose shadows we live, and it has become increasingly difficult to imagine ourselves influencing anything.

There are actually things we can do to moderate the ill effects of these megasystems. We could, for example, regenerate the spirit of populism, the one native American movement that understood and challenged the industrial revolution's assault on freedom. We could start treating our largest corporations more like public utilities, demanding, as we did once, that they function in the public interest, convenience, and necessity. We could press for real anti-trust enforcement, for public members on the boards of large companies and elected corporate regulatory commissions. We could create an American Association of Working People—modeled more on the AARP than on the AFL-CIO—to organize the masses of non-unionized employees of America into an effective political lobby. We could create state and city banks, countering the redlining of America's financial institutions by providing loans to excluded home-buyers and small businesses. And we could encourage as public policy the growth of cooperatives and community or worker-owned companies. In short, we could finally recognize that much of today's political struggle is not between conservatives and liberals, but between corporatism and democracy.

There are also things we could do to moderate the excessive power of the modern presidency, a position so bloated that it undermines the Constitution, obscures its alternatives, and daily forces its monomaniacal presence upon us. But here the task is more difficult and more subtle, because it involves not only laws and regulations but our own view of the matter. The power of the president rises and falls with our willingness to grant that power. It is the same power possessed by Madonna and Jesse Jackson and Mother Teresa and Rush Limbaugh.

To be sure, the media plays an extraordinary role in determining our views, but we retain the choice should we desire to exercise it. Nothing in the Constitution speaks to whether we must believe in a mythic presidency and the tyranny such a faith inevitably produces. Imagine, for example, if we taught our schoolchildren the dangers of excessive power in government with the same assiduousness that we teach the dangers of drugs; if we encouraged safe democracy as well as safe driving; if our children learned how to discern the inner meaning of a White House news release as well as that of a poem; if more than 50 percent of our Ivy League students knew the names of their own senators as well as that of the chief executive. Such circumstances would, I think, lead to a different sort of presidency.

Reforms like these, however, speak primarily to controlling power rather than transferring it. Can the latter really happen? Well, it has in the past. From the American revolution to the underground railroad, to the organizing of labor, to the drive for universal suffrage, to the civil rights, women's, peace, and environmental movements, every significant political and social change in this country has been propelled by large numbers of highly autonomous small groups linked not by a bureaucracy or a master organization but by the mutuality of their thought, their faith, and their determination. There is no reason it cannot happen again.

What is lacking is not devolutionary theory, nor grand schemes, nor even useful experiments, but rather a practical politics of devolution. We need to apply these theories and experiences to the everyday politics of ordinary citizens. If we do, I think we will be surprised to discover where the American mainstream really flows.

The Rules of the Game

A good place to start is with the rules of the game. We live in one of a declining number of countries that use the demonstratively undemocratic winner-take-all electoral system. A winner need only be first, not necessarily the choice of the majority of voters. Nor is there any serious provision for political parties other than the two major ones. This latter defect has been elevated to a virtue by the obeisance paid it not only by representatives of the two parties but by the media, which quickly warns that any retreat from political duopoly will result in "instability"—a phrase that does not readily spring to mind when one considers Germany, Norway, Switzerland, and the Netherlands, all countries with a multi-party system. As election scholar Douglas Amy notes, in America "you have the right to vote, you just don't have the right to be represented."

In fact, when you look at the major democracies of the world, including the new ones of the former Soviet bloc, you find that the United States is electorally largely in the company of countries that once formed the British Empire. Even here there are defections: New Zealand has recently moved toward proportional representation, and the Australian senate uses preferential voting.

The American system fails on a number of counts:

• *It does not provide for a majoritarian decision.* For example, both the present and the former mayor of Washington were chosen by less than 35 percent of the vote in primaries that were tantamount to election. Clinton was elected with only 43 percent of the vote, and in only one state did *any* presidential candidate receive a majority of the popular vote. The center-right parties got only 39 percent of the votes in the 1993 French elections but 80 percent of the seats. In Canada, the Progressive Conservatives in 1993 won 16 percent of the vote, but no seats.

• *It clearly discriminates against minorities and minority views.* The district system used for elections to the House, for example, has traditionally produced underrepresentation of Latinos and blacks. The attempt to squeeze civil liberties into the district voting system has resulted in the degrading and ineffective anomaly of "minority districts," a sort of separate-but-equal politics that guarantees decennial attempts at gerrymandering. Further, non-geographically defined or underrepresented groups—such as gays or women—are not helped by such artificial machinations. For example, while women make up only about 10 percent of the American Congress, they constitute at least a third in Scandinavian countries, and over 20 percent in the Netherlands.

The difference can be seen dramatically in those countries that use both systems. In the German Bundestag, half the members are elected by proportional representation. Of these, 29 percent are women. The other half of the Bundestag is elected by district on a winner-take-all basis. Only 7 percent of these seats are held by women. An almost identical result holds in Australia, where the upper house uses PR and the lower uses winner-take-all.

As Helena Catt of New Zealand's Electoral Reform Coalition has explained, under proportional representation, "when parties prepare their lists they will strive to select balanced teams of candidates with broad appeal to voters. It will be very obvious if a party puts up a team with few women on it."[12]

• *It discourages voting.* If you are a minority by race, sex, or inclination, there is little opportunity for your views to be heard, let alone represented under the American system. This contributes

to the extraordinarily high level of voter apathy in the U.S. compared to those countries with proportional representation. For example, the *Washington Post*'s Lou Cannon reported that in the first
round of the 1993 voting for mayor in Los Angeles, only 4 percent
of the city's 918,000 adult Latinos cast ballots.

• *It gives too much importance to personalities and too little
to issues.* With only two parties pretending to represent the country's entire political spectrum, it is nearly impossible for either
party to propose a coherent program or even a new idea. Too
many intraparty compromises have to be made. Since the political
parties don't have much ideological meaning, it is inevitable that
American elections tend to focus excessively on the personalities
of the candidates. We end up talking about draft dodging, for
example, while avoiding any real debate over health care. As Will
Rogers noted, "We only get to vote on some man; we never get to
vote on what he is to do."

• *It is not flexible.* The genius of a well-working democracy
is its ability to adapt to new social conditions and values. The first-
past-the-post and district election system places an artificial barrier
in the way of the country adjusting to new realities. When combined with election laws cynically protective of the existing major
parties, these barriers become a broad moat around the status quo,
almost guaranteeing that change will be dilatory and quarrelsome
at best, and chaotic and violent at worst.

Fortunately, there are few constitutional bars to correcting this
situation. The Constitution does not mandate congressional or legislative districts, nor does it prevent the preferential election of
senators. By state action, larger states could switch to proportional
representation for their legislatures and for the U.S. House now.
By congressional action, the House of Representatives could be
enlarged—despite our enormous population growth it is still the
same size as in 1910—to allow other states to do likewise. And
while the electoral college would need to be abolished by constitutional amendment, nothing in the Constitution prevents the use
of proportional representation in choosing electors.

There are a variety of specific ways that America could improve its elections. Each has advocates who can verge on the fanatical. There are, as well, political scientists and statisticians who can offer comprehensive, if sometimes opaque, analyses of the effect of each of the systems, factoring in such matters as strategic voting (i.e., the voter trying to get an edge on the system through, say, bullet voting when several votes are allowed).

Then there are the non-objective considerations. Can the public understand the system? Does it seem intuitively fair? Whose ox gets gored?

New Zealand dealt with all these problems by naming a national commission to study and present to the public, in clear and unbiased fashion, the major alternatives. The result was a vote for the German system, which combines the virtues of the district system and proportional representation. By contrast, France in 1986 handled the matter as pure politics. The Socialists killed PR because they thought they could do better with a run-off system. Seven years later this came back to haunt them, as center-right parties with only a plurality of votes won an overwhelming majority of legislative seats.

Given the vagueness of the Constitution on the matter, we have the option of testing out various systems. One state might choose the German approach, another pure PR, another preferential voting, and so forth. Presumably, over time, the virtues and defects of each would become clearer.

Any of the standard alternatives would more closely approximate real democracy than our present system by ending gerrymandering, giving more voice to minorities, increasing voter turnout, and providing a forum for issues not heard about in our current two-party campaigns.

To understand the various possibilities, it helps to make a distinction between single-office contests (the presidency or mayor of a city) and multi-seat contests (Congress or a city council). Here are the major alternatives for single-office contests:

- *First-past-the-post:* This is our current system. Under it, in a three-way race, for example, the winner might theoretically get as few as 33.5 percent of the votes.
- *Run-offs:* In a single-office contest, a run-off system—as used in the American South and in France—is at least arguably better than the first-past-the-post now common in the U.S. One of the major problems with run-offs, however, is the expense of holding a second election and the falloff in voter turnout.
- *Preferential voting (also called the alternative vote):* In the classic system of preferential voting, if no one wins a majority of the votes, the votes of the least successful candidate are redistributed according to his or her supporters' second choice. Let us imagine that an election produced the following results:

Karen South:	3,700
Kwami East:	3,400
Maria Norte:	2,200
Bill West:	700

Under the current system, South would be the winner even though she fell quite short of a majority (5,001 votes). In typical preferential voting, the votes of the last-place West would be redistributed according to his voters' second choice. Since this would still not produce a majority for any candidate, the votes of Maria Norte would be redistributed in like manner. Given the closeness of the race, either South or East might win in this instance.

There is also a variation of preferential voting known as the Bucklin System. In it, if there is no clear winner, all the second-place votes of all the candidates are added to the first-place votes.

- *Approval voting:* Under this system, used by a few professional associations but as yet untested in a major political context, voters get to check off every candidate of whom they approve, but not in order of preference. Advocates claim this produces a fairer result, although there is the practical question of whether voters wouldn't prefer to rank the candidates.

Here are the major choices for multi-seat elections:

- *District and at-large elections:* This typically American form of election is responsible for many of the least appealing aspects of U.S. politics. The main virtue of district voting is that the district has someone with power at the seat of government. But it also leads to gerrymandering, minority disenfranchisement, and intensely parochial decisions on the part of legislators. The typical legislator spends more time fixing problems for constituents than acting as a legislator. Geography is considered more critical than race, sex, economics, age, ideology, and so forth.

At-large elections, in which the voter has as many choices as there are seats available, leads to the majority of a community magnifying its power to the exclusion of minorities, and has been frequently subject to successful assault in the courts on civil rights grounds.

- *Proportional representation:* Typically, various parties produce lists of candidates between which the public chooses. These lists can be either "open" or "closed." In the latter, the party determines the order of the candidates; in the former, voters have some influence. Under PR, if the Sunny Day Party wins 45 percent of the vote, it gets 45 percent of the seats in the legislature. In most cases there is a minimum threshold and the legislature is broken up into multi-member districts, within which the proportional representation occurs, thus allowing PR and regional concerns to work in tandem.
- *Single transferable vote:* This is essentially the principle of preferential voting applied to a multi-member body. Voters rank the candidates, and those surpassing a mathematically derived quota are considered elected. To determine the other victors, the choices of the least successful candidate are distributed to the other candidates. This is the system that has been used for years in Cambridge, Massachusetts, and is used in Ireland.
- *Mixed proportional representation:* This is the system used

in Germany, in which half the legislature is selected by district and half by PR. It is the system recently adopted by New Zealand after public consideration of the various alternatives.

Strange as proportional representation may seem to us, it has a history in this country going back to the progressive era, when nearly two dozen cities used it—including New York, Sacramento, and Cleveland. It disappeared not because it was ineffective, but because the urban elites and machines didn't like it, just as the French socialists killed PR in their country because they thought they could gain more power without it.

The story of Cincinnati is instructive. Theodore Berry, a black member of the Cincinnati city council, won election in 1953 under proportional representation. Because he was the highest vote-getter among council members, local tradition declared he should have become mayor, but his election was blocked. In 1957, opponents of Berry convinced the city to do away with PR entirely. Berry was finally elected mayor under a conventional voting system in the 1970s, two decades after a major American city could have had its first black mayor.

The ways in which government, working on behalf of the two major parties, rigs the rules for elections is mind-boggling. There is a whole newsletter, *Ballot Access News,* devoted to following the efforts by citizen groups to overturn them—challenging petition requirements, filing deadlines, registration rules, and so forth. One of the least noticed but most important are strictures against third parties temporarily allying themselves with major parties on fusion slates as a means of increasing their power. These anti-fusion laws not only fly in the face of normal definitions of democracy, but some specifically violate international human rights agreements such as those in the Helsinki Accords.

The Senate poses a special problem, since its unique nature is determined by the Constitution. As it stands, women, Latinos, and blacks constitute 61 percent of the American population, but make up only 7 percent of the U.S. Senate. If the Senate were a school district, it would be under court-ordered busing. If it were a private club, you'd want to resign from it before you ran for public office. Without altering the Constitution, it is difficult to democratize the Senate, but not impossible. For example, the admission of the District of Columbia and Puerto Rico as states would improve the minority composition of the Senate. Splitting large states like California, Florida, and New York into two or three states—all possible without a constitutional amendment—would increase the electoral chances of minorities and women. In fact, a strong case can be made for granting statehood to ten or twenty of the largest metropolitan areas in order to correct the egregiously anti-urban discrimination inherent in the current composition of the Senate.

With such measures, the smaller voices of this country could be heard within the political system rather than only through the media or by protest or violence. As an Ashtabula, Ohio, newspaper said in 1915 after that town's first election conducted by proportional representation: "The drys and the wets are represented, the Protestants and the Catholics; the business, professional, and laboring men, the Republicans, Democrats, and Socialists; the English, Swedes and Italians are represented. It would be hard to select a more representative council in any other way."[13]

Natural and Constitutional Rights

Fair elections, however, are only the start. A central problem is to give back to the people their natural and constitutional rights—starting with the forgotten amendments of the Bill of Rights, namely the Ninth and Tenth:

Amendment Nine: "The enumeration of the Constitution, of certain rights, shall not be construed to deny or disparage others retained by the people."

Amendment Ten: "The powers not delegated to the United States by the Constitution, nor prohibited by it to the States, are reserved to the States respectively, or to the people."

Together, these amendments should be bulwarks protecting our natural rights and repelling authoritarian federal government.

But habit, the lack of civic education, media ignorance, and the stealthy usurpation of power by Washington have conspired not only to deprive us of the benefits of these amendments but to conceal the fact that they even exist.

Beyond the question of rights are also some practical reasons for a dramatic devolution of political power in the United States. Under our present overcentralized system:

* Citizens lack access to politicians, and politicians, responsible for oversized political units, rely heavily on bureaucrats or "experts" who are unresponsive to the citizen.

* The expense and difficulty of making changes in the political structure is magnified. From civic committees to militant demonstrations, from community organizing to riots, citizens in recent years have experimented with a variety of methods to achieve the political change they could not achieve within the political system. They have had minimal success.

* Both the politician and the bureaucrat become scornful of the democratic process as they become less dependent upon it. The citizens become more scornful of the democratic process as it apparently fails them.

* The citizens' contact with politicians increasingly comes through the images of the media rather than through direct or even second-hand contact.[14]

We need alternatives to our failing centralized systems. And we need a way to function at a human level, with our thoughts and actions and words ecologically connected to reality rather than to propaganda and myth. We need, in short, a way to fly under the radar of America's military-industrial-media complex.

Here are a few ways it could happen:

Neighborhood Government

Real neighborhood government would not be merely advisory. It would include the power to sue the city government, to incorporate, to run community programs and business, to contract to provide services now offered by city hall, and to have some measure of budgetary authority over city expenditures within its boundaries. Not the least among its powers should be a role in the justice system, since it is impossible to recreate order in our communities while denying communities any place in maintaining order. We should move closer to the "small republics" that Jefferson dreamed of, communities where every citizen became "an acting member of the common government, transacting in person a great portion of its rights and duties, subordinate indeed, yet important, and entirely within his own competence."

Budgetary authority (not the actual money) could be granted over 1 percent of a community's pro rata share of a city's budget. In D.C., this would mean an extraordinary $1 million for a neighborhood of 20,000 people. Federal revenue sharing of a similar magnitude would produce another million dollars for each such community in the country. Consider what could be done in your own community for $2 million a year, and then try to figure out what happens to the money now.

While one community might choose to spend its money on education, another might choose more police patrols or recreation facilities. There would be mistakes, but they would be *our* mistakes, easier to understand and to rectify. Further, by permitting error, we would again also be permitting genius.

Neighborhood government also offers an antidote to the chronic gap between government and governed, There is, after all, little reason to cling to the notion that the solution to our problems is to spend more money on a form of government that has increasingly shown its incompetence. To say that because the crime rate is rising sharply we should therefore double the size of the same police force that has thus far been unable to cope with it; to reward with more concentrated power a city government that has spent decades on absurd, disruptive, and cruel planning; to continue to vest the power of educating our children in an administrative system that appears to lag as far behind the human intelligence norm as the children it miseducates do in reading and math—surely this can have little logical justification.

Neighborhood government is another way. It is not some utopian scheme but a pragmatic approach. It is, in fact, contemporary large-city governance that is utopian, in that there is no empirical evidence that it works. It is under this form of government that we generally find the worst crime, the worst education, the worst health, the worst pollution, and the highest unemployment.

Neighborhood government is pragmatic economically. We know, for example, that the per capita costs of government begin to soar as jurisdictions increase in size. Further, the larger the jurisdiction, the greater the tendency to deal with problems through the application of money and bureaucracy. Imagination narrows into a budget item; the specific offspring of the budget item becomes far less important than the fact that it costs X dollars.

Small government works differently. It tends to pay more attention to detail and substance. I recall attending a PTA meeting at which the chaos produced by major teacher reassignments was discussed. It did not take long before someone pointed out that while we must deal with citywide issues, we must also continue to teach the children no matter what happened. A committee was quickly formed to seek volunteers to help fill in the gaps caused by the transfers. Big government doesn't work that way.

To be sure, neighborhood government takes time. I know. For two years I was a neighborhood commissioner dealing with politics at its most minute level. On one occasion, I spent five hours at a meeting attempting to mediate a dispute over where a recreation center's tennis backboard should be placed. But I do not begrudge the time nor the hassles; it was one of the great experiences of my life. Besides, there was no need for term limits; I happily retired after one.

Neighborhood government is also pragmatic politically. Much political dissatisfaction comes from the inability of residents to make their concerns felt at city hall. Problems are specific; big-city government by its nature is general. If you don't fit the average or the generalized model, you get left behind.

Back in the early seventies, Senator Mark Hatfield made the remarkable proposal that citizens be allowed to funnel a portion of their tax dollars to neighborhood organizations. In defense of this profoundly radical idea, he cited some figures that dramatically show how some of the nation's social problems can be broken into smaller and more manageable parts:

> If, for example, every church and synagogue were to take over the responsibility of caring for ten people over the age of 65 who are presently living below the poverty level there would be no present welfare programs needed for the aged. If each church or synagogue took over the responsibility for 18 families who are eligible for welfare today, there would not be any need for federal or state welfare programs to families. If each church and synagogue cared for less than one child each the present day care program supported by federal and state funds would be totally unnecessary.

Community Control of Public Schools

Under the headline PARENTS TELL DC SUPERINTENDENT: CUT BUREAUCRACY, NOT 430 TEACHERS, the *Washington Post* reported that a parents' group had calculated that in 1979 the D.C. school system had 114,000 students and just over 500 administrative employees. By 1991 the student population was down to 83,000, but central staff was up to more than 1,000.

Such absurdities cannot be handled effectively by playing endless budgetary cat-and-mouse games with administrators whose primary function and skill is keeping their own jobs. The problem needs to be addressed directly through community control and the dismantling of school bureaucracies. In the sixties there was a strong movement for community control, but because it came largely from minority communities and because the majority was not adequately distressed about public education, it faltered. The issue has recently revived; it shows strength and should be pushed.

Community Justice

The decline of the American city is intimately related to the problem of crime. One need not get into a chicken-and-egg argument to recognize that the failures of urban policy contribute to crime and crime contributes to the failure of cities. The question is: How do we interrupt this destructive cycle? The conventional answers—more police and more jails—not only haven't worked, they are beginning to bankrupt a number of cities.

There are other things that could be done, but none are more important than restoring the community to the center of our attempts to obtain social order. Most law and order stems from personal and community values or from peer pressure of one sort or another. Yet our prescription for law and order ignores such influences, using as their surrogate vastly overextended police departments and courts.

Consider what happens today. A young person engages in some minor offense such as vandalism or fighting and we call the cops. The city police immediately remove the offender from the very community against which the offense has been committed. From that point on, the community is ignored; the offense becomes one against the larger and far more abstract city. It is small wonder that so many youths fail to learn what living in a community entails.

There is no substitute for organic social order, as even totalitarian countries have discovered. To create this organic system, we must return to the community and build our justice system up from it. Community courts and neighborhood constables are one way of recreating community law and order. Community courts could deal with misdemeanors using such correctives as community work and various forms of restitution. They must, however, represent the community and not merely be in it, as is the case with a number of current decentralized court experiments.

Neighborhood constables or sheriffs would have the power of arrest and would become a symbol not of the city's law and order, but of the community's. Strange as this idea might seem, downtown business districts and shopping malls regularly practice it; their constables are called security guards. Neighborhoods should be entitled to similar protection.

States' Rights

While maintaining federal preeminence in fields such as civil rights and the environment, we need to be strong advocates of states' rights on issues not properly the federal government's. We need, for example, to end the current practice by the federal government of passing laws mandating state or local action, but without the funds to accomplish it. In particular we should oppose the use of federal green-mail—forcing states and localities to take legislative measures at the risk of losing federal funding—as a clear end run around the 10th Amendment of the Bill of Rights. As the Supreme Court noted in *Kansas v. Colorado,* this amendment "discloses the widespread fear that the national government might, under the pressure of supposed general welfare, attempt to exercise powers which had not been granted." It might, has, and today does, with great regularity.

Such talk greatly offends many liberals who persist in their faith in the beneficence of big government. They have slipped into the trap of defending a theory that defies the teachings of common eyesight. Many liberals think that to talk about a smaller government is to consort with reactionaries. In fact, while Reagan talked of getting government off our backs, one of his first acts was to eliminate the Carter-originated office of neighborhoods. The government stayed on our backs; it was just that more of it was in military and police uniform. To date, neither political party has seriously considered devolving political power.

Revenue Sharing

A similar liberal blind spot leads to a chronic indifference to government waste. It's not that liberals really favor waste, they're just afraid that if you start talking about it, the next thing you know they'll want to do away with social security. As with the issue of centralized authority, this liberal neurosis discredits many worthy ideas whose major problem may be only that they are being conducted inefficiently or by the wrong people at the wrong level.

One of the best ways to reduce the federal government while maintaining an adequate flow of funds for needed programs is through revenue sharing, yet another victim of that great phony decentralizer, Ronald Reagan. Whatever the problems of malfeasance or nonfeasance at the local level, they are almost guaranteed to be less than the misuse of these funds at the federal level. As Congress's own auditor, Comptroller General Charles Bowsher, told a Hill hearing, "There are hardly any [federal] agencies that are well managed."

In contrast, much of the best government is at the state and local level. It could do even better without the paperwork and the restrictions dreamed up in Washington to fill the working day. And even when that doesn't prove true, you don't have to drive as far to make your political anger known.

Decentralizing the Federal Government

The existing federal government could be greatly decentralized. There are a number of federal agencies that already are. Interestingly, these agencies are among those most often praised by the public. The National Park Service, the Peace Corps, the Coast Guard, the Soil Conservation Service, and U.S. attorneys all have dispersed units with a relatively high degree of autonomy and a strong sense of turf responsibility by their employees. A further example can be found within the Postal Service. While many complain about mail service, you rarely hear people gripe about their own mail carrier, who is given a finite federal task in a finite geographical area.

I stumbled across this phenomenon while serving in the Coast Guard. At the time, the Guard had about eighteen hundred units worldwide but only three thousand officers, many of the latter concentrated on larger ships and in headquarters units. Thus there were scores of units run by enlisted personnel who rarely saw an officer. Yet the system worked extremely well.

It worked because once competent individuals had been assigned and training and adequate equipment had been provided, there was relatively little a bureaucratic superstructure could do to improve the operations of a lifeboat or loran station. Similarly, a former Peace Corps regional director told me that in his agency's far-flung and decentralized system, there was no way he could control activities in the two dozen countries under his purview. Despite this generally presumed liability, the Peace Corps became one of the most popular federal programs of recent times. As with education, a bureaucracy in such circumstances can do itself far more good than it can do anyone in the field.

Can the success of these decentralized agencies be replicated, say, in housing or urban development? Why not give it a try? Why not have federal housing policy administered by fifty state directors, who like U.S. attorneys would be politically acceptable to the state and who would be given considerable leeway in the mix of programs they could fund and approve? Why does it surprise us that responsible people given responsibility might act responsibly? Is it because we no longer study human nature and "act accordin' "?

At least one major corporation found that such autonomy works. Johnson and Johnson, the *Wall Street Journal* reports, has averaged a 13 percent annual growth in its earnings per share over the past decade. It has 166 units around the world, each largely autonomous, "its contact with headquarters largely limited to reporting results. This places authority in the hands of managers nearest the marketplace, and frees top management to focus on broad trends."

Economic Citizenship

Our economics need to devolve as well, in part because in small-scale economics, market forces can be mediated by such non-economic factors as altruism, cooperation, initiative, and sense of responsibility. As Jonathan Rowe has said of Korean family-run groceries, "A family operates on loyalty and trust, the market operates on contract and law."

Small business not only has been the country's major producer of new jobs, but micro-businesses—those with fewer than twenty employers—created 47 percent of the new jobs between 1984 and 1990.[15] Small business is more likely to hold on to its jobs, less often damaging to the environment, and less physically harmful to its workers.

And it can be productive in surprising ways. *Regardies Magazine,* for example, did a study of what basketball player Patrick Ewing had produced for Georgetown University in return for his scholarship. Adding in everything from the obvious (ticket sales) to the not so obvious (a big jump in application fees to GU), *Regardies* found Ewing returning the university a profit many times over cost. No Fortune 500 company can make that claim.

We tend to underestimate the importance of small and unconcentrated business because political and media attention tends to follow size and power. Yet a Wharton Econometrics Forecasting Associates analysis a few years back found that bowling contributed roughly half as much to the American economy as did local mass transit. Health club memberships were even more important than bowling. In aggregate, amusement and recreation was a larger industry than textiles or apparel or coal mining. The sports industry was almost as big as auto manufacturing.

Obsessed with trade policy and domestic macro-economics, we tend to ignore other economies at home, both legal and illegal. For example, a 1988 estimate put the nation's underground economy at $380 billion a year, including drugs, prostitution, and numbers, various forms of tax dodging, and unreported cash-based transactions. Hazel Henderson, author of *Creative Alternative Futures,* estimated the drug trade at $45 billion alone, almost as great as the sports and auto industries. Writing in the newsletter *Green Revolution,* Henderson noted: "*Business Week* points out rightly that this rapidly-growing subterranean economy not only discredits much traditional macro-economic analysis, but also accounts for much of its large error factor in measuring GNP performance, levels of total employment, rates of saving, investment and productivity—all of which are significantly understated."

Similarly, assuming that poor urban communities can be changed only by bringing them into the larger marketplace through such devices as urban renewal or enterprise zones, we have ignored the importance of creating self-reliant economies within these neighborhoods. The economic problem of such communities is not just an absolute lack of money, but what happens to it. Since the War on Poverty, little attention has been given to devices such as community credit unions, cooperatives, and community-owned businesses that recycle and leverage money within neighborhoods. The potential is substantial. For example, zip code 20032, one of the poorest in D.C., has a per capita income of $9,039. By American standards that's not much, but it's greater than the per capita gross domestic product of Israel, and almost as much as those of Italy and the United Kingdom. The total household income of this one poor neighborhood is $370 million a year.[16] What happens to that $370 million after it gets to the neighborhood is vital to what happens to the people who earn it. At present, much of the $370 million simply flows through the community as though through a sewer.

The self-generating economy has a long history in America. Many of the country's early communities were largely self-sufficient. This self-sufficiency, however, disappeared with the concentration of industry and land. One study a few years back of the difference between the economics of a typical Ohio farm and that of an Amish farmer in the same state revealed the striking importance of land ownership. The research found that while an Amish farmer was making money on a bushel of corn, the conventional farmer was not. Lack of land debt, while not the only reason, was a major factor. In fact, much of what is known as the farm problem is not agricultural at all, but stems from the way we have permitted land ownership to be managed in this country. Many rural communities could be much more self-sustaining if freed from some of their debt burden.

In cities, one can easily find self-generating economies, although we seldom recognize them as such. The explosion of the legal profession, for example, reflects in no small part the ability of lawyers to create jobs for each other. The whole yuppie phenomenon can be seen as a self-generating economy: yuppies creating artificial needs for other yuppies, and with some selling and others buying items that fulfill these needs.

There is also the economy that Hazel Henderson calls the "counter-economy"—the non-monetarized economy—which she says is "still invisible to most economists and policy makers. It is based on . . . altruism, volunteering, community and family cohesiveness, cooperation, sharing, respect for the environment and the rights of future generations, and conservation of all resources—human and natural." The economic effect of this economy is enormous. For example, the UN's International Labor Organization, studying the role of women in the non-monetarized segment of the economy, has reported that women globally work 47 percent of all productive hours, but receive only 10 percent of the world's wages and own only 1 percent of the property. Orio Giarini, a futurist economist, claims that 80 percent of all the world's capital investment is not monetarized.

Not only does our infatuation with the Fortune 500 and international trade blind us to our other economies and their contribution to our economic well-being, we often actually work against them. Legislators are prone to write regulatory measures with only big business in mind, ignoring the effects their actions will have on a mom and pop firm. In part this is because the legislators, like many of the activists pressing the measures, have never experienced the problems of running a small business or because they are lawyers, trained to serve a large corporate bureaucracy that can handle any amount of paperwork.

For example, over the past few years my town has lost thousands of jobs through the simple expedient of overregulating (or overenforcement of the laws regarding) street vendors, gypsy cabs, artist studios, street performers, interior decorators, and home occupations. It would appear that every time someone thinks of a good way to make money outside of working for a major corporation, a city council member comes up with a law to make it as difficult as possible. The result is a reduction in employment, more "illegal" activity, and a growing tendency toward concentration in the particular industry involved, since it is the powerful who are best equipped to deal with the regulatory morass.

Thus the economic space between being homeless and being a junior partner is slowly emptied. Employment choices are limited; innovation and entrepreneurship are penalized; and workstyles are homogenized. That so many choose to ignore the rules and drive their gypsy cabs or run their illegal business from their homes is a tribute to the staying power of American economic initiative, but at some point we should start discussing why this has to be so. A politics of devolution would be the politics of small business, of self-generating economies, of cooperatives and neighborhood or worker-owned companies, and of other commercial activity that revitalizes and serves communities rather than merely draining them.

Planning for People

Most political, economic, and physical planning in this country is done to achieve abstract goals and aggregated results. The problem is that net progress can be, for many, a gross disaster. For example, if a community in one year experiences 100 murders and 110 births, it would record a net population increase, yet few would cheer the fact. Nonetheless, at the national level we regularly debate issues—NAFTA is a good example—as though the net result renders insignificant any pain created in its achievement.

Such Darwinian analysis has been traditionally applied to military adventures; battlefield cemeteries are a monument to it. We also long considered the environment only in net terms, until we finally realized that not only had we been adding wrong, but you couldn't ever really counterbalance destruction. So we began to think ecologically, another way of saying that the means are the end and that there is no free lunch.

Then there is the character of the planners themselves. In *The Uses of Disorder,* Richard Sennett says of urban planners: "Their impulse has been to give way to that tendency, developed in adolescence, of men to control unknown threats by eliminating the possibility of surprise. . . . Buried in this hunger for preplanning along machine-like lines is the desire to avoid pain, to create a transcendent order of living that is immune to the variety, and so to the inevitable conflict, between men."[17]

It is this impulse that drives Ira Magaziner to try to decide every health policy issue while he is still at the White House, that forces citizens into the sterile boxes and spaces of the planned city, and that creates order where the average human would much prefer a little serendipity and freedom.

Although citizens have regularly protested planning that excludes or minimizes their interests, there is not yet a politics aimed at changing the nature of planning itself or that fosters effective citizen counterplanning. That counterplanning can have an impact has been demonstrated by such groups as Urban Ecology, whose international conferences on cities have produced far more imaginative and useful ideas than would have come out of HUD or the average city planning office. The Other Economic Summit regularly shows up at meetings of world leaders to witness the existence of an alternative economic reality. Citizen groups sometimes leap ahead of city officials, planning a portion or all of their neighborhood before downtown tells them what it's going to look like.

But there is still a long way to go. To give just one example, the American city was designed on a couple of premises now widely considered to be not only faulty but anti-social. One was the presumption of clean fuel; the other was the presumption that men would go to work and women would stay home. We separated work from home and men from women and called it the suburban ideal.

Today we attack these presumptions, yet we have not connected our beliefs and our politics to our planning. We do not, for example, design cities that physically reflect the changed role of women. We continue to leave such matters to those we call experts, those trained in the profession that made the mess in the first place. This has to change. The deprofessionalization of planning in all its forms is absolutely essential for a decent politics.

Living Together

A politics of devolution—a politics of the manageable—could also offer badly needed alternatives to the ethnic problems that plague us, many of which stem from our forced existence in huge systems that deny us other than group identity.

It's not polite to say so, but the cause of civil rights is in trouble. Much of this is due to forces over which civil rights activists have little control, such as the rightward drift of both political parties and a growing culture of meanness exacerbated by the country's economic problems.

Yet the advocates of thirty years ago faced even worse obstacles and still managed to raise an exceptionally powerful, focused, and moral voice on behalf of human justice. Today, instead, we find civil rights laws increasingly enmeshed in arcane legalisms, civil rights politics transferred from the street and the pulpit to the courtroom and the attorney's office, a growing if often needless conflict between civil rights and those of free speech, a persistence of deep segregation in places ranging from central cities to Ivy League campuses, administrative excesses by university officials in the name of a diversity constantly proclaimed but rarely achieved, a failure to even discuss discrimination in some of its more virulent forms such as in housing and public transportation, and a sense that the one true commonality flourishing among Americans is that they all feel they're being screwed.

For multiculturalism to work, there have to be people working for it. For all the talk, the constituency for multiculturalism is surprisingly small. What does exist is an enormous, diverse, and growing constituency for implacable jingoistic monoculturalisms. Yugoslavia on the installment plan.

Relying on the law as our offense and defense, preferring litigation to negotiation, indifferent to the intercultural relations we claim to want, unskilled and apathetic in dealing with the practicalities of diversity, and stymied by mutual self-righteousness, multiculturalism may turn out to be a far less pleasant condition than many of its advocates imagine, a place not of peace and justice but only of more hate, violence, and lawsuits.

As long as the scale in which we function is so immense that we can recognize each other only by our ethnic channel number, by our ethnic ID, there is not much hope. Trapped in our large systems, we not only make broad assumptions based on sex and ethnicity, we become obsessed with the very distinctions we claim shouldn't matter. For example, our laws against discriminatory practices inevitably heighten general consciousness of race and sex. The media, drawn inexorably to conflict, mentions race five times as often as taxes in covering urban politics, according to one study. And the very groups that have suffered under racial or sexual stereotypes consciously foster countering stereotypes as a form of protection.

If humans were truly moral, the concept of race wouldn't even exist. It has no biological, and only a limited taxonomic, justification, serving largely as an excuse for one group of humans to do harm to another. Still, our desire to separate ourselves from those unlike us is much deeper than we are willing to admit. As Ruth Benedict pointed out, a great many tribal names mean simply "the human beings." Outside the tribe are no human beings. "We are not," she surmised, "likely to clear ourselves easily of so fundamental a human trait."

Once we accept the unpleasant persistence of human prejudice, once we give up the notion that it is merely social deviance controllable by sanctions, we drift away from a priggish and puritanical corrective approach toward one that emphasizes techniques of mitigating harm, toward what Andrew Young has called a sense of "no fault justice," and toward emphasizing countervailing human qualities that can serve as antibiotics against hate and fear. We move from being victims to being survivors. We start to deal with some of the real problems of creating a multicultural community; we actually start to envision it, to build it not on false politeness but upon realistic interdependence.

Such communities, the sine qua non of a functioning America, will not be constructed by laws, pronouncements from deans of freshmen, or civil rights leaders. Nor can we continue to treat multiculturalism like some overbearing parent saying to her toddler, "Now go make friends with that nice Nancy." It didn't work when we were six and it's not working much better now.

Multicultural communities will be constructed not by the hustlers of the diversity trade but by a growing local and personal regard for common sense, fairness, and, yes, reasonable self-interest. The new multicultural community will work because it is jointly and severally proud of itself, leaving behind the self-hate that so often accompanies the hatred of others. It will work because there are adequate jobs for people of every group—thus eliminating one of the primary causes of ethnic triage, and it will work because our educational system will teach not a prudish diversity but simply the way the world really is, which, among other things, is very diverse. Our children will learn to enjoy and incorporate this diversity, and as they do so will undoubtedly find it odd that their elders couldn't get any closer to the matter than a rigid and legalistic sensitivity.

Perhaps this is why ethnic restaurants are among the most successful practitioners of multiculturalism in America. Why is it so hard for universities to deal with multicultural issues while the Arab carry-out across from my office offers a "kosher hoagie"? It is, in part, because most of us are like Bismarck, who said when offered German champagne that his patriotism stopped at his stomach. It is also that the ethnic restaurant offers a fair multicultural deal: a good living for the owner in return for good food for the patrons.

For multiculturalism to work, we need a willing suspension of our politics as well as the creation of places where this can happen, both neutral places and places where we can participate in another culture that will leave us feeling that something good has happened. Outside of restaurants and ethnic nightclubs, this is now rarely available in America. We are not taught the pleasures of diversity, only its problems and burdens. We are seldom invited to enjoy other cultures, only to be sensitive toward them and—unspoken—to feel sorry for them. Thus, inevitably, we tend to think of multiculturalism in terms of conflict and crisis.

The restaurant analogy is not trivial. Political scientist Milton L. Rakove credits Irish dominance in Chicago partially to the fact that the Irish ran saloons that "became centers of social and political activity not only for the Irish but also for the Polish, Lithuanian, Bohemian and Italian immigrants. . . . As a consequence of their control of these recreational centers of the neighborhoods, the Irish saloon keepers and bartenders became the political counselors of their customers, and the political bosses of the wards and, eventually, of the city." As one politician put it, "A Lithuanian won't vote for a Pole, and a Pole won't vote for a Lithuanian. A German won't vote for either of them—but all three will vote for an Irishman."[18]

Cutting the Cost of the Middle

Government programs have come to contain enormous hidden subsidies for various intermediaries. Give a government grant to an academic researcher, and the university takes 30–50 percent off the top. Give a college student a loan, and it has to be funneled through financial institutions that skim off a piece of the action. Give someone national health insurance under the Clinton plan, and big insurance companies will take their cut. Want to bail out a failing industry? Don't put up government equity, just guarantee credit so that banks can make risk-free loans.

Sometimes the superfluous middle is right on the government payroll. Many liberals cling to the notion that federal housing funds are used for housing, agriculture funds for farmers, and so forth. In fact, an extraordinary percentage of these moneys is used to maintain a superstructure to carry out poor housing policy or bad farm policy. A basic principle of a devolutionary politics should instead be to get the money to the streets (or to the farms) as quickly—and with as few intermediaries—as possible.

The Clinton educational loan program is an excellent example of how this goal can be achieved. Yet the same White House took precisely the opposite approach on health care; its plan includes an enormous subsidy of the big insurers. Meanwhile, neither major party shows any interest in direct assistance for housing—such as a shared equity program—preferring instead elaborate policies that quietly and effectively funnel aid to various housing and financial interests.

Seizing the Time

Finally, a politics of devolution would demand the freedom and time to practice it. As one activist artist told me, "You don't have time to organize anything in this economy." Barbara Brandt of the Shorter Work-Time Group of Women for Economic Justice notes that the time that men and women are spending at work has actually increased over the past twenty years. And *Time* wrote, "When Arlie Hochschild studied working couples in the San Francisco area . . . she found that 'a lot of people talked about sleep. They talked about sleep the way a hungry person talks about food.' "[19]

Shorter-workweek advocates such as Brandt, Harvard economist Juliet Schor, Eugene McCarthy, Benjamin Hunnicutt, and William McGaughey are on the cusp of a major revolution, one that challenges not only political and economic concentration but tyranny over time. The twelve-to-eighteen-hour workday was, after all, the product of the industrial revolution. As that revolution is replaced by whatever is happening to us now, our archaic allocation of time must be examined as well. And not merely the time Americans spend on the job. Time can also be a hidden form of inflation, as when jobs and shops are moved farther from one's home or one is forced to wait longer for service in a store. In each such case, someone benefits financially by the time you are forced to waste.

The shorter workweek not only is crucial for economic and psychological reasons and to more fairly distribute jobs and income, it also would allow a shift in our cultural priorities. We would once again—as was the case through most of human history—be able to consider the needs of our communities and families as part of our "work," and not something we are always too tired or too important or too busy to do.

Even if many Americans do not understand the relationship of time to their other concerns, corporate America clearly does. Brandt quotes a 1990 survey of two hundred CEOs, more than half of whom said they expected their managerial employees to work an average of fifty to fifty-nine hours a week in order for their companies to compete internationally. In another survey, three hundred leading CEOs were overwhelmingly negative to the idea of a shorter workweek. Said one: "I cannot imagine a shorter work week. I can imagine a longer one both in school and at work if America is to be competitive in the first half of the next century."

Coming Home

These are just a few examples of how a politics of devolution might begin to come about. Such a politics is needed if for no other reason than that it is our best defense against the increasing authoritarianism of government, the monopolization of economic activity, the dictatorship of time, and the regimentation of human behavior. It is also needed because without it, politics becomes little more than a choice between two increasingly interchangeable propaganda machines.

In the 1960s, Robert McNamara declared, "Running any large organization is the same, whether it's the Ford Motor Company, the Catholic Church or the Department of Defense. Once you get to a certain scale, they're all the same."

And so, increasingly to our detriment, they are. In 1993 we "changed" administrations, but, unless challenged by a new politics, this will largely leave unchanged that which is administered.

We must learn and teach, and make a central part of our politics, that while small is not always beautiful, it has—for our human ecology, our liberties, and our souls—become absolutely essential.

Politics, of course, is not a neat place. A young legislator once asked Earl Long whether ideals had any place in politics. "Hell yes," said Ol' Earl, "you should use ideals or any other damn thing you can get your hands on."

Politics is the sound of the air coming out of the balloon of our expectations, and it is the music of hope. Vaclav Havel says that genuine politics is "simply a matter of serving those around us, serving the community, and serving those who will come after us." James Michael Curley put it this way: "Wherever I have found a thistle, I endeavored to replace it with a rose."

Politics is laundry lists and dirty laundry, new hospitals and old hates, finding out what others think about it, and the willing suspension of our closest beliefs in order to get through the next month or year. It is, suggested one writer, a matter of who gets what, when, where, and how. Not least, as Paul Begala says, "it is show business for ugly people," a theater in which each voter and candidate writes a different morality play.

In the end, the only test of political faith is when it is put to work. It is a test that is graded on a curve—not by its proximity to perfection but by its improvement over all previous, adjacent, and potential imperfections. Havel says, "It is not true that a person of principle does not belong in politics; it is enough for his principles to be leavened with patience, deliberation, a sense of proportion, and an understanding of others." This is the part of politics that doesn't appear in any platform. Done badly, it becomes demagoguery and manipulation. Done well, it makes every voter a part of the office the politician holds. It is a standard to which every person in office, including our presidents, can be held.

We started by talking a lot about Bill Clinton, but as we got closer to what was really bothering us, he began to fade. Like much of the American system today, what he has to say keeps wandering from what is in our hearts. It is a curious thing to think of someone so powerful, but when you come right down to it, Bill Clinton is often, well, irrelevant. As a conscious, sometimes manic, and often not very skilled reflection of our desires, he is in the end mostly waiting for us to tell him what to do.

We don't usually give ourselves credit for such power, but it is there whether we choose to use it or not. If we choose, we can move empires. John Adams understood this. The American Revolution, he said, "was effected before the war commenced. The Revolution was in the minds and hearts of the people. . . . This radical change in the principles, opinions, sentiments and affections of the people was the real American Revolution."[20]

This book has been about reviving our rights before, as Jefferson put it, they expire in convulsion, about recovering our democracy before it is "reinvented" beyond recognition. It has been, in a sense, a letter from the battlefront of the American dream, part of the endless conversation and debate that keeps democracy from becoming something else.

I have offered a few suggestions but no panaceas. That's all right, because the moment democracy is safe from its own destruction, it is no longer a democracy. As Eugene Debs told his followers, he would not lead them to the promised land because if he could, someone else could lead them out again.

We cannot be free if we turn our politics over to Bill and Hillary Clinton, Ross Perot, Bob Dole, or Rush Limbaugh. And we cannot be free without risking failure. The walls that we have increasingly built around ourselves in the name of safe streets, economic security, or acceptable speech, merely isolate us further from that which we profess to seek.

Finally, we cannot be free if we cannot retrieve the aspect of politics that once made it a natural, integral, and pleasurable part of our lives, and if it now becomes so distant or so dirty or so cruel that we would rather not even think or speak about it. Someone else, to our great danger, will fill our silence.

NOTES

INTRODUCTION

1. Extrapolated from table 7 in Henry C. Gilliam, *U.S. Beef Cow-Calf Industry,* Agriculture Economic Report 515, U.S. Department of Agriculture, 1984.

2. *Washingtonian,* 5/93.

1. AUDITION

1. Details of events surrounding the 1988 convention come from contemporary news accounts, as well as Charles F. Allen and Jonathan Portis, *The Comeback Kid: The Life and Career of Bill Clinton* (New York: Birch Lane Press, 1992). Also Jim Moore, *Clinton: Young Man in a Hurry* (Fort Worth: The Summit Group, 1992).

2. Some of the information on the Harriman sessions comes from the *Washingtonian* and *Time.*

3. Quoted in Eugene McCarthy, *Up 'til Now* (New York: Harcourt Brace Jovanovich, 1987), p. 123.

4. *New Yorker,* 8/2/93.

5. *Washington Post,* 2/3/93.

6. *Washington Post,* 6/22/93.

7. *New York Times,* 11/22/92.

8. Quoted in Bernard Bailyn, *The Ideological Origins of the American Revolution* (Cambridge: Harvard University Press, 1967), p. 3.

9. Robert Axelrod, *The Evolution of Cooperation* (New York: Basic Books, 1984), p. 84.

10. Ibid., p. 87.

11. Marion Elizabeth Rodgers, ed., *The Impossible Mencken* (New York: Anchor Books, 1991), p. 256.

12. *Vanity Fair,* 10/93.

13. *Money,* 7/92.

14. CNN, 5/13/93.

15. *New York Times,* 10/9/93.

16. Quoted in *Washington Post,* 5/25/93.

17. *Time,* 8/16/93.

18. *Washington Post,* 8/12/93.

19. Pauline Marie Rosenau, *Post-Modernism and the Social Sciences* (Princeton: Princeton University Press, 1992), p. 128.

20. Ibid., p. 119.

21. Ibid., p. 96.

22. Marshall Blonsky, *American Mythologies* (New York and Oxford: Oxford University Press, 1992), p. 50.

23. Ibid., p. 57.

24. Ibid., p. 301.

25. Joel Krieger, ed., *The Oxford Companion to Politics of the World* (Oxford: Oxford University Press, 1993).

26. *Liberal Education,* Summer 1993.

27. As quoted by Jeramiah Creedon in the *Utne Reader,* July/August 1993.

28. *Utne Reader,* July/August 1993.

29. *New York Times,* 7/5/93.

30. Blonsky, p. 439.

31. *Spy Magazine,* 8/93.

32. *Time,* 5/24/93.

2. SHOWTIME

1. *Washingtonian,* 7/93.

2. *New York Times,* 7/5/93.

3. Polling data from *New York Times,* 11/5/92.

4. *New York Times,* 5/1/93.

5. *Polling Report,* 6/28/83.

6. *Washington Post,* 4/28/93.

7. *Washingtonian,* 5/93.

8. *Spy,* 8/93.

9. The Eisenhower story comes from Eugene McCarthy; the Packwood incident was described by the *Washington Times,* 6/30/93.

10. *Spy,* 5/93.

11. *Washington Post,* 6/4/93.

12. Quoted by *Left Business Observer,* 4/26/93.

13. Kenneth S. Davis, *FDR: The New Deal Years* (New York: Random House, 1979), p. 304.

14. Jack W. Germond and Jules Witcover, *Mad as Hell: Revolt at the Ballot Box, 1992* (New York: Warner Books, 1993), pp. 9–10.

15. Gordon S. Wood, *The Radicalism of the American Revolution* (New York: Vintage Books, Random House, 1993), p. 275.

16. Thurman W. Arnold, *The Folklore of Capitalism* (New Haven and London: Yale University Press, 1957), p. xv.

17. Ibid., p. 171.

18. Richard Rothstein, "The Left's Obsessive Opposition," in *The American Prospect,* Fall 1993.

19. Ibid., p. xv.

20. *Washington Post,* 11/18/93.

21. *New Yorker,* 11/29/93.

22. *Washington Post,* 11/13/93.

23. Ibid.

24. *Washington Post,* 10/21/93.

3. IN SEARCH OF CLINTONISM

1. Jonathan Lynn and Antony Jay, eds., *The Complete Yes Minister: The Diaries of a Cabinet Minister by the Right Hon. James Hacker MP* (London: BBC Books, 1987), p. 9.

2. *Newsweek,* 11/1/93.

3. *Washington Post,* 5/2/93.

4. Blonsky, p. 450.

5. Ibid., pp. 45, 50.

6. *U.S. News & World Report,* 10/26/92.

7. *New York Times,* 8/24/93; *Washington Post,* 9/4/93.

8. See Moore and *The Nation,* 11/23/92, among others.

9. *U.S. News & World Report,* 12/13/93.

10. See Mimi Abramovitz and Frances Fox Piven, "Scapegoating Women on Welfare," *New York Times,* 9/2/93, among others.

11. Quoted in *The Nation,* 5/24/93.

12. *U.S. News & World Report,* 12/13/93.

13. *New York Times,* 10/15/93.

14. Margaret Canovan, *G. K. Chesterton: Radical Populist* (New York and London: Harcourt Brace Jovanovich, 1977), p. 44.

15. Ibid., pp. 45–47.

16. Ibid., p. 53.

17. Center for Political Studies, University of Michigan, and *Los Angeles Times,* quoted in *Time,* 7/19/93.

18. Based on a study of the indices of the transcript firm Journal Graphics.

19. *What You Can Do for Your Country,* Report of the Commission on National and Community Service, 1993.

20. Pacific News Service.

21. *New York Times,* 5/15/93.

22. *Newsweek,* 8/9/93.

23. Associated Press, 12/14/92.

24. *New York Times,* 8/4/93.

25. *New York Times,* 4/29/93.

26. Lester Brown et al., *State of the World* (New York and London: W. W. Norton and Co., 1993), pp. 127, 130.

27. *Urban Transport International,* March/April 1992.

28. *Washington Monthly,* 9/93.

29. *The Nation,* 3/22/93.

30. *Washington Times,* 5/26/93.

31. *New York Times,* 7/18/93.

32. *American Prospect,* Spring 1993.

33. *Washington Post,* 5/9/93.

34. *Fortune,* 5/17/93.

35. A. Ernest Fitzgerald, *The Pentagonists* (Boston: Houghton Mifflin, 1989), pp. 308–310.

36. Adrian Lyttelton, *The Seizure of Power* (Princeton: Princeton University Press, 1987), pp. 354–360.

37. William Shirer, *The Rise and Fall of the Third Reich* (New York: Simon and Schuster, 1960), p. 259.

38. *New York Times,* 9/29/93.

39. *Toward Freedom,* December 1992/January 1993.

4 . THE CLUB

1. Quoted in Phil Duncan, ed., *Politics in America: 1990* (Washington: Congressional Quarterly Inc., 1989), pp. 2–3.

2. USA Today/CNN Poll, 7/27/93.

3. Jeremy Rifkin and Carol Grunewald Rifkin, *Voting Green* (New York: Doubleday, 1992), pp. 288–292.

4. Arnold, p. 156.

5. *Time,* 12/6/93.

6. Sources include contemporary newspaper accounts and reports of the Center for Public Integrity.

7. *New York Times,* 2/5/93.

8. *Miami Herald,* 7/5/87.

9. Alan Taylor, " 'The Art of Hook and Snivey': Political Culture in Upstate New York during the 1790s," *The Journal of American History,* 3/93.

10. David Walls, *The Activist's Almanac* (New York: Simon and Schuster, 1993) p. 28.

11. Ibid., pp. 273–274.

12. Quoted in William Greider, *Who Will Tell the People* (New York: Touchstone, 1992), p. 107. Reich's calculation appeared in the *Harvard Business Review,* May–June 1981. While the figure may seem excessive, Greider in his book says, "A decade later, Reich's head-count doubtless understates reality."

13. *Washington Times,* 11/26/93.

14. Greider, p. 48.

15. Tip O'Neill with William Novak, *Man of the House* (New York: Random House, 1987), p. 324.

16. *New York Times,* 11/1/93.

17. *The Nation,* 7/8/91.

18. *Time,* 5/3/93.

19. *The Nation,* 7/19/93.

20. *New York Times,* 11/28/93.

21. *New York Times,* 5/23/93.

22. *Newsweek,* 5/3/93.

23. Pacific News Service, 4/26/93.

24. *Washington Times,* July 14, 1993.

25. *L.A. Times,* 5/28/93.

26. *Environmental Action,* Summer 1993.

27. Speech before the Wisconsin Psychiatric Association Legislative Institute Conference, 3/26/93.

28. Donald A. Ritchie, *Press Gallery: Congress and the Washington Correspondents* (Cambridge: Harvard University Press, 1991), p. 7.

29. Statistic from the *Village Voice,* 7/20/93.

30. *Extra!,* July/August 1993.

31. *Washington Post,* 7/11/93.

32. For some years I have sat on the board of the Fund for Constitutional Government, which has helped to support a number of these groups as well as assisting journalists investigating stories the mainstream media won't touch.

33. A labor dispute at the Williamsburg Inn forced a further retreat of the retreat to Leesburg, Va. See *Roll Call,* 2/7/93.

34. *Washington Times,* 9/17/93.

35. *Washington Post,* 9/1/93.

36. *Washington Post,* 7/9/86.

37. *Washingtonian,* 8/93.

38. *New York Times,* 11/27/93.

39. Austin H. Kiplinger with Knight A. Kiplinger, *Washington Now* (New York: Harper and Row, 1975), p. 339.

40. Greider, p. 57.

41. Perry Miller, *The Life of the Mind in America* (New York: Harcourt, Brace and World, 1965), p. 100.

42. Ibid., p. 102.

43. Thorstein Veblen, *The Theory of the Leisure Class* (New York: Mentor, 1953), p. 156.

44. *Indices: A Statistical Index to District of Columbia Services,* December 1992.

45. Tennessee Williams, *Camino Real* (London: Secker and Warburg, 1958), p. 14.

5. SIGNS ALONG THE HIGHWAY

1. Data from the *Washington Post* and *Congressional Quarterly.*

2. Quoted in *NetNews,* November/December 1993. *NetNews* is the newsletter of the Institute for Global Communications.

3. *Washington Times,* 10/18/93.

4. David Osborne and Ted Gaebler, *Reinventing Government* (New York: Penguin Books, 1993), p. 327.

5. Wood, p. 167.

6. David Kemmis, "Living Next to One Another," in *Parabola: The Magazine of Myth and Tradition,* Winter 1993.

7. Quoted by Fitzgerald, p. 314.

8. Michael Zuckerman, *Almost Chosen People: Oblique Biographies in the American Grain* (Berkeley and Los Angeles: University of California Press, 1993), p. 303.

9. James L. Huston, "The American Revolutionaries, the Political Economy of Aristocracy, and the American Concept of the Distribution of Wealth, 1765–1900," *American Historical Review,* 10/93.

10. Wood, p. 320.

11. Howard Zinn, *A People's History of the United States* (New York: Harper Perennial, 1980), p. 249.

12. Pacific News Service.

13. *New York Times,* 9/5/93.

14. *Wired,* Premier Edition, 1993.

15. *New York Times,* 9/5/93.

16. Henry Cisneros, ed., *Interwoven Destinies: Cities and the Nation* (New York: W. W. Norton, 1993), p. 86.

17. Children's Defense Fund.

18. Zuckerman, p. 303.

19. Center for New Priorities.

20. Kathryn Schneider Smith, *Port Town to Urban Neighborhood: George Washington of Washington, D.C. 1880–1920* (Washington: The Center for Washington Area Studies of the George Washington University, 1989), p. 34.

21. Government of the District of Columbia Department of Regulatory Affairs, *Instructions for Filing Application for Retailer's License Class "F" or "G."*

22. Quoted in *American Journalism Review*, 6/93.

23. Davis, pp. 306–308.

24. Families against Mandatory Minimums.

25. *The Nation*, 11/15/93.

26. National Drug Strategy Network, *Newsbriefs*.

27. *Washington Post*, 6/15/93.

28. *Time*, 11/8/93.

29. Urban Ecology.

30. Cisneros, p. 89.

31. Ibid., p. 174.

32. *Washington Times*, 10/12/93.

33. MTV Rock the Vote Survey, 1992.

34. *Washington Post*, 5/18/93.

35. Ibid., 10/9/93.

36. *Maine Sunday Telegram*, 9/12/93.

37. Thomas Jefferson, *Notes on Virginia*, quoted in Bernard Mayo, ed., *Jefferson Himself* (Charlottesville: University Press of Virginia, 1970), pp. 83–84.

38. *Washington Times*, 6/4/93.

39. Quoted in the *Washington Times*, 7/15/93.

40. Quoted in the *Washington Post*, 10/12/93.

41. *New York*, 5/5/93.

42. *New York Times*, 5/31/93.

43. *Time*, 12/6/93.

44. Robert Axelrod, *The Evolution of Cooperation* (New York: Basic Books, 1984), p. 114.

6. BRINGING POLITICS HOME

1. Sam Smith, *Captive Capital* (Bloomington: Indiana University Press, 1974), p. 284.

2. *Atlantic Monthly,* 8/92, and the National Center for Urban Ethnic Affairs.

3. See William Riordon, *Plunkitt of Tammany Hall* (New York: E. P. Dutton, 1963).

4. Milton L. Rakove, *Don't Make No Waves, Don't Back No Losers* (Bloomington: Indiana University Press, 1975), pp. 118–120.

5. *Washington Post,* 11/7/93.

6. *Washington Post,* 10/24/93.

7. Centers for Disease Control.

8. Canovan, pp. 40–41.

9. Steven J. Wolin and Sybil Wolin, *The Resilient Self* (New York: Villard Books, 1993), p. 13.

10. Ibid., p. 20.

11. Ibid., pp. 59–60.

12. Center for Voting and Democracy.

13. Quoted in *Blueprint for Social Justice,* April 1993.

14. Smith, p. 284.

15. Small Business Administration.

16. Bureau of the Census, 1990 Neighborhood Demographics Report.

17. Richard Sennett, *The Uses of Disorder* (New York: Vintage Books, 1970), p. 96.

18. Rakove, pp. 32–33.

19. Barbara Brandt, "Less Time for Our Jobs, More Time for Ourselves," Paper published by Women for Economic Justice, 32 Rutland St., Boston MA 02118, 1993.

20. Bailyn, p. 160.

BIBLIOGRAPHY

Allen, Charles F., and Jonathan Portis. *The Comback Kid: The Life and Career of Bill Clinton*. New York: Birch Lane Press, 1992.

Arnold, Thurman W. *The Folklore of Capitalism*. New Haven and London: Yale University Press, 1957.

Axelrod, Robert. *The Evolution of Cooperation*. New York: Basic Books, 1984.

Bailyn, Bernard. *The Ideological Origins of the American Revolution*. Cambridge: Harvard University Press, 1967.

Blonsky, Marshall. *American Mythologies*. New York and Oxford: Oxford University Press, 1992.

Brown, Lester, et al. *State of the World*. New York and London: W. W. Norton and Co., 1993.

Cahn, Edgar, and Jonathan Rowe. *Time Dollars*. Emmaus: Rodale Press, 1992.

Canovan, Margaret. *G. K. Chesterton: Radical Populist*. New York and London: Harcourt Brace Jovanovich, 1977.

Cisneros, Henry, ed. *Interwoven Destinies: Cities and the Nation*. New York: W. W. Norton, 1993.

Duncan, Phil, ed. *Politics in America: 1990*. Washington, D.C.: Congressional Quarterly Inc., 1989.

Fitzgerald, A. Ernest. *The Pentagonists*. Boston: Houghton Mifflin, 1989.

Germond, Jack W., and Jules Witcover. *Mad as Hell: Revolt at the Ballot Box, 1992*. New York: Warner Books, 1993.

Greider, William. *Who Will Tell the People*. New York: Touchstone, 1992.

Kiplinger, Austin H., with Knight A. Kiplinger. *Washington Now*. New York: Harper and Row, 1975.

Krieger, Joel, ed. *The Oxford Companion to Politics of the World*. Oxford: Oxford University Press, 1993.

Lynn, Jonathan, and Antony Jay, eds. *The Complete Yes Minister: The Diaries of a Cabinet Minister by the Right Hon. James Hacker MP*. London: BBC Books, 1987.

Lyttelton, Adrian. *The Seizure of Power*. Princeton: Princeton University Press, 1987.

Mayo, Bernard, ed. *Jefferson Himself*. Charlottesville: University Press of Virginia, 1970.

McCarthy, Eugene. *Up 'til Now*. New York: Harcourt Brace Jovanovich, 1987.

Miller, Perry. *The Life of the Mind in America*. New York: Harcourt, Brace and World, 1965.

Moore, Jim. *Clinton: Young Man in a Hurry*. Fort Worth: The Summit Group, 1992.

Osborne, David, and Ted Gaebler. *Reinventing Government*. New York: Penguin Books, 1993.

Rakove, Milton L. *Don't Make No Waves, Don't Back No Losers*. Bloomington: Indiana University Press, 1975.

Rifkin, Jeremy, and Carol Grunewald Rifkin. *Voting Green*. New York: Doubleday, 1992.

Riordon, William. *Plunkitt of Tammany Hall*. New York: E. P. Dutton, 1963.

Ritchie, Donald A. *Press Gallery: Congress and the Washington Correspondents*. Cambridge: Harvard University Press, 1991.

Rodgers, Marion Elizabeth, ed. *The Impossible Mencken*. New York: Anchor Books, 1991.

Rosenau, Pauline Marie. *Post-Modernism and the Social Sciences*. Princeton: Princeton University Press, 1992.

Sennett, Richard. *The Uses of Disorder*. New York: Vintage Books, 1970.

Shirer, William. *The Rise and Fall of the Third Reich*. New York: Simon and Schuster, 1960.

Smith, Kathryn Schneider. *Port Town to Urban Neighborhood: George Washington of Washington, D.C. 1880–1920*. Washington: The Center for Washington Area Studies of the George Washington University, 1989.

Smith, Sam. *Captive Capital*. Bloomington: Indiana University Press, 1974.

Veblen, Thorstein. *The Theory of the Leisure Class*. New York: Mentor, 1953.

Walls, David. *The Activist's Almanac*. New York: Simon and Schuster, 1993.

Williams, Tennessee. *Camino Real*. London: Secker and Warburg, 1958.

Wood, Gordon S. *The Radicalism of the American Revolution*. New York: Vintage Books, Random House, 1993.

Zuckerman, Michael. *Almost Chosen People: Oblique Biographies in the American Grain*. Berkeley and Los Angeles: University of California Press, 1993.

INDEX